CHRIST-CENTERED
Exposition

AUTHOR **Tony Merida**

SERIES EDITORS **David Platt, Daniel L. Akin, and Tony Merida**

CHRIST-CENTERED
Exposition

EXALTING JESUS IN

EXODUS

HOLMAN
REFERENCE

NASHVILLE, TENNESSEE

SERIES DEDICATION

Dedicated to Adrian Rogers and John Piper. They have taught us to love the gospel of Jesus Christ, to preach the Bible as the inerrant Word of God, to pastor the Church for which our Savior died, and to have a passion to see all nations gladly worship the Lamb.

—David Platt, Tony Merida, and Danny Akin
March 2013

TABLE OF CONTENTS

SERIES INTRODUCTION

Augustine said, "Where Scripture speaks, God speaks." The editors of the Christ-Centered Exposition Commentary series believe that where God speaks, the pastor must speak. God speaks through His written Word. We must speak from that Word. We believe the Bible is God breathed, authoritative, inerrant, sufficient, understandable, necessary, and timeless. We also affirm that the Bible is a Christ-centered book; that is, it contains a unified story of redemptive history of which Jesus is the hero. Because of this Christ-centered trajectory that runs from Genesis 1 through Revelation 22, we believe the Bible has a corresponding global-missions thrust. From beginning to end, we see God's mission as one of making worshipers of Christ from every tribe and tongue worked out through this redemptive drama in Scripture. To that end we must preach the Word.

In addition to these distinct convictions, the Christ-Centered Exposition Commentary series has some distinguishing characteristics. First, this series seeks to display exegetical accuracy. What the Bible says is what we want to say. While not every volume in the series will be a verse-by-verse commentary, we nevertheless desire to handle the text carefully and explain it rightly. Those who teach and preach bear the heavy responsibility of saying what God has said in His Word and declaring what God has done in Christ. We desire to handle God's Word faithfully, knowing that we must give an account for how we have fulfilled this holy calling (Jas 3:1).

Second, the Christ-Centered Exposition Commentary series has pastors in view. While we hope others will read this series, such as parents, teachers, small-group leaders, and student ministers, we desire to provide a commentary busy pastors will use for weekly preparation of biblically faithful and gospel-saturated sermons. This series is not academic in nature. Our aim is to present a readable and pastoral style of commentaries. We believe this aim will serve the church of the Lord Jesus Christ.

Third, we want the Christ-Centered Exposition Commentary series to be known for the inclusion of helpful illustrations and theologically driven applications. Many commentaries offer no help in illustrations, and few offer any kind of help in application. Often those that do offer illustrative material and application unfortunately give little serious attention to the text. While giving ourselves primarily to explanation, we also hope to serve readers by providing inspiring and illuminating illustrations coupled with timely and timeless application.

Finally, as the name suggests, the editors seek to exalt Jesus from every book of the Bible. In saying this, we are not commending wild allegory or fanciful typology. We certainly believe we must be constrained to the meaning intended by the divine Author Himself, the Holy Spirit of God. However, we also believe the Bible has a messianic focus, and our hope is that the individual authors will exalt Christ from particular texts. Luke 24:25-27,44-47; and John 5:39,46 inform both our hermeneutics and our homiletics. Not every author will do this the same way or have the same degree of Christ-centered emphasis. That is fine with us. We believe faithful exposition that is Christ centered is not monolithic. We do believe, however, that we must read the whole Bible as Christian Scripture. Therefore, our aim is both to honor the historical particularity of each biblical passage and to highlight its intrinsic connection to the Redeemer.

The editors are indebted to the contributors of each volume. The reader will detect a unique style from each writer, and we celebrate these unique gifts and traits. While distinctive in approach, the authors share a common characteristic in that they are pastoral theologians. They love the church, and they regularly preach and teach God's Word to God's people. Further, many of these contributors are younger voices. We think these new, fresh voices can serve the church well, especially among a rising generation that has the task of proclaiming the Word of Christ and the Christ of the Word to the lost world.

We hope and pray this series will serve the body of Christ well in these ways until our Savior returns in glory. If it does, we will have succeeded in our assignment.

David Platt
Daniel L. Akin
Tony Merida
Series Editors
February 2013

ACKNOWLEDGMENTS

Before saying thank you to some important individuals and my local church, I must recognize my bride, Kimberly, who is (in the words of Jonathan Edwards) "my dear companion." She is involved in all my endeavors in some way. She not only supports and encourages me, but also challenges me by her own respected ministry, particularly with her work of seeking justice, correcting oppression, bringing justice to the fatherless, and pleading the widows' cause (Isa 1:17). In addition to being my beloved bride, best friend, and ministry partner, she is also an incredible mother to our five adopted children (James, Joshua, Angela, Victoria, and Jana). I am grateful to God for blessing us with this wonderful mini-van full of kids and for sustaining us through the challenges of parenthood. To my children, I praise God for you all. I love to watch you sit on the front row taking notes, and I love having our table talks at dinner (where my weekly sermons get preached first!). I pray that you will know, delight in, and glorify our Redeemer faithfully.

I also want to acknowledge Imago Dei Church. Your love for the gospel motivates me to expound the Christ-centered Scriptures passionately. As we read the Scriptures weekly, and as you respond by saying "Thanks be to God," I feel enormous gratitude to God for giving me the privilege of shepherding you. Our study through the book of Exodus provided the heart and soul of this commentary, and I dedicate this book to you.

Along with this acknowledgement, I want to say thank you to the other elders at Imago Dei, who share in the shepherding and teaching ministry with me. The unity we share is evidence of God's grace. I am grateful for your friendship and partnership in the gospel.

Next, I also want to say thank you to Aaron Lumpkin, my diligent and intelligent student assistant. I am indebted to you for your research and thoughtful feedback on this commentary.

I want to also acknowledge Dr. Danny Akin. He not only invited me to serve on the faculty at Southeastern Baptist Theological Seminary, but also invited me to be part of the Christ-Centered Exposition series. I am out of my league with both of these responsibilities. Regarding this particular project, I must say that I feel more comfortable on a baseball diamond or on a basketball court than with writing commentaries, but I am grateful for the opportunity to take a rip (or shot).

For the reader, I recommend that you always read more than one commentary on a book of the Bible that you are studying. Be sure to do this regarding Exodus. I am glad you picked up this commentary, but I should point you to some others who helped me along the journey. I am especially indebted to Douglas Stuart for his Exodus commentary; to Philip Ryken for his Christological emphasis in the *Exodus* volume of the Preaching the Word series; to Christopher J. H. Wright, for his powerful work *The Mission of God*; and to Russell Moore whose "Exit Strategy" study provided a wonderful example both of how to expound Exodus Christocentrically and of how one might expound large portions of Exodus at a time. Other biblical theologies, such as *God's Glory in Salvation through Judgment* by James Hamilton and *Kingdom through Covenant* by Peter J. Gentry and Stephen J. Wellum, were very helpful as well.

I want to say thanks to Jeremy Howard and the B&H team for agreeing to publish this work. What a joy to serve with folks who desire to get Word-saturated resources into the hands of others—for the good of the nations, the edification of the church, and to the glory of King Jesus.

Tony Merida

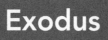

Exodus

Introduction to Exodus

"Exodus" means "a going out," or "departure" (taken from the Septuagint and the Greek noun *exodos*). A true masterpiece, the book of Exodus provides the historical account of God's deliverance of His people from Egypt's cruel slavery. The narrative captivates and challenges us. We should not see it as a tale from the distant past but as an eternally important and relevant story for our lives.

You may not think about Egypt that much in your everyday life (although the country has been in the news at the time I write this). Some of us grew up with that memorable song "Walk like an Egyptian" by the Bangles from 1986. It was not a song that took Egypt seriously.

My wife and I visited Egypt recently on a layover. We took a quick, eight-hour tour of Cairo. We saw the Great Pyramid of Giza, which is the only one of the Seven Wonders of the World still standing. It was the tallest man-made structure for 3,800 years. It is as tall as a 50-story skyscraper, though built around 2560 BC. We enjoyed seeing the pyramids and the museum with King Tut's property. Egypt continues to be a fascinating place to visit for historical reflection, but it is not a great superpower.

In the period of Exodus, however, Egypt was a serious superpower. People feared Egypt. Egypt had mighty Pharaohs, they built great projects such as the pyramids, and they were in touch with dark power. While scholars debate different aspects of the historical situation, there is evidence (in addition to the Bible) that Egypt was enslaving a Semitic people in the decades leading up to the exodus, as noted in Papyrus 348, which dates back to Ramses II. This document speaks of using the "Apiru *(hapiru)* to drag stones to the great pylon." Some think there may be a connection between the word "Apiru" and *Ibri*, the word from which we get the word *Hebrew* (Ryken, *Exodus*, 21).

Traditionally, Moses is viewed as the main author of the *Pentateuch* (the first five books of the Bible, also called "The Five Books of Moses"), though he might not have written everything (e.g., Deut 34). When Jesus quoted from Exodus (Mark 7:10; 12:26), He attributed such verses to Moses. We therefore should hold to Moses as the primary author, writing under the inspiration of the Spirit (2 Pet 1:20-21; 2 Tim 3:16-17).

The historical events seem to occur during the Late Bronze Age (1550–1200 BC; Hill and Walton, *A Survey of the Old Testament*, 40). More specifically, the exodus event probably took place in 1446 BC (Kaiser, "Exodus," 287–93). Evangelical scholars usually hold to either a later date, 1260 BC, or an earlier date, 1446 BC. The earlier date seems best given the internal evidence in 1 Kings 6:1 and Judges 11:26.

As we will see, chapters 1–18 provide the story of God's deliverance of the Israelites from Egypt, and chapters 19–40 show us the glory of God at Sinai.

Why Exodus?

Why would you want to study this book? Let me mention four reasons.

First, we need to know God better. We meet the living God in Exodus! Think of Psalm 66:5-7:

> *Come and see the wonders of God;*
> *His acts for humanity are awe-inspiring.*
> *He turned the sea into dry land,*
> *and they crossed the river on foot.*
> *There we rejoiced in Him.*
> *He rules forever by His might;*
> *He keeps His eye on the nations.*
> *The rebellious should not exalt themselves.*

Come and see! We will see that God wills to be known and glorified. We will see a God who is "merciful and gracious, slow to anger, and abounding in steadfast love and faithfulness" (Exod 34:6 ESV). In encountering this holy God we should, like Moses, bow down and worship (34:8).

Second, we need to understand God's redemption better. Exodus is a picture of the Gospel, and we will seek to understand Exodus in relation to Jesus. There are a number of reasons for this. In Luke 24 Jesus explained the Old Testament "beginning with Moses and all the Prophets . . . concerning Himself in all the Scriptures" (v. 27). "Moses" here is short for the Pentateuch, which includes Exodus! Earlier, in Luke 9:31, when Jesus talked with Moses and Elijah on the Mount of Transfiguration and Luke says that Jesus spoke about His "death," (lit. His "departure,") the word there is *exodos*, the Greek word for "exodus." Jesus' triumphant death and resurrection was the greater exodus. Jesus would pass through the waters of death in order to deliver His people from bondage to their sin and take them to the new heavens and new earth. In the New Testament,

Jesus is also referred to as "our Passover Lamb," using terminology from Exodus (1 Cor 5:7). Also realize there are more than just a few verses that invite us to read Exodus with Christ-centered lenses. The gospel appears everywhere in pattern, type, theme development, and foreshadowing. Through these and many other features, Exodus shows us redemption (cf. Col 1:13-14; 1 Pet 1:18-19; Jude 5). Christopher J. H. Wright in *The Mission of God* reminds us of God's model of redemption:

> How big is our gospel? If our gospel is the good news about God's redemption, then the question moves on to, How big is our understanding of redemption? Mission clearly has to do with the redemptive work of God and our participation in making it known and leading people into the experience of it. If, as I am seeking to argue throughout this book, mission is fundamentally God's before it is ours, what is God's idea of redemption? The scope of our mission must reflect the scope of God's mission, which in turn will match the scale of God's redemptive work. Where do we turn in the Bible for our understanding of redemption? Already it will be clear enough that in my view it will simply not do to turn first to the New Testament. If you had asked a devout Israelite in the Old Testament period, "Are you redeemed?" the answer would have been a most definite yes. And if you had asked "How do you know?" you would be taken aside to sit down somewhere while your friend recounted a long and exciting story—the story of exodus.
>
> For indeed *it is the exodus that provided the primary model of God's idea of redemption,* not just in the Old Testament but even in the New, where it is used as one of the keys to understanding the meaning of the cross of Christ (Wright, *Mission,* 265; emphasis added).

As Wright says, Exodus provides the primary model of redemption in the Old Testament and New Testament, and it stands as one of the keys for understanding the cross and salvation. Notice some of the similarities between Israel and believers today:

- Like Israel, we are saved from something (from slavery to sin) for something (to witness and to worship). This idea of being delivered "out of Egypt" gets recorded many times in the Bible (Exod 3:10; 3:17; 20:2; Ps 81:10; Matt 2:15; Jude 5).

- Like Israel, we are saved by the blood of a lamb (Exod 12; 1 Pet 1:18-19; Rev 5).
- Like Israel, we have been saved, and we are now sojourners and a holy priesthood, seeking to glorify God in word and deed until we reach the promised land (1 Pet 2:4-12).

With this in mind, we can say that, in a sense, the exodus story is our story.

Third, we need to understand God's mission (and ours) better. The mission of the church does not begin in the Great Commission (Matt 28:16-20). It begins well before this important text, in the Old Testament. Here we see God concerned about physical injustice as well as spiritual deliverance. We need to be a people who care about the enslaved, both physically and spiritually. Wright says it well: "*Exodus-shaped redemption demands exodus-shaped mission*" (Wright, *Mission of God,* 275; emphasis in original). The exodus gives us not just a model of redemption, but also a model of mission.

Finally, we need to draw lessons for living out our faith on a daily basis. We have examples to avoid and examples to follow in Exodus (1 Cor 10:11). A number of practical topics should interest us:

- Taking care of the unborn
- Racism and murder
- How God can use weak, ordinary people
- The importance of singing praise
- The nature of true community
- How to rely on God's presence daily
- Delegation and the need to take counsel from others
- Obeying God's word
- The issue of idolatry and true worship

As we journey through this amazing book, we will seek to understand and apply the exodus story historically, theologically, Christologically, missiologically, and practically. Let the journey begin!

Redemption and Mission

EXODUS 1–2

Main Idea: God's determination to free Israel from oppression so that they could worship Him calls us to practice a similarly integrative model of mission.

I. **The Need for Redemption (1:8-22)**
  A. Political slavery (1:8-10)
  B. Economic slavery (1:11-14)
  C. Social slavery (1:15-22)
  D. Spiritual slavery (1:8–2:25; 9:1)
II. **The Mediator and Redemption (2:1-22)**
  A. The birth of a Moses (2:1-10)
  B. The growth of Moses (2:11-15)
  C. The flight of Moses (2:15-22)
III. **God's Motive of Redemption (2:23-25)**
IV. **The Mission of the Redeemed**
  A. Let us care for urgent physical needs.
  B. Let us care for urgent spiritual needs.

The opening verses of Exodus connect the book directly to Genesis, which ended with the death of Joseph around 1805 BC. The first half of the book focuses on Israel's departure from Egypt: the historical setting (1:1–2:25); Moses's leadership (3:1–6:30); miraculous signs and judgment (7:1–15:21); and Israel's journey (15:22–18:27). The second half covers the events at Mount Sinai: the Ten Words and the laws (19:1–23:19); instructions for entering the land (23:20-33); the confirmation of the covenant (24:1-18); instructions for, and later the execution of, building the tabernacle (25:1–31:18; 35:1–40:38); and the breach of the covenant, Moses' intercession, and the renewal of the covenant (32:1–34:35).

In Genesis 12:2-3 God made His covenant with Abraham, promising to make him into a great nation, that through this people all nations on earth might be blessed. Exodus continues talking about God's relationship with this people and this grand covenantal purpose.

Further, Exodus fits within the context of the first five books of the Bible (the Pentateuch) and should be read in light of this context. From this context, one can broaden out and observe how Exodus fits beauti-fully into the bigger story of the Bible. Many foundational promises, themes, and truths emerge from this book of Holy Scripture.

One might reasonably ask, "Why were the Israelites in Egypt?" Consider two related reasons. First, Joseph, Jacob's son, was taken to Egypt because his jealous brothers sold him into slavery. He gained favor in the eyes of Pharaoh and ended up helping to save lives by stock-piling food. In the ensuing famine, all the earth came to Egypt to buy grain (Gen 41:57). Second, during this famine, his family went to Egypt, and Joseph provided food for them (Gen 42). The family ended up resettling in the Nile Delta. Seventy entered Egypt (see Gen 46:3-27), and from there they grew and grew!

In verse 7 we see the Israelites following the command God had given in the garden to "be fruitful and multiply" (Gen 1:28). God had later told Jacob, "I am God Almighty. Be fruitful and multiply. A nation, indeed an assembly of nations, will come from you, and kings will descend from you" (Gen 35:11). Eventually, the Israelites filled Egypt (Exod 1:7,20). In Exodus 12:37 we read that their number expanded to six hundred thousand men, plus women and children!

"Redemption" is one of the greatest themes in Scripture. Later, we will see the meaning of this term more fully (*ga'al*, Exod 6:6; 15:13). As the Redeemer, God came to Israel's rescue, protected them, and restored them.

The Need for Redemption
EXODUS 1:8-22

In verses 8-22 we find four reasons Israel needed redemption.

Political Slavery (1:8-10)

In Egypt, the Israelites were immigrants. They came to Egypt as refugees. Things started out favorably, but as the text says, the new ruler in Egypt "had not known Joseph" (v. 8). Now the Israelites lived in fear because they were discriminated against. Pharaoh said, "Let us deal shrewdly with them" (v. 10). As a result of discrimination, God's people had no political freedom. Because of the rising Israelite population, they were perceived as a threat to Pharaoh, and this prompted his evil actions. Pharaoh's harsh treatment would soon come to an end, however, and God would eventually make Israel into a great nation.

Economic Slavery (1:11-14)

Pharaoh used Israel for slave labor. Notice the language: "heavy burdens" (v. 11 ESV), "oppressed" (v. 12), "worked the Israelites ruthlessly" (v. 13), "bitter with difficult labor," and "They ruthlessly imposed all this work on them" (v. 14). These phrases describe their enslavement. The Egyptians used the Israelites for construction projects (e.g., building Pithom and Raamses) and for agricultural projects. In comparison to the Nazi regime, we see that Pharaoh does not go as far as Hitler. Why? He knows that he needs them—but not all of them.

The injustice we read about here bears some resemblance to our day. People of power continue to abuse the weak for their own devilish reasons. Some report upwards of thirty million slaves in the world today (NotForSaleCampaign.org). Tragically, human trafficking is now the second largest organized crime in the world. What motivates this atrocity? Two of the main roots of this evil include sexual perversion and financial greed. Despite the existence of injustice like this, we believe that God remains a God of justice standing on the side of the oppressed. God's people should also aim to glorify Him by imitating His character. The Scriptures describe God and His justice in many ways:

> The mighty King loves justice. (Ps 99:4)

> The Lord executes acts of righteousness and justice for all the oppressed. (Ps 103:6)

> [He is] executing justice for the exploited
>   and giving food to the hungry.
> The Lord frees prisoners.
> The Lord opens the eyes of the blind.
> The Lord raises up those who are oppressed.
> The Lord loves the righteous.
> The Lord protects foreigners
>   and helps the fatherless and the widow,
>   but He frustrates the ways of the wicked. (Ps 146:7-9)

Later, God instructed His people to act for others the same way He acted on their behalf:

> He executes justice for the fatherless and the widow, and loves the foreigner, giving him food and clothing. You also must love the foreigner, since you were foreigners in the land of Egypt. (Deut 10:18-19)

Learn to do what is good. Seek justice. Correct the oppressor. Defend the rights of the fatherless. Plead the widow's cause. (Isa 1:17)

Isn't the fast I choose: To break the chains of wickedness, to untie the ropes of the yoke, to set the oppressed free, and to tear off every yoke? Is it not to share your bread with the hungry, to bring the poor and homeless into your house, to clothe the naked when you see him, and not to ignore your own flesh and blood? (Isa 58:6-7)

One of the roles of the Redeemer (*go'el*) in the Old Testament was to restore economic stability to a family member, and God acts in this way. God ultimately gave Israel a land for themselves (Exod 6:8).

Social Slavery (1:15-22)

As the story goes on, we see how the Egyptians acted brutally and violently against the Israelites. This began with Pharaoh's evil decision in verses 15-16. He initiated a state-sponsored genocide that demanded the killing of all the male Hebrew babies. This reminds us of the Deliverer who survived the ruthlessness of another dictator. Just as Moses lived in spite of the genocide, so Jesus lived through the baby-killing leadership of Herod (Matt 2:16).

Then Pharaoh told the midwives, or birthing nurses, Shiphrah and Puah, that when they saw a child on the "birthstool" (ESV) and it was a boy, to kill him. "Birthstool" is a difficult word to translate. Some say it means a "stone"—meaning they would give birth on a stone. Some say it means "a basin," where they would wash the baby off, implying that one would drown the baby. Another option is that the "stones" represent "what you look for to see if it is a boy" (Russ Moore, "Exit Strategy"). Whatever it means, the command is clear: kill the boys. But why did Pharaoh do this? It seems that he attempted to slow the growth of the Israelites and to make them fear him.

Now they lived in constant terror. Think about it. Nine months of dread. Remember, ultrasounds did not exist. On delivery day, the "It's a boy" report devastated parents.

However, God would deliver them out of this eventually. The final, most devastating act of judgment that God would inflict on Egypt was the death of firstborn sons (Exod 4:23). The Passover would forever remind God's people of God's redemption. And later, when Israel would become a new society, one of the things that they would emphasize was social justice and the sanctity of human life—the latter being something our culture still does not embrace.

After Pharaoh's decision, look at the two midwives' decision (1:17-22). These two women heroically did not listen to the king. Instead, they "feared God" (vv. 17,21). While they did fear the king, they feared the King even more! Pharaoh realized what they had done and called them in for questioning: "Why have you done this?" (v. 18). They told him the Hebrew women were "vigorous." Essentially, the Hebrew women gave birth before the midwives could even say, "Push!" They just kept having babies in the most remarkable way. Now, some argue that they lied, and God was not pleased with them. But did they lie? We do not have their entire statement recorded, but what we do have is factual: they said, "These women are vigorous." Even if they did not give complete testimony in Pharaoh's court, I think this is an example of "We must obey God rather than man" (Acts 5:29). The text is honoring these women, who lived up to their names (Shiphrah—"beautiful one," and Puah—"splendid one"). Pharaoh was overstepping his bounds.

Next observe God's decision regarding the midwives. We read in Exodus 1:20, "God was good to the midwives." To what extent did God deal well with the midwives? He blessed them with families (v. 21).

We should remember that these women did something for us. Because they rescued the babies, we will be raised from the dead! How so? If you do not have these women, you do not have Moses, the exodus, David, Mary, or Jesus. The women are so important that Moses even mentioned them by name, yet you do not see the name of Pharaoh anywhere in this text. ("Pharaoh" means "Great House," just as "White House" personifies the US president.) Pharaohs wanted their names remembered. They built pyramids to be remembered. Yet the only names remembered are those who feared God and protected life.

In hearing the midwives' response, Pharaoh became infuriated. He demanded that all boys born to Hebrew women were to be thrown into the river. He likely chose the river for two reasons. First, it was convenient. Everyone lived on the Nile, and the clean up would have been easy. The Nile was a source of water and a conveyance for sewage, for the mighty current took away waste. Second, the Nile was viewed as a god, so this shifted the blame. Egyptians viewed the Nile as a giver and taker of life; thus, they might have thought they were doing the will of the gods.

In seeing this, we should recognize a biblical pattern: God takes a place of death and turns it into a place of life and salvation. Think about Noah and the flood; Jonah and the sea/fish; the Red Sea and God's people; and how Jesus' tomb became the place of life. All of these stories point to God's divine power to take death and bring life.

Spiritual Slavery (1:8–2:25; 9:1)

Pharaoh appears in archaeological records with the snake on his crown. It makes us think of the promise in Genesis 3:15, where we read of the enmity between the triumphant seed of the woman over the opposing seed of the serpent. Pharaoh lived out the serpent role by killing boys. Egypt was the enemy of God, and God must deliver Israel so that "they may worship [Him]" (Exod 9:1). This story shows us a cosmic, spiritual battle, not just a battle between Moses and Pharaoh.

God's goal, then, included more than simply getting His people out of Egypt. He wanted to get Egypt out of His people. Luke underscored this truth in Acts 7:39. Stephen, in recounting the exodus and the events thereafter, said, "In their hearts [the Israelites] turned back to Egypt." Even after leaving Egypt, Israel faced the temptation of turning their backs on God. In Exodus 4:22-23 we read of this spiritual purpose: "Let My son go so that he may *worship* Me" (emphasis added). Pharaoh blocked this purpose by oppressing the Israelites. Despite Moses' repeated request for Pharaoh to allow Israel to make a journey into the wilderness "that we may sacrifice to [worship] the LORD our God" (3:18 ESV; 5:8), he denied it, and Israel's suffering continued.

God's desire extended beyond liberating Israel from political, economic, and social slavery. He desired worshipers. He wanted Israel (like Adam) to know and worship Him. Further, He wanted to use Israel to make worshipers from all nations. Therefore, God responded to all of the dimensions of Israel's slavery. He did not just free them from social-economic-political oppression and let them worship any god. Neither did He just free them spiritually without changing their awful situation.

God continues to be concerned for physical freedom, and especially spiritual freedom. Wright says, "Although Exodus stands as a unique and unrepeatable event in the history of Israel, it also stands as a paradigmatic and highly repeatable way God wishes to act in the world, and ultimately will act for the whole creation" (Wright, *Mission*, 275).

Some of us have not experienced the enslavement of these first three forms (political, social, and economical); but everyone understands this last form (spiritual slavery). We need spiritual deliverance. But some around the world, victims of human trafficking for example, are enslaved in all four ways. We must seek to deliver them in every way. One of the things I love about ministries like International Justice Mission is that they have related powerful stories of rescuing enslaved children physically and spiritually.

The Mediator and Redemption
EXODUS 2:1-22

In order to free people to worship Him, God raised up a mediator, a deliverer, a savior, named Moses. Let us take a look at Moses.

The Birth of a Moses (2:1-10)

Despite the circumstances, a Levite woman bore her son and kept him for three months. When it became too dangerous to hide him, she placed him in a basket and set him afloat in the Nile. The "basket" in this instance is the same word in Hebrew (*tebah*) used to describe Noah's ark (Gen 6–9), the only other place it is found in the Bible. The basket was probably a covered papyrus box, maybe with air holes. She for some reason put him in a little boat, like Noah, that was sealed with pitch. Every Hebrew would have caught the significance of this word. Just as God's hand of grace was on Noah, a deliverer, bringing salvation, so it was with the deliverer Moses.

Imagine this scene: Moses floats down the dangerous Nile! God sovereignly cares for this little boy. God keeps Moses from crocodiles, starvation, and drowning. When the daughter of Pharaoh finds him, she takes "pity on him." Perhaps she says something like "aww," the way others react when they see a little one. God used the nurturing instinct in her life to take care of Moses. And by God's grace, Moses was nourished and taught by an Israelite—his mother, it seems—as an infant (vv. 7-9). God raised up a deliverer, right under Pharaoh's nose!

This brings us to an important principle. We may think that things are falling apart sometimes, but remember God's mysterious providence. God works out His perfect will in amazing ways. Trust in Him.

The daughter of Pharaoh gave the child the name Moses, "to draw out," thinking "I drew him out of the water" (v. 10). What a perfect name, given the fact that God would use Moses to draw His people out of Egypt!

The Growth of Moses (2:11-15)

Notice the time that passes between verses 10 and 11. Moses grew up. A number of similarities exist between Moses and the greater Savior, Jesus. Let me point out a few:

- Like Moses, Jesus was born to be a Savior and was rescued from an evil ruler at birth (Matt 2:16).

- Like Moses, He sojourned in Egypt: "Out of Egypt I called my Son" (Matt 2:15).
- Like Moses, "silent years" occurred before His public ministry.
- Like Moses and the Israelites who wandered for 40 years in the wilderness, Jesus spent 40 days in the wilderness (Matt 4:1-11).
- Jesus went to a high mountain and gave "the law," His sermon (Matt 5–7), much like Moses did on Sinai.

Of course, Jesus transcends Moses. Jesus is without sin, and Jesus is fully God. Thus, it should not surprise us when we see Moses fail for all the mediators in the Old Testament failed at some level. But Jesus did not.

As the Story continues, we find that when Moses "had grown up," he witnessed the brutal assault on one of his people, the Hebrews. Luke told us that this was when Moses was 40 years old (Acts 7:23). Seeing this, "he struck the Egyptian dead" (Exod 2:12). While some may say that Moses had the right to kill him as a son of Pharaoh, his own conscience reveals to us that he knew it was wrong for before he acted, he looked around, and after he acted, he "hid [the Egyptian] in the sand." This act reveals that Moses still had a lot to learn before he would be ready to lead the Israelites out of Egypt.

It was not only wrong for Moses to kill the man, but it was wrong for him to attempt to begin leading the people out of Egypt without God's instruction. In Acts 7:25 Stephen tells us that Moses assumed that "his brothers would understand that God would give them deliverance through him, but they did not understand." This attempt led to the rejection of his leadership (Exod 2:13-14). Moses should have waited for God's instructions.

On a more positive note, Moses' act revealed that he desired to be associated with the people of God rather than the Egyptians. Hebrews 11:23-26 says this:

> By faith, after Moses was born, he was hidden by his parents for three months, because they saw that the child was beautiful, and they didn't fear the king's edict. By faith Moses, when he had grown up, refused to be called the son of Pharaoh's daughter and chose to suffer with the people of God rather than to enjoy the short-lived pleasure of sin. For he considered the reproach because of the Messiah to be greater wealth than the treasures of Egypt, since his attention was on the reward.

Ryken notes that the same word used to describe the exodus event is used here to tell of Moses' going "out to his own people" (v. 11).

Essentially, "before Israel could go out of Egypt, Moses needed to go out of Egypt, emotionally if not yet physically" (Ryken, *Exodus*, 60).

The Flight of Moses (2:15-22)

Moses became an outlaw on the run! As he fled, he ended up in Midian (v. 15). The Midianites' name came from the fourth son of Abraham by his second wife, Keturah (Gen 25:2). Some of the teachings of Abraham possibly continued with the Midianites. Josephus tells us that the Midianites lived around the Gulf of Aqabah, which is at the north end of the Red Sea, about 120 miles south-southwest of the Dead Sea in the wilderness.

While Moses was at a well in Midian, the daughters of the priest of Midian came to get water. During their visit, some shepherds came and "drove them away" (v. 17). Moses acted to combat this injustice. But this time he did not kill anyone. Instead, he acted only to drive them away—a contrast to the previous episode in Egypt. We begin to see Moses act as a righteous deliverer. He not only rescued them but also "watered their flock" (v. 17). Moses began displaying servant leadership. This act of service got him rewarded with not only bread but also with marriage! So Moses married Zipporah and had a son, Gershom.

The book of Acts explains that Moses spent 40 years in Midian. Someone said, "Moses was 40 years in Egypt learning something; 40 years in the desert learning to be nothing; and 40 years in the wilderness proving God to be everything" (in James Boyce, *Ordinary Men*, 59). Think about that. He spent two years of preparation for every one year of ministry. By living in the wilderness, he learned to rely on God. By having a family, he learned to lead, guide, and discipline those he loved. By working with the Midianites, most likely as a shepherd, he developed skills to help him lead the Israelites out of their enslavement.[1]

Of course, I do not want to imply that God selected Moses because he was so gifted and talented (see the next two chapters!). Moses depended on God's power and grace for victory. But these experiences in the wilderness did have a shaping effect on his life. Remember, God wastes nothing. He often prepares us for the next chapter of life with the present chapter's experiences.

---

[1] Ultimately, we understand that God led the flock: "You led Your people like a flock by the hand of Moses and Aaron" (Ps 77:20; cf. Ps 78:52).

God's Motive of Redemption
EXODUS 2:23-25

Verse 23 begins with an important fact: "the king of Egypt died." This meant Moses could return to Egypt as a prophet and not as a fugitive (see 4:19). Despite the change in government, the slavery remained severe. We read, "their cry for help ascended to God." Picture the intense grief, distress, and agony here in these cries (cf. Ps 130:1-2; Lam 2:18; Rom 8:26). The verbs in this section show us God's motive for acting on their behalf.

First, consider God's knowledge of the oppressed. When the people cried out, He *heard* their cry. Not only did He hear it, He also *saw* or looked at their oppression, and He *took notice*, meaning He knew or was concerned (vv. 24-25). God heard. God saw. God knew. God's ability to see and to hear appears throughout Scripture. Think of Psalm 34:15: "The eyes of the LORD are on the righteous, and His ears are open to their cry for help." God's exhaustive knowledge or omniscience also appears often in Scripture. When the Scripture says that God "knew," it means that He knew all about them. God was intimately aware of their agony. And because God knows, He acts.

Second, "He remembered His covenant with Abraham" (v. 24). God's covenantal memory gets underlined here. God remembers His unbreakable promise of salvation. To "remember" something means to bring it to the front burner and act on it. The term "covenant" appears for the first time in Exodus here. It appears 25 times in Genesis. The best definition of "covenant" may be in *The Jesus Story Book Bible*: "a never stopping, never giving up, unbreaking, always and forever love" (Sally Lloyd-Jones, *Story Book*, 36).

As mentioned above, Exodus and Genesis go together. In Genesis, God declared His intention to bless Israel and to fulfill His covenant to Abraham. Later in Exodus, Moses will appeal to God's covenant as he intercedes for Israel (chs. 32–34). At the right time, God remembered His covenant to make a people from all nations and sent Jesus. If you belong to God through Jesus Christ, you belong to His eternal covenant, "his never stopping, never giving up, unbreaking, always and forever love." These motives, as Wright suggests, perpetually motivate God throughout the Bible. God's purpose of redemption and mission given to Abraham continues in Exodus. This same God continues on the same mission of reclaiming worshipers today.

The Mission of the Redeemed

I believe Wright points us in the right direction for applying Exodus when he says, "*Exodus-shaped redemption demands exodus-shaped mission.* And that means that our commitment to mission must demonstrate the same broad totality of concern for human need that God demonstrated in what he did for Israel. . . . [O]ur mission must be derived from *God's mission*" (*Mission,* 275–76; emphasis in original). We mentioned under the first point that God would deliver His people from (1) social-political-economic slavery and (2) spiritual slavery. I contend that we too must share these same concerns. We must respond to urgent physical and spiritual needs around the world.

Let Us Care for Urgent Physical Needs

As we think about applying the mission in Exodus, allow me to draw on some of the insights of Wright again. One should avoid having spiritualized application *only* in Exodus, meaning *evangelism with no social action*—that is, so emphasizing the spiritual freedom in Exodus that we neglect real physical needs. We cannot allow ourselves to miss the social-political-economic dimension in Exodus. Do not forget, these were real people being enslaved by a real ruler, and they could not worship when they were lugging mud all day, seven days a week.

Today, millions of young girls are enslaved and are raped multiple times a day for profit to satisfy the cravings of wicked people. This reality is sickening and maddening, and it demands a response from God's people.

While *proclamation* remains the most important task of the church, this does not mean that kingdom citizens should neglect practical acts of mercy and justice. Plus, in some cases people cannot hear our message until they are liberated from physical injustice. Let me ask you, can girls who are being sexually abused multiple times a day hear the good news? Tragically, they cannot. Should we not fight to free them (and other victims of injustice) so that they may hear our message?

I believe the impulse that drives people to go to unreached peoples to share the gospel is the same impulse that calls them to care for victims of injustice: love. Justice is love going public. If we really love people, we will tell them the gospel while we care for their physical needs. Further, often the darkest places of injustice are the same places that have little gospel witness. If we lovingly go to the dark places, we will have opportunity to bring freedom—both physical and spiritual freedom.

Five issues help us remember to keep an emphasis on justice and mercy ministry here in Exodus.

First, Israel needed freedom not because of "their sin" but because of "Egypt's sin." To be clear, Israel was sinful—dreadfully sinful. But the exodus and the later exile of Israel have differences. God sent Israel into exile in Babylon because of their sin. "But there is no hint whatsoever that Israel's suffering in Egypt was God's judgment on sin" (Wright, *Mission*, 278). In Exodus an outside force oppressed them. Therefore, being delivered out of slavery to our sin is not exactly the same thing as Israel getting delivered from their slavery. We should make this application, but it is not the only application for us to make. The exodus shows God's victory over outside powers of injustice, violence, and death. We cannot miss this.

Second, the New Testament does not replace the physical aspects of the exodus with the spiritual aspects of it. It *extends* the physical aspects and the spiritual aspects. The Greatest Command and the Great Commission encompasses both emphases—word and deed ministry.

Third, God has not changed. We should not make the mistake of thinking that God was concerned about real injustice then, but not now. Think of how many laws were given related to justice and how many Psalms speak of it. Remember that in His teaching, Jesus railed on the Pharisees who had their religious sacrifices but denied the "more important matters" of mercy and justice (Matt 23:23; cf. Matt 25:35-36; Jas 1:27). Further, the love and justice of God were on full display at the cross (Rom 3:21-26). The justice of God will also be magnified in the end of all things (Rev 20:11-15). God is just, and His people are to imitate Him.

Fourth, it is wrong to think that what God did for Israel is not what God wants or will do for other people. To think, "Yeah, God freed Israel from oppression, but that was Israel," is to miss God's purpose for choosing Israel in the first place: to be a blessing to the nations. And He chose them and acted on behalf of them *so that people might know what He is like.* While God did not free everyone in the Near East, this does not mean that He did not know about them or that He was not concerned about oppression elsewhere. God always opposes violent oppressors. For us, Israel stands as a model as to how God works in the world.

Further, the Old Testament shows that God acts for those who cry out under oppression. Psalm 33 goes from the "exodus" character of God to the universal claim of His love (v. 5) and on to the fact that all of human life is under His gaze (vv. 13-15). Psalm 145 says something similar: "His compassion rests on all He has made" (v. 9). Amazingly, in

Isaiah 19 even Egypt itself is scheduled for a redemptive blessing: "When they cry out to the LORD because of their oppressors, He will send them a savior and leader, and he will rescue them. . . . Egypt will know the LORD on that day. . . . He will hear their prayers and heal them" (Isa 19:20-22). So Israel stands distinct, but God's liberation of Israel is not limited to them. Instead, Israel serves as an example of God's mercy and justice for all to see.

A final reason we should not miss the call to social action is that the midwives are honored for their act. They serve as examples for us to follow in protecting the weak and vulnerable. We need an army of people like these ladies to care for orphans, widows, the unborn, and victims of injustice.

Let Us Care for Urgent Spiritual Needs

The second mistake to avoid in applying Exodus is the view that is limited to the social-political-economic situation *only*, meaning *social action with no evangelism*—that is, being so focused on these social dimensions that the spiritual dimension gets lost. Some forms of liberation theology take this view. They are solely devoted to the issue of freeing those in oppression.[2]

This socialized approach is the opposite problem of the spiritualized approach. The socialized approach ignores the spiritual purpose of Exodus and disregards the New Testament connection of the exodus to the cross and the saving work of Jesus.

Remember, God wanted to free Israel that they might worship Him! As a royal priesthood, they were formed, like Adam (the garden priest), to worship God. A spiritual freedom was at the heart of their physical release. Israel's deepest problem involved "Egypt inside of them"—a persistent tendency to return to their previous wretched condition. After Israel went free, they fell into sin in their hearts— idolatry—and got sent into exile. So, we should want to free people from physical oppression, but ultimately we should work to free them spiritually.

Therefore, we need *an integrative model of mission.* That is, a balanced, fully biblical, missional model. The integrative model takes into account the same broad totality of concern that God has for people. Let us do *evangelism* to see people saved from bondage to sin and death.

---

[2] Many times, it is debatable whether what they call oppression is really oppression.

Let us also *care for the oppressed* by fighting for justice for the physically enslaved and showing mercy to those in need.

To summarize, you could say that Christians should care about alleviating both types of human suffering: temporal suffering and eternal suffering—and especially eternal suffering!

Welcome to Exodus. May God help us to understand our redemption better, and may He help us to understand our mission better.

Reflect and Discuss

1. What are some examples of economic slavery today that are comparable to Pharaoh's exploitation of Israel? What can a Christian do about these things?
2. What are ways that fear is used in some cultures to control populations? How does the gospel address fear?
3. How does this account of God's providence in protecting baby Moses encourage you?
4. How has Moses' experience growing up as a Hebrew in Pharaoh's palace been portrayed in the movies? What do you think it might have been like?
5. Why did Moses' first attempt to help the Hebrews fail? What were the practical, social, and spiritual reasons?
6. How has God prepared you for ministry? Have you learned your most valuable lessons in a "palace" or a "desert" or a "wilderness"?
7. In what way is God's gracious mission in Jesus Christ also seen in the book of Exodus?
8. Of the ministries you support, which ones focus on social action and which ones on spiritual action? Does each ministry have the proper balance?
9. What did Jesus say and do about social, political, and economic oppression in His day?
10. Why is the social mission sometimes a necessary precondition to the spiritual mission? How does Matthew 11:5 express an integrative model of missions?

I AM Has Sent Me

EXODUS 3–4

Main Idea: Because of who God is, He graciously uses imperfect people to accomplish His perfect will.

I. **Moses' Call and Commission (3:1-10)**
    A. God reveals Himself (3:1-6).
    B. God reveals His plan (3:7-10).
II. **Moses' Excuses and God's Responses (3:11–4:17)**
    A. Lack of credentials (3:11-12)
    B. Lack of content (3:13-22)
    C. Lack of converts (4:1-9)
    D. Lack of communication skills (4:10-12)
    E. Lack of commitment (4:13-17)
III. **Moses' Journey and God's Faithfulness (4:18-31)**

If you could change one thing about yourself, what would it be? Intelligence? Height? Better hair? My one-of-a-kind friend, Benjie, posed this question to a congregation. During his message on Exodus 3–4, he said with his unforgettable, high-pitched, North Georgian accent, "I'd change the way I talk. I hate the way I talk." He then proceeded to describe how people poke fun at him about his accent. He used this example to connect us to this passage.

Exodus 3–4 shows us, among other things, how God can use weak, imperfect vessels by His power, for His glory, and for the good of others. It shows us how "God can hit a straight lick with a crooked stick." Remember what Paul says: "[God] is able to do above and beyond all that we ask or think according to the power that works in us" (Eph 3:20). As we will see, Moses will show himself to be a living example of this verse.

We last left the story with Israel crying out with groans to God because of their slavery. Here we will examine the calling and commissioning of Israel's mediator-leader, an imperfect man, Moses.

Moses' Call and Commission
EXODUS 3:1-10

God Reveals Himself (3:1-6)

Chapter 3 begins by setting the scene of what is about to occur. Moses was leading the flock belonging to Jethro. This seems to be the same individual named as "Reuel" in 2:18. It was not uncommon to have two names in this time period, but some think Reuel was Jethro's father. "Jethro" means "his excellency," so it could have been a title of some sort. Notice: they were at Horeb, which is called "the mountain of God." This is a natural name for the mountain because of what happened there: God showed up. It seems to be the same place as Mt. Sinai, where Moses later received the Ten Commandments. God drew Moses to this place in order to reveal Himself to him.

Moses was "shepherding the flock" (v. 1). It is important to note that Egyptians did not think highly at all of shepherds (see Gen 46:34). It is also important to recognize the shepherding pattern being set here. Moses spent 40 years as a shepherd in Midian. David was also a shepherd who was taken from the sheepfolds to become king. God loves to use shepherds! He even refers to Himself as a shepherd (Ps 23:1; Ezek 34:13). Ultimately, salvation would come through Jesus, the good shepherd, who laid down His life for His sheep (John 10:11).

In verses 2-4 we find a unique encounter with the "Angel of the LORD." This was not a fluffy little angel in a golden diaper. He appeared out of the fire. He is also referred to as "the LORD" in verse 4. The messenger spoke *as God* not simply *for God*. This is what theologians call a "theophany," an appearance of the invisible God. Many throughout church history, especially the early church fathers, believed appearances like this were pre-incarnate appearances of Christ.

Moses was first drawn in by the burning bush. What an amazing sight! Before Moses' eyes, he saw a bush burning without being consumed. The "fire" is representative of God's holy presence. Fire appears later in Exodus and in other Scripture—in a pillar of fire that leads God's people, fire at Mt. Sinai, in the tabernacle, and the Day of Pentecost. When God forbade idolatry later in Deuteronomy, Moses said, "For the Lord your God is a consuming fire, a jealous God" (Deut 4:24). The author of Hebrews used this language also in describing how to worship (Heb 12:29). Fire is appropriate because we know that we are drawn to fire and amazed by fire, but we also tell children, "Don't play with fire." Fire is to be taken seriously. And so is God. He is holy.

Now we must ask, "How might we be accepted by God if He is so holy?" The sacrifices in the Old Testament are pointing to the ultimate sacrifice, Jesus. Only in Jesus can we be in God's presence. He is our "righteousness, sanctification, and redemption" (1 Cor 1:30). "He chose us in Him, before the foundation of the world, to be holy and blameless in His sight" (Eph 1:4).

The bush "was not consumed" (v. 2). Moses was seeing something mysterious. While it burned, it was not consumed. This is a picture of the never-ending power of God, the One who upholds the universe. God never runs out of fuel!

Then "God called out to him from the bush, 'Moses, Moses!'" (3:4). God called Moses by name. This is significant for all who are called to salvation have experienced God's personal summons. Jesus said, "Zacchaeus." Peter said that God "called [us] out of darkness into His marvelous light" (1 Pet 2:9). God did not have to call us, but He did, in His mercy. God wills to be known and worshiped. Our natural response should be, "Here I am," like Moses (and Samuel and Isaiah).

As Moses began to approach the bush, God said, "Do not come closer. . . . Remove the sandals from your feet" (v. 5). To show the gap between a holy God and sinful man, He says, "Do not come closer." Again, it is only through Jesus that we draw near (Heb 10:19-22).

As an act of respect and reverence, which is still practiced in many settings today, Moses took his shoes off. In the book of Joshua, a similar experience happened to Moses' follower, and he is told the same thing (Josh 5:13-15). God then identified Himself with the patriarchs: "I am . . . the God of Abraham" (v. 6). Before He entered a relationship with Moses, He entered a relationship with them. God was alluding to His covenant relationship that we spoke of earlier (2:24). God was also giving Moses a bit of personal history of Himself. The God of the burning bush was not an unknown God; He was the God who acted on behalf of these earlier persons. Notice that He does not say "I *was* the God" but "I *am* the God." This indicates that God's people never really die; they are part of an eternal relationship with God. When Jesus was proving the resurrection to the Sadducees, He quoted this verse. He said, "Haven't you read . . . in the passage about the burning bush? . . . He is not God of the dead, but of the living" (Mark 12:26-27).

So they exchanged names. That is the first step in forming a relationship. They met each other. Have you met Jesus Christ? Paul says we Christians have come to know God, or rather to be known by God (Gal 4:9). When Moses encountered God, the Scripture says he "hid his face" (v. 6). He was in the presence of the Holy One. It was an awesome scene. Now, as believers through Christ, we do not have to hide our face, for we are hidden with Jesus the Messiah (Col 3:3).

God Reveals His Plan (3:7-10)

God is a sending God. Notice three parts to this commission: (1) God's motive, (2) God's purpose, and (3) God's plan. *God's motive* is especially seen in verses 7 and 9. "I have observed . . . have heard . . . I know about their sufferings. . . . The Israelites' cry . . . has come to Me. . . . I have also seen the way the Egyptians are oppressing them." Previously, we mentioned how God was moved by an intimate knowledge of the slavery of His people (2:23-25). It appears again here. God hears the groans of people who genuinely cry out to Him. In Luke 18, the tax collector beat his breast and cried out, "Turn Your wrath from me—a sinner!" (v. 13). Jesus said that the man "went down to his house justified" (Luke 18:14).

Many of us are turned off by what people refer to as "the sinner's prayer." We are turned off by it because it seems that some people use it like a "hocus pocus" sort of thing. It seems that people think if you say the magic words then you can be saved. Russ Moore told about a guy who tricked a man into reading the prayer on a tract by claiming that his eyesight was too bad to read it! The guy went on to read the copyright date and everything. Then the witness pronounced the man a Christian (Moore, "Exit Strategy"). That is crazy. That is not what a real sinner's prayer that God hears is all about. A prayer that God hears is when a person genuinely cries out to God for mercy and forgiveness in repentance and faith. If you will cry out to Him, He will hear you and save you. It is not about a magical formula. It is about crying out over the misery of your sin and begging Jesus for mercy.

Notice also *God's purpose*. His purpose is to transfer His people. He will take them out of Egypt and put them in a place with milk and honey (3:8). It is a land occupied by other nations, and they will have to conquer them later. God is going to save them from something (slavery) for something (worship and witness). That is exactly what has happened to us in the gospel.

Finally, see *God's plan*. After revealing His great purpose of redemption, God told Moses the plan: "You're it." God says, "I am sending you"

(v. 10). God is a sending God. Throughout the Bible, God sends people on different assignments covering a variety of issues. Joseph was sent to save lives in a famine (Gen 45:5-8). Here Moses was sent to deliver people from oppression and exploitation (3:10). Elijah was sent to influence the course of international politics (1 Kgs 19:15-18). Jeremiah was sent to proclaim God's word (Jer 1:7). Jesus said that He was sent "to proclaim freedom to the captives and recovery of sight to the blind, to set free the oppressed, to proclaim the year of the Lord's favor" (Luke 4:18-19). The disciples were sent to preach and demonstrate the power of the kingdom (Matt 10:5-8). Paul and Barnabas were sent for famine relief (Acts 11:27-30), then they were sent for evangelism and church planting (Acts 13:1-3). Titus was sent to put a messed up church in order (Titus 1:5). God is a sending God, and there are a number of holy missional efforts in which one may be involved: church planting, justice, church revitalization, and caring for the hungry. Do you have a holy ambition?

Moses' Excuses and God's Responses
EXODUS 3:11–4:17

Moses makes five excuses for not obeying God's mission. These stand out by the words "but" and "if" (3:11,13; 4:1,10). This section shows that God is enough. Moses was insufficient but God is self-sufficient. God responded to each of Moses' excuses and questions with statements about His own sovereignty and power. This section is so deeply encouraging. If you feel as though God is sending you to do something beyond yourself, the key is to take your eyes off of your failures and weaknesses. Get a vision of God.

Lack of Credentials (3:11-12)

Moses' first argument was about himself. "Who am I?" probably implies that he did not have the ability to perform such a task. He asked, "Have you considered my resume? The last 40 years, I've been in a wilderness." Think about it. While he used to be a prince, he is a lowly shepherd now. He is now asked to go to the most powerful person in the world and tell him to let his slaves go free. This would be sort of like a car mechanic declaring war on Canada! Imagine a guy in coveralls carrying a wrench going up to the president and saying, "Let everyone go."

Not only did Moses not have the ability, but he really did not have the reputation either. He was not well thought of by the Israelites. His first task would be to talk to the elders, but he doubted they would listen to him.

In response, God started with promises: "I will certainly be with you." Throughout the Bible this is what God's leaders have needed. It is the non-negotiable for serving God. Think about Joseph, Moses, Joshua, Gideon, Jehoshaphat, and the disciples (Matt 28:18-20). God was with them all. Then God promised a sign saying, "you will all worship God at this mountain." God intended to bring His people back to this mountain to sing His praises.

Lack of Content (3:13-22)

Moses' next big question was "what shall I say?" Moses asked, "What is [Your] name?" (v. 13). It was obviously important to know who God is, especially if you are going to tell a group of people that God sent you. Obviously only saying "I heard a voice in a bush" would not be sufficient. Moses wanted to go with God's authority. What a response God gave him! Let us break verses 13-22 down into two parts.

First, God told Moses to tell them His name (vv. 14-15). God revealed His name "Yahweh" in verse 15 (corresponding to the four Hebrew consonants *YHWH*, translated "LORD" in most English Bibles). It is connected with the verb *hayah*, "to be," mentioned three times in verse 14, which is rendered "I AM" in English.

Great mystery exists here. No one knows for certain how to pronounce *YHWH*, and the meaning is mysterious also, but the meaning seems to be related to the idea of this verb "to be." God *is*. He is central. He has no beginning. He causes everything to be. He is God. Does it move you when you hear, "Tell them I AM sent you"? God is saying that He is absolutely central. "For from Him and through Him and to Him are all things" (Rom 11:36). Is He central in your life? Is He central in your marriage? Is He central in your ministry? God tells Moses that the most important thing about his mission is God Himself!

Behold, the greatness of your God! God is saying that He is self-existent. As Tozer says, "[God] needs no one, but when faith is present he works through anyone" (Tozer, *Knowledge*, 36). God is self-existent and self-sufficient. He needs no air, no sleep, and no food. He does not need us, but we need Him! God is not like the Egyptian false gods. He was and is the one true God on whom all things depend.

God is majestic in mysteriousness. We will never have Him totally figured out. God is not a book you read and then put on your shelf.

God is not a class you take. God is eternal and unchangeable. He says, "I AM." He is the same yesterday, today, and forever. He is not getting better or worse. He is infinitely perfect.

Jesus Christ referred to Himself as "I am." When He was trying to convince the religious leaders that He was the Savior, He said, "Before Abraham was, I am" (John 8:58; cf. other "I am" statements). Then they wanted to stone Him. Do you believe that Jesus Christ is the God of Moses? Jesus Himself said, "If you do not believe that I am He, you will die in your sins" (John 8:24). He is not merely a teacher or moral example, but God. The Bible presents Him as Thomas confesses Him to be: Lord and God (John 20:28).

Second, God also instructed Moses to tell them His word (vv. 16-22). God told Moses that he was to go to the elders and report what God had told him. Moses was learning what it means to be a prophet: to declare what God has said. Notice how God told him that the elders "will listen to what you say" (v. 18). This is not the last time God would promise Moses that people would respond to his message. I know in our day you hear people talking like Christianity will collapse. No, God has a people. Some will respond. Paul says, "God's solid foundation stands firm" (2 Tim 2:19).

God assured Moses that the elders would listen. The "elders" were those entrusted with leadership of the community. They played an important role in the life of Israel throughout Exodus (e.g., chs. 18; 24). In much the same way, the New Testament teaches a plurality of elders who shepherd God's flock (Acts 20:17-35; 5:17; 1 Pet 5:1-5; Titus 1:5-9).

Notice also that they were going to say, "Let us go on a three-day trip into the wilderness so that we may sacrifice to Yahweh our God" (3:18). Again, you see how God's people were enslaved spiritually and wanted to be freed to worship (7:16; 8:1,20; 9:1,13; 10:3). It is unclear why they only asked for three days. It may be an ancient Near East expression to mean a long journey of an indefinite period of time. What is important about the trip is the purpose: worship. Even though the elders would listen, God reminded Moses that Pharaoh would not—at least, not initially. God told Moses that in response to Pharaoh's refusal, He would have to intervene with His "strong hand" performing wonders (3:19-20).

After God performed these wonders, the Egyptians would allow the Israelites to plunder them (vv. 21-22). What is going on here? God said, "Before you go out of Egypt, I want you to take the women shopping!" God was setting another pattern: the idea of conquering and taking the spoils. Paul later said that after Jesus Christ conquered our greatest enemies of sin and death, "He took prisoners into captivity; He gave gifts to people" (Eph 4:8). What is amazing is that the Israelites are simply told to ask for it. God is fighting the battle for them, which is another pattern. Also noteworthy is that these precious metals will be used to construct the tabernacle (Exod 35:4-9,20-29).

So, what do we tell people as God's missionaries? We tell them who God is, and we tell them what God has said. This includes what He has done in the past, what He is doing in the present, and what He will do in the future.

Lack of Converts (4:1-9)

Even though God just told Moses that the elders *will* believe him, Moses lacked trust and confidence. Moses asked, "What if they won't believe me?" (v. 1). Moses was struggling to understand that God makes converts. His responsibility was to trust God and deliver the message.

In 4:2-9, God responded in His grace by providing Moses with three signs of God's power: over creation, over people, and over elements in nature. Moses would take his staff and throw it to the ground. When he did so, it would become a serpent, and when he picked it up, it would return to being a staff. Why did God accommodate Moses in this way? "[S]o they will believe that Yahweh, the God of their fathers, the God of Abraham, the God of Isaac, and the God of Jacob, has appeared to you" (v. 5).

We might be able to discern a few lessons from this scene. First, notice God's *authority*. He told him to "grab it by the tail." You do not pick snakes up by the tail (or at least I do not!). Many believe that the snake was a cobra. While this is uncertain, we know that as a general rule, you do not mess with snakes. The vicious cobra represented the national god in lower Egypt. I think what God was showing Moses here was God's great authority over evil, and indeed, over the evil one. At the cross, Jesus crushed Satan's head. And throughout the Bible there is a running rivalry between God's people and the enemy. What symbol was on Pharaoh's head? A snake. All over Egypt, there were pictures of cobras—on walls, helmets, and monuments. Moses was learning something about divine authority here.

We can also learn a lesson of *humility*. Moses learned about the nature of his leadership with this staff. Moses did not have a scepter. He had a staff. That is leadership in the kingdom of God. He has authority over the evil one, but He does not rule like a dictator, but as One who sacrifices for His people, like a shepherd.

Notice also that the staff served as a sign of *God's presence*. This staff would also go on to be a visible sign that God was with Moses.

Not only would Moses use the staff, but he would also put his own hand in his cloak. When he pulled it out, it would be covered in leprosy; then, when he put it back in and pulled it out again, it would be healed—this was the second sign (vv. 6-7). It was a sign of God's power over sickness and death of people.

The third sign was this: Moses would take water from the Nile and pour it on the ground. When he did, it would become blood on the dry ground (v. 9). This sign was a pointer to the plagues to come.

What sign do we have? Our sign is an empty tomb! (Matt 12:39-40). The empty tomb is the sign that Christianity is true, and so is God's Word. Our God is not dead; He is alive!

Lack of Communication Skills (4:10-12)

This excuse was about Moses' inability to speak well (v. 10). What exactly was Moses' speaking problem? We do not know. People speculate it could have been *psychological*. Maybe Moses was shy and scared to death to speak in public, like some of my students in "Sermon Delivery" class (or as John Piper used to be in college). A student once told me that he was excited but "scared to death." He asked, "Can I go first?" Whenever someone delivers their first sermon, they often say something like "I am a nervous wreck." That is good in a sense. Our fear should not paralyze us, but we should feel desperate for God's help. Our confidence should not be in ourselves; it must be in God (2 Cor 3:5).

Others speculate that it was an *educational* issue. Maybe Moses failed rhetoric! Perhaps he thought he was not smart enough to persuade the ruler. Maybe he thought he was *too old*. Or it could be the flip side for some of you, like Jeremiah, who thought he was too young. Others have speculated with other possibilities. Maybe there was a *vocal* problem— he had a speech impediment of some type. Others claim it was a *verbal* problem. Perhaps he was referring to the language of Egypt that he lost after being in the wilderness for 40 years. Finally, some say that it might have been *exaggerated humility*. Is he saying something like Paul: "I am the worst of [sinners]" (1 Tim 1:15), or I am "the least of all the saints" (Eph 3:8). There probably was an element of this in Moses.

What is clear is that Moses did not think of himself as the best of orators. He felt insufficient to perform such a task by himself. The Corinthians did not think Paul was much of a speaker either (2 Cor 10:10; 11:6), yet he was the most effective preacher-missionary in history! How? He said,

> *When I came to you, brothers, announcing the testimony of God to you, I did not come with brilliance of speech or wisdom. For I didn't think it was a good idea to know anything among you except Jesus Christ and Him crucified. I came to you in weakness, in fear, and in much trembling. My speech and my proclamation were not with persuasive words of wisdom but with a powerful demonstration by the Spirit, so that your faith might not be based on men's wisdom but on God's power.* (1 Cor 2:1-5)

Paul said that he came in weakness, depending on God's power. Moses had to learn to do the same—and so do we.

In response, God basically told Moses two things: "That is irreverent" and "That is irrelevant." Concerning irreverence, God said, "Who made the human mouth?" (Exod 4:11). God was telling Moses that He formed him for a purpose. God is saying, "Do you think I do not know about your perceived weaknesses? It is precisely because of those weaknesses that I want to use you so that I may get the glory."

Then God addressed the irrelevance of the objection. God said, "I will help you speak and I will teach you what to say" (v. 12, cf. Jer 1:4-10). God is looking for reporters, not orators. We do not have to make fine speeches; we just give the news.

Moses' problem was that he was thinking too much about himself. Notice "I," "I," "I." God was saying, "It is not about you!" It is about I AM. It is about making God's word known. We should seek to glorify God with our abilities as well as with our disabilities. This reminds me of the last stanza of Cowper's *There Is a Fountain* (emphasis added):

E'er since by faith I saw the stream
Your flowing wounds supply,
Redeeming love has been my theme,
And shall be till I die.

Then in a nobler, sweeter song
I'll sing your pow'r to save,
When this poor, lisping, stamm'ring tongue
Lies silent in the grave.

Moses was to use his "poor, stamm'ring tongue" and declare God's word as a faithful prophet.

Lack of Commitment (4:13-17)

This final excuse was not so much an excuse as it was Moses' desperate plea to pass the responsibility to someone else. He was out of excuses. Every one of his questions had been answered in stunning ways. Now he basically said, "Here I am, send someone else."

God responded with anger (v. 14a), but He was gracious here as well. He gave Moses some help by sending Aaron (vv. 14b-16). God said, "He will be your spokesman." They were cospeakers, so to speak. Aaron was an encourager as well. Moses eventually did the vast majority of the speaking. And then God reminded Moses about the signs He would perform to validate the message (v. 17).

Moses' Journey and God's Faithfulness
EXODUS 4:18-31

Before Moses left for Egypt, he asked Jethro to let him go see if his people the Hebrews were still alive. Why he did not mention his commissioning from God is unclear. After receiving Jethro's blessing, he took his wife and his sons. He also took the staff of God with him to Egypt, signifying God's presence.

In verse 21 we see an important phrase that will be mentioned in coming chapters: "I will harden [Pharaoh's] heart so that he will not let the people go" (4:21; 7:13,22; 8:15,32; 9:12,35; 10:1; 14:8). There is so much that can be said that we will address later with this idea. For now, just notice that God, in hardening Pharaoh's heart, is able to fully showcase His power over the enemies of His people.

After God told Moses this, He instructed him to explain the sonship of Israel to Pharaoh (vv. 22-23). God wanted to free His son to worship Him. In fact, the firstborn is a theme that runs throughout the Scripture, from Adam to Abraham to David to Jesus to all the saints (Ps 89:26-27; Jer 31:9; Rom 8:29; Col 1:15,18; Heb 1:6; 12:23; Rev 1:5). Of course, this appeal insulted Pharaoh. He believed that he alone was the "son of the gods." Yet God told Moses that He would kill Pharaoh's firstborn son if he did not let His firstborn son go (Exod 4:23).

As the story continues, we encounter some of the strangest verses in the Old Testament in verses 24-26. Out of nowhere, it seems, God "sought to put [Moses] to death" (v. 24)! It is apparently because his firstborn son was not circumcised (v. 24). Moses was to keep the requirement given to Abraham, namely circumcising his sons (Genesis 17). God was remembering His covenant and the sign of His covenant. Zipporah seems to have acted faithfully, overcoming her headstrong husband, and Moses' life was saved by her act. She did the circumcision instead of Moses here (Exod 4:25). She was showing him that we are only right with God through blood and His covenant promises. Apart from the shedding of blood, Moses was no different from the Egyptians. (For a variety of interpretations on this passage, see Stuart, *Exodus*.) Likewise, as Christians we know that apart from blood and a new heart (circumcision of the heart), we are no different from unbelievers.

As the journey to Egypt continued, Aaron was now sent (v. 27). He was told to meet Moses, and he obeyed God's call. Aaron and Moses went before the elders of Israel and told them of what God had done in their lives, thus fulfilling what the Lord had commanded them. And just as God promised, the elders believed (vv. 29-31). God was faithful. Moses worried about this meeting, but it proved an easy win since it was God's plan.

The chapter ends with a doxology. Even before their freedom, they knew that God was worthy of worship and exaltation. They worshiped God because He "paid attention to" the people of Israel in their misery (4:31; cf. 3:16). What an awesome word in the Bible of redemption: "pay attention" (KJV says "visit"). In the Greek version of the Old Testament this is the word from which we get the idea of a "bishop" or "pastor." It is the same word that is used in James 1:27, which tells us to "look after orphans and widows in their distress." It means to get involved, to shepherd. Throughout redemptive history, God is the God who pays attention to His people; He looks after His people; He gets involved in the situation and rescues them (see Gen 21:1; 50:24; Ruth 1:6; Matt 25:36; Luke 1:68; 7:16). God's gracious attention should lead to God-glorifying exaltation. Praise God, for He has paid attention to us in our affliction.

He has come to us in our slavery and freed us, through Christ. And now, as His people, we are called to pay attention to those in affliction—those with physical and spiritual needs. Do you know this God? This God has come to us in Jesus, the One who said, "I am the door. I am the vine. I am the way, the truth, the life. I am the light of the world. I am the resurrection and the life." Do you know Jesus Christ?

Not only must we know God through Christ, but we must also elevate our view of God. You will not attempt great things for God if you do not have a great vision of God. From these chapters we see that He is holy, self-sufficient, eternal, mysterious, glorious, and gracious.

In knowing God and elevating your view of God, realize that God accomplishes His purpose through weak vessels. Because of this, you can stop making excuses and start trusting His promises. This is one of most encouraging passages in Scripture. Look at who God uses! He can use you as well.

Reflect and Discuss

1. If you could change one thing about yourself, what would it be? How could God accomplish His plan through you without changing anything?
2. Why did God use a lot of shepherds? What are the skills and virtues of a competent shepherd that are also valuable in a leader of persons?
3. How is it possible to say the words of "the sinners prayer" without being saved? What is the difference between speaking magic words and genuine repentance?
4. Think of people you know whom God has sent on various assignments. What were their assignments? Which of your skills might God be able to use?
5. Moses asked, "Who am I?" God replied, "I will certainly be with you" (3:11-12). How does this exchange encourage you to tackle any task God gives you?
6. What does "I AM" express about the nature of God? How is that encouraging to those He sends on mission?
7. What was the ultimate purpose of God delivering Israel from slavery (3:12,18)? What is the ultimate purpose of our salvation? What results are secondary?
8. Moses was given three tangible signs of God's power; we have the historical sign of the empty tomb. What is the advantage of a tangible sign? How is the empty tomb even better?
9. Name some ways that a lack of talent in speaking can actually be an asset in ministry.
10. In what sense was the nation of Israel God's firstborn son? In what sense are Christians firstborn sons of God? In what sense is Jesus the firstborn Son of God?

Fighting Discouragement with Gospel Promises

EXODUS 5:1–7:5

Main Idea: When obedience results in suffering, we can be encouraged by reminding ourselves of the gospel promises of our sovereign God.

I. **Discouragement (5:1-22)**
   A. Moses speaks to pharaoh (5:1-3).
   B. The king refuses to listen (5:4-9).
   C. An awful situation: bricks without straw (5:10-14)
   D. You have made us stink (5:15-21).
   E. Moses cries out (5:22).

II. **Gospel Promises (6:1–7:5)**
   A. God is in control (6:1).
   B. God keeps His covenant (6:2-5).
   C. God saves (6:6–7:5).
   D. Acting on the promises

So far we have seen Moses go from royalty in Egypt to humble shepherd in the wilderness. Then he met the great I AM. This holy, eternal, self-sufficient God—the God of Abraham, Isaac, and Jacob—commissioned Moses to go to Pharaoh and bring out the children of Israel from Egypt. Moses made a series of excuses for not following God's plan. He asked, *Who am I?* and *What shall I say?* and *What if they will not believe me?* After God answered each of these questions magnificently, Moses had two "Oh Lord!" moments. He said, "Please, Lord, I have never been eloquent" (4:10), and "Please, Lord, send someone else" (4:13). It is only after God gave Moses his companion, Aaron, as a cospeaker, that they returned to Egypt. Upon their return, they spoke to the elders, and the elders believed, just as God said they would.

Now in chapters 5–6, they approach Pharaoh to fulfill their mission. What follows is a very important pattern for all who attempt to obey God. *Obedience to God's call does not mean everything will be easy.* It may mean hardship, suffering, and persecution. There may even be times you say, "Why, Lord?" When Moses met with Pharaoh and had no success, he asked, "O Lord, why have You caused trouble for this people?

And why did You ever send me?" (5:22). When Moses followed God, things actually seemed to get worse!

Have you ever suffered hardship *even though* you are obeying God? Maybe you are a young Christian kid in high school who is seeking to follow Jesus. Is it easy? Have some of your peers tempted you to follow their sinful lifestyles? Have they labeled you a "holy roller" or a "geek" or just a "weird kid?" When you follow God's Word, do others mock you? That is a tough place to be.

Maybe you are a single lady who desires to be married, but you have certain standards for a husband based on Scripture. Have others ever tried to get you to lower your standards and go out with some guy who is wealthy and/or attractive, even though he is not committed to following Jesus? Obeying Jesus in your singleness is difficult.

Have you ever been an employee that has known about someone breaking a company policy or even the law? Did you report this? If so, when you did the right thing, did people think better or worse of you? They might have labeled you a troublemaker.

I know of adoptive couples that have experienced waves of trouble after adopting children. Some are now dealing with behavioral issues, attachment issues, academic issues, and many other challenges. I know of a few couples that experienced great financial trouble postadoption because the father has lost his job. These couples pursued God's will, did what they thought was right, yet they are facing hardship.

Recently, I heard of a young kid playing baseball who had an accident. Those present thought that he broke his arm, but they later discovered that he actually had a tumor. Before this tragic discovery, several of his family members had become Christians. The joy in this family over these conversions quickly turned to grief.

I know of many pastors who followed God's call to pastor a particular church but have met great opposition since arriving. Some pastors have preached the Bible faithfully but have seen little response and no growth. "Why did You ever send me, Lord?" might enter the mind of such pastors.

What about this example: You and your family leave your life behind in the States and head for the mission field. When you get there, your wife contracts a rare disease. Maybe you would wonder, "Why Lord? Didn't You send us here?"

Obeying God is not a pain-free life. It does not mean you will be popular. It does not mean you will be immune from awful problems in a fallen world, like cancer. It does not mean you will not encounter serious spiritual warfare and times of despair. You can expect problems. So the question is *not*, "Will we ever have moments of discouragement?" The question *is* this: "How can I deal with deep discouragement?" When I seek to live out God's Word and things do not work out the way I expect, where do I go for help, strength, and sanity? The answer to this practical, real-life question lies in Exodus 5–6. We will learn that *we fight discouragement with Gospel promises.*

Moses was in the center of God's will, yet he met serious opposition. So after a period of grief and questioning, God spoke to Moses in chapter 6 providing him with some awesome promises that strengthened him for the task ahead. One key section in this passage, indeed in all of Exodus, is 6:6-8, where God gave Moses a number of "I will" promises. These promises are about God's amazing grace.

Before we examine this, we should be reminded that the gospel is not just for unbelievers. It is definitely for unbelievers, but it is for Christians also. Paul wrote in Romans 8 about God's promises of redemption in the context of human suffering. You fight discouragement, despair, and suffering with promises. Paul ended Romans by saying, "Now to Him who has power to strengthen you according to my gospel" (16:25). God strengthens us by the gospel. You cannot go anywhere else to get the type of strength you need.

Discouragement
EXODUS 5:1-22

Moses Speaks to Pharaoh (5:1-3)

At the start, we find Moses and Aaron obeying God's instruction. They asked for a "festival . . . in the wilderness" (v. 1) This initial request was modest, reflecting a Near Eastern approach, although more was being sought (Stuart, *Exodus*, 161). More importantly, they were following God's call in Exodus 3:18. Then Pharaoh asked, "Who is Yahweh?" (v. 2). The book of Exodus answers this question. "I am Yahweh/the LORD" is a major theme in the book. God acted so that people knew He is the great I AM (6:7; 7:5). Pharaoh's question shows not only an acknowledgement problem, it also shows an attitude problem. The second part of the question is ". . . that I should obey Him?" In other words, he asked, "Who is your god that I should take Him seriously?" Pharaoh is about to experience firsthand why he should take Yahweh seriously.

Despite his questions and audacity, Moses and Aaron persisted. They said, "God . . . has met with us" (v. 3). They made their plea, asking that they "may sacrifice." Here we again see the language of worship being used. They also added, "or else He may strike us with plague." It seems that they were implying that if Pharaoh did not let the people go, the consequences would be horrific for both Egypt and Israel. This, of course, is manifested in the coming plagues. Here Pharaoh received his warning! But he refused to obey the Lord's word.

Moses and Aaron were bold with their request before Pharaoh. The phrase "God . . . has met with us" reminds us of a passage in Acts 4:13:

> *When they observed the boldness of Peter and John and realized that*
> *they were uneducated and untrained men, they were amazed and knew*
> *that they had been with Jesus.*

Where did the apostles' boldness come from? It came from being with Jesus. Think of Hebrews 11:27:

> *By faith [Moses] left Egypt behind, not being afraid of the king's*
> *anger, for he persevered, as one who sees Him who is invisible.*

In a similar fashion, we endure by relying on Him who is invisible. The early church gathered for prayer and as a result they "were all filled with the Holy Spirit and began to speak God's message with boldness" (Acts 4:31). Does this not occur for believers today as well? We have the Spirit of God living in us. This reality should bring holy boldness. Unfortunately for Moses, after he spoke boldly and the results were not what he expected, he got dejected. And the Lord had to keep reminding him of the promises. Do not forget the Lord's promises.

The King Refuses to Listen (5:4-9)

Pharaoh would not listen, despite what Moses and Aaron had said. Instead, he thought this whole thing was a distraction. He was incensed by the whole proposal. As a result, Pharaoh decided to make things worse for Israel. He now said (1) they would not be given straw (5:7), yet (2) they must produce the same number of bricks. Pharaoh did not think they were working hard enough, so he gave them more to do, thinking that they would not have idealistic dreams of going into the wilderness to worship if they were busy working. In fact, he not only gave them more to do but also made the conditions worse. He told the taskmasters and the foremen to make it worse and to ignore their cries.

An Awful Situation: Bricks without Straw (5:10-14)

Israel was already in bondage. They were slaves. They had built great cities and worked on agricultural projects. They were oppressed socially, economically, and politically. Now it went from bad to worse. They were in great need of mercy.

In verses 10-13 we see the slave drivers doing as Pharaoh demanded. The people were scattered throughout Egypt to find straw for bricks. Egyptians used sun-dried mud bricks for all kinds of things, so the requirement was great. Ancient historical pictures display great brick making in Egypt.

Now in verse 14 the foremen, who were apparently Israelites in middle management, were beaten because the people had not supplied as many bricks as before. Can you imagine this lifestyle? It is incredibly hot, with temperatures often over a hundred degrees. They are wearing little aprons. They have no hats and few water breaks. They are stuck in the muck all day. Many surely died of exhaustion, dehydration, or heat stroke. This is an awful picture of slavery!

You Have Made Us Stink (5:15-21)

As the story continues, the foremen turned to Pharaoh in protest because they did not understand why they were being beaten. They were caught in the middle. Perhaps they thought the slaves should be beaten instead of them. Pharaoh refused to listen, and the foremen were in despair. You can see why the foremen would go to Pharaoh, but it seems like they should have instead turned to God for deliverance. It was His face they should have been seeking, not the one who put them in bondage in the first place. Do you take your problems to God in prayer? Cry out like the psalmist:

> LORD, hear my prayer; listen to my plea for mercy.
> I call on You in the day of my distress, for You will answer me.
> (Ps 86:6-7)

Not only did they go to Pharaoh instead of God, they also lashed out at their leaders. They said, "You have made us reek in front of Pharaoh" (5:21). The beat-up foremen were looking to blame someone, so why not Moses and Aaron? This is a common theme throughout the Pentateuch: Israel complained against leadership. Ultimately, the people will do the same to Jesus, the greater prophet, and they will crucify Him (Acts 7:51-53).

Moses Cries Out (5:22)

Because the people rejected Moses, he cried out to God wanting to know why this was happening. He did not understand why obedience made things worse. Moses was rightly disappointed, but he should not have been shocked for God told him that Pharaoh would not listen (3:19; 4:21). Nevertheless, he was discouraged because of the terrible situation. From verse 22, notice how Moses is beginning to question (1) God's *goodness* ("why have You caused trouble for this people?"), (2) God's *purpose* ("why did You ever send me?"), and (3) God's *actions* ("You haven't delivered Your people at all"). Moses reminds us of ourselves. Moses was an imperfect sinner, like us. He was a man in desperate need of God's mercy and grace, like us. Here, he is at a crisis of belief.

On a positive note, at least Moses was addressing God. He cried out *to God*. It was an honest groaning before the Lord. Moses' complaint is like the prayers in the Psalms, as people lamented and cried out (see Ps 77). It is okay to cry out with questions. Even Jesus, while on the cross, cried out, "Why have You forsaken Me?" (Matt 27:46). These questions are not sinful. They just need to be humble, honest, and faithful. Ask God your questions! But do not ask sinfully or rebelliously. And remember, God does not have to answer our questions (He never answered all of Job's!), but He does hear our questions.

So that is what chapter 5 is all about. At times, life brings deep discouragement, pain, trouble, questions, and harsh slavery. It can be a stinking mess. Moses was following God, but things actually got worse. How do you fight this discouragement? You fight it with promises. That is what chapter 6 is about.

Gospel Promises
EXODUS 6:1–7:5

Promises provide us with hope of what is to come. In the midst of darkness, promises remind us of the glory of God. Here we find that God gave Moses three awesome reminders. These truths are timeless. As a result, we need to dwell on them daily as well.

God Is in Control (6:1)

As the story continues, God assured Moses that there is only One sovereign, and it is not the man with the snake on his head. God never answered the question "Why?" He simply reminded Moses that His plan would not be thwarted. He reminded Moses that He is in control. Many believers believe in God's sovereignty theologically, but practically they are emotional train wrecks! They have not worked this truth down deep into their hearts.

God is working all things for His people's good. He is always using circumstances to shape us into His Son's image. We do not always know what He is doing. The Israelites were enslaved for four hundred years. Should Moses think that God should act immediately? God could have sizzled Pharaoh any time, but He has His own ways of doing things in His own time.

This story reminds me of my dad. For the majority of his life, he was an unbeliever. I prayed for him regularly. Then at age 59, after a period of reading and searching, my dad stood up in front of his congregation and said, "I believe Jesus Christ is the Son of the living God." Then I had the privilege of baptizing him. It was one of the greatest moments of my life. He began attending a small group, going over to the pastor's house, and reading Christian books. After about six months, he said, "I've read the whole Bible." He is continuing to grow as a new believer.

A few months later he called me, with obvious concern in his voice, and said that his factory was closing down. My dad worked in this factory my whole life—35 years. He only missed two days of work this whole time. He was devastated. In a small town without many good paying jobs, the whole town was devastated. The management decided to move the factory to make more money, taking virtually no one with them. My dad was concerned not just for himself but also for everyone else. He was one of the senior guys in the plant and was about two years from retirement.

When we were visiting during Thanksgiving, he was telling me what he did on that day he received the news about the shutdown. He said, "I went outside, I sat on the porch, and I opened the Bible to Psalms, and I read Psalm 55:22." It says, "Cast your burden on the LORD, and He will sustain you; He will never allow the righteous to be shaken." He said, "That verse hit me right between the eyes. I knew everything was going to be okay."

Six months earlier my dad would have never done this or said this. But God changed his life. Nevertheless, following this awesome experience of grace, he faced a difficulty he had not faced in 35 years! What truth comforted him? This truth: God is in control. He sustains us. Fight discouragement with this truth.

God Keeps His Covenant (6:2-5)

God kept repeating these things. God wanted His people to remind themselves of His promises. For us, this is the idea of preaching the gospel to ourselves every day. Once again, God mentioned these two great motives of redemption: (1) His covenant and (2) His knowledge of the oppressed (cf. 2:23-25; 3:6-7).

God said that He would keep His unbreakable promise of salvation. The psalmist said, "[God] remembers His covenant forever" (105:8). One can trace this glorious theme throughout Scripture. Ultimately, God kept His covenant in Jesus. In Christ, we are part of an eternal covenant, established by Christ's own blood. Because of this, we can find peaceful rest during life's discouraging times. We have a Savior who died, rose, ascended to the Father, and now intercedes for us. He is forever faithful to His people. Remember His covenant.

God Saves (6:6–7:5)

We should pay careful attention to the "I will" statements in 6:6-8 and 7:3-4. They can be grouped into five gospel words or five words of salvation. I want to pair these five gospel words with New Testament references. What I love about Exodus is that it is *so visual*. We are watching theology unfold. God is going to do all of this. All He asks His people to do is know that He is Yahweh. Salvation is all of God.

The first truth we should note is liberation. "I will deliver you from the forced labor of the Egyptians and free you from slavery to them" (6:6). This is a picture of salvation. God is going to bring His people out of slavery. He is going to deliver them. God liberated the people from bondage through the mediator Moses. This would be accomplished by grace through faith for it was not something that they had earned. The purpose of this liberation was that they might worship the Almighty God. And, as we will see in Exodus 15, the people celebrated their liberation.

Of course these gospel truths are taught in the New Testament as well. In Exodus, we see a picture of what is to come. For instance, Paul said Jesus "gave Himself for our sins to rescue us from this present evil age" (Gal 1:4). On a similar level God set us free, from spiritual slavery and our inability to keep the law, through the mediator Jesus Christ. This occurs only by grace through faith, for we have not earned this. The purpose of our release is worship as well. We were made to worship, and only though this liberation can we truly worship.

There is an "already–not yet" dimension to our salvation. Israel was looking forward to these promises. For us, in one sense, they have happened to us "already," but we also look forward to the "not yet" when Jesus will set us free for good and forever from this age. Paul said, "For I consider that the sufferings of this present time are not worth comparing with the glory that is to be revealed to us" (Rom 8:18). God gives us a word that we will suffer in this life. Do not be surprised when you get cancer. Do not be surprised when you lose your job. What God has promised us is resurrection from the dead. We are set free, but we still dwell in this body in a fallen world, and we are awaiting ultimate, final liberty.

The next gospel concept we should recognize is redemption. In 6:6 it says, "I will redeem you with an outstretched arm and great acts of judgment." What a gospel word this is! Tim Keller says, "There is no more basic word in the Bible than redemption" ("Getting Out"). With the exception of Jacob's blessing in Genesis 48:16, this is the first occasion that the Bible uses the language of redemption (Wright, *Mission*, 266). Later it is also used in Exodus 15:13, where they are singing of God's redemption. In both cases it is the Hebrew verb *ga'al.* The participle form of the verb is *go'el.* God is the "Redeemer."

The word carries the idea of "purchasing," but there is more to it than that. "Redeem" in Hebrew often communicates that there is a privilege or duty of a close relative. The *go'el* was a member of the wider family who acted to protect the family when they were in some particular types of situations. The *go'el* was the "kinsman protector" or "family champion" (Wright, *Mission*, 266). This was seen in many situations. If a member of the family was murdered, the *go'el* would see to it that the guilty person was brought to justice (Num 35). If a kinsman fell into debt and was forced to sell land, a better-off kinsman (a kinsman protector) would take the responsibility to purchase the land in order to keep it in the family. If the situation was so bad that the debtor had to offer himself and his family into bonded labor, the kinsman protector would act to rescue them from servitude (Lev 25). If a man died without a son to inherit his name and property, it was the kinsman's job to take the deceased man's widow and seek to raise an heir (Deut 25:5-10; Ruth 3:12-13; 4:1-12).

God is the ultimate *go'el*, the family protector, the family champion! God is an eligible *go'el*! He is going to *ga'al* (redeem) His people. In Exodus, God was coming to the aid of His people. His relatives were in bonded labor, spiritual slavery, and He was coming to defend, intervene, avenge, and rescue them. He was coming to redeem them with justice. As the text says, "[God] will redeem you with an outstretched arm and great acts of judgment" (Exod 6:6). He was also coming to ensure that the ultimate family heir would be preserved. Ultimately, this people would bring forth Messiah, the ultimate Redeemer.

In Galatians, Paul put redemption and the family dimension of adoption together. He said in 4:4-7,

> *When the time came to completion, God sent His Son, born of a woman, born under the law, to redeem those under the law, so that we might receive adoption as sons. And because you are sons, God has sent the Spirit of His Son into our hearts, crying, "Abba, Father!" So you are no longer a slave but a son, and if a son, then an heir through God.*

In your discouragement, remember that you have a Redeemer! Jesus, your kinsman protector, your family champion, has intervened in your misery. He has paid the price to relieve you from your greatest debt, from your most desperate situation. He paid it with His own blood, with His own life. And now we will sit at His table. We will live in His place forever. Soon, we will know the riches of our redemption. When our *go'el*, Jesus, comes again in majesty to complete the final act of redemption, all of our problems that we encountered here will seem as nothing.

The third gospel concept for us to consider is adoption. "I will take you as My people, and I will be your God. You will know that I am Yahweh your God, who delivered you from the forced labor of the Egyptians" (Exod 6:7). This verse shows us the familial nature of salvation. It reminds us of the doctrine of adoption. God was going to take Israel as His people. He had already called them His "son" (4:22). This is a display of God's matchless love. Paul said of God's choice of Israel, "to them belong the adoption, the glory, the covenants, the giving of the law, the temple service, and the promises" (Rom 9:4). In redemption, God has rescued us from a dreadful situation, but there is more! Through adoption, God brings us into His family. This is privilege! John said, "Look at how great a love the Father has given us that we should be called God's children. And we are!" (1 John 3:1).

My friend Dennis Omondi and his bride live in Kenya. Their adoption story was recently on MSNBC. They told the story of Benjamin. Benjamin was thrown into an 18-foot hole in a Nairobi slum. This hole was the public toilet. A passing stranger heard his cry and spent two hours digging down into the muck to rescue him from death. Benjamin was taken in by New Life Home Trust and eventually placed into the loving family of Dennis and Allison.

What a picture of what God did for Israel! What a picture of what He has done for us! We were in a pit and are now in the arms of the Father, who "redeems your life from the Pit; He crowns you with faithful love and compassion" (Ps 103:4). "He brought me up from a desolate pit, out of the muddy clay, and set my feet on a rock, making my steps secure. He put a new song in my mouth, a hymn of praise to our God. Many will see and fear and put their trust in the LORD" (Ps 40:2-3). I encourage you to meditate on your sonship daily. God has brought you out of a pit and placed you in His eternal family. Bless His holy name!

The fourth gospel concept is inheritance. "I will bring you to the land that I swore to give to Abraham, Isaac, and Jacob, and I will give it to you as a possession" (Exod 6:8). God was promising His people that they would possess a country. This promise was first mentioned to Abraham (Gen 12:7). Later, in the book of Joshua, we will see the people entering, conquering, and inhabiting the land. These people had nothing. They were slaves in Egypt. But God is going to give them an inheritance. He is going to give them the promised land—all by His grace. They did not earn it.

The New Testament applies this idea of inheriting the promised land to the believers' hope in the new heavens and new earth. By Jesus' resurrection, we have "inheritance that is imperishable, uncorrupted, and unfading, kept in heaven for you." (1 Pet 1:4). Peter said this inheritance is awesome ("imperishable, uncorrupted, and unfading") and assured ("kept in heaven for you"). Jesus told us the meek will inherit the earth (Matt 5:5). One reason we should live generously in this life and not covet is that our heaven is later. Do not covet—you own the earth!

In your difficult hour, savor the gospel like Dietrich Bonhoeffer. Just 24 hours before Bonhoeffer was executed, he gathered some prisoners and held a worship service. He chose as one if his texts 1 Peter 1:3-12, which speaks of the believer's "living hope" (Metaxas, *Bonhoeffer*). What an example for all of us of meditating on the gospel in our dark hours!

John Newton said that the way the Christian might endure trials is by considering the doctrine of glorification, which includes inheritance. Newton said the Christian should not complain, murmur, or despair in light of all that is coming. He said we should imagine a man who inherited a really large estate, worth millions, and he had to go to New York City to get it. As he journeyed there, his carriage broke down, leaving him to walk the last one mile. Can you imagine that man saying, "My carriage is broken, my carriage is broken," kicking and complaining in disgust when he has only a mile to go to receive a million? Christian, we only have a few miles to go! (Piper, "Children, Heirs, and Fellow Sufferers"). Rest in God's promises and faithfulness!

We have just examined four wonderful aspects of salvation: liberation, redemption, adoption, and inheritance. God made all these promises saying, "I will save you." He has sent His Son to do everything we need to be saved. Paul said, "For every one of God's promises is 'Yes' in Him" (2 Cor 1:20). God revealed Himself to the Israelites and to us. All that was left for Israel was to know and trust the Lord as Savior. Have you done this?

Despite these amazing promises, Moses and the people struggled to believe (Exod 6:9-13,26-30). The people of Israel were unmoved. It says it was because of their "broken spirit and hard labor" (6:9). We can sympathize with them. Ryken says, "They were so broken that they would not listen to the promise of freedom" (176). Spurgeon said,

> Some cannot receive Christ because they are so full of anguish, and are so crushed in spirit that they cannot find strength enough of mind to entertain a hope that by any possibility salvation can come to them. . . . the mere struggle to exist exhausted all their energy, and destroyed all their hope. . . . I do not wonder that a great many are unable to receive the gospel in this city of ours, because their struggle for existence is awful. I am afraid that it gets more and more intense, though even now it passes all bounds. If any of you can do anything to help the toil-worn workers, I pray you, do

it. . . . And yet, dear friend—if such a one has come in here tonight—I pray you do not throw away the next world because you have so little of this. This is sheer folly. If I have little here, I would make sure of the more hereafter. ("Saddest")

Sometimes people are so wounded it is hard for them to put everything together. It is hard for them to hear. Sometimes people are so mentally and emotionally crushed, they cannot get it. We have been applying Israel's situation to victims of human trafficking. Many are crushed by physical slavery, so much so that they will have a hard time believing. We need to deliver them physically and spiritually.

In verses 10-13 God told Moses to go back to Pharaoh, and Moses' response was one of unbelief and despair. Moses responded to God with confusion. He could not understand how Pharaoh would listen if the Israelites would not. He believed he was a "poor speaker," possibly implying that he had a speech problem or that he considered himself unclean to speak. Moses is like many of us who are tempted to give up. But once again, God persisted. God commanded them to listen and obey. Once again, after this genealogy, there were more gospel promises that fueled him to action.

Next we find an excursus (6:14-25). Notice that this section is framed with the phrase "the heads of their fathers' families" (vv. 14,25). Genealogies always show us the importance of individuals. God knows our names. This particular section is provided to allow the reader to know who Moses and Aaron are and where they came from. It provides us with a list of only three of Jacob's sons: Reuben, Simeon, and Levi. Moses and Aaron are not the sons of the firstborn, Reuben, but of Jacob's third son Levi. Likewise, Moses was not the firstborn son, yet God chose him to lead the people out of Egypt, with his older brother Aaron serving as his own prophet. Thus, Moses was chosen in God's grace and election. He was not one who deserved the birthright or the blessing, but he received it from God Almighty nonetheless. Remember, the tribe of Levi was not given the inheritance but instead were scattered (Gen 49:5-8).

It was through Moses and Aaron that eventually God would call the Levites back to His service as priests and ministers over the people of Israel and the tabernacle (Num 3:1-10). There was nothing in and of themselves that brought them there, only God's own election and appointment of them. They served and worshiped day and night (1 Chr 9:33), often doing tasks that might at times seem mundane or insignificant. What a word for us who serve in the church: from helping set up to cleaning up to welcoming guests or serving in child care, it all matters! And as the Levites show, it is worship to God!

The fifth and final gospel concept is judgment and mercy. "But I will harden Pharaoh's heart. . . . I will put My hand on Egypt" (Exod 7:3-4). To counter Moses' discouragement, God reminded Moses of who was in control. Verses 1-5 are about the fact that God is the only God. It was essential for Moses to know and walk in this truth. In verses 1-7 Moses was fulfilling the role of a mediator. He was God's representative. Pharaoh considered himself to be "god," but here God put Pharaoh in his place by saying Moses was "like God to Pharaoh." This does not mean that Moses was divine. Instead, he represented God. Moses prepared the way for Jesus, who was God, the true Mediator. Jesus was called the prophet greater than Moses (Deut 18:18; Acts 3:22; 7:37; Heb 3:3). Aaron was like the "prophet's prophet." Similarly, when Jesus ascended to heaven, He gave us the prophetic ministry of speaking His gospel. We are His ambassadors. And remember, all of this was happening while Moses was a senior citizen (Exod 7:7)!

Then, in verses 4-5, we read an "I will" statement. In the middle of this promise, God said He would lay His hand on Egypt in judgment. Why was He doing this? That they might "know that [He is] Yahweh" (v. 5). God's glory would be seen in His judgment and in His mercy. Notice there are two ways to "know Yahweh." First, you may know Him by experiencing His mercy in salvation (6:6-8). Second, you may know Him by experiencing His wrath in judgment (7:4-5). Everyone will eventually acknowledge that He is God (Phil 2:10-11). God will deal with His enemies either by "drowning them" or by redeeming them through the cross. Here in Exodus the Egyptians were rejecting God's word. In Isaiah 19 there is a promise that Egypt will one day be God's people. This is what we want for God's enemies. We want them to know the real God as Savior. We do not want to have the attitude of James and John when the Samaritans refused to believe (Luke 9:54) or Jonah's attitude toward the Ninevites (Jonah 3:10–4:1). We want God's enemies to become God's people.

Now, there is a period of time in which God is waiting for those of you who do not know Him. God will have mercy on you. Trust Him as Savior today! Believe in the God who mercifully frees sinners, redeems sinners, adopts sinners, and promises an inheritance to sinners.

The text shows us that Pharaoh's heart was hardened. We see a tension here in Exodus. On the one hand, the Lord is sovereign over everything that was going on here. On the other, Pharaoh is held responsible for refusing to listen. We need to remember that the Bible warns us about hardening our hearts to God's word. Psalm 95 used this idea to warn Israel in its worship (95:8), and the book of Hebrews used Psalm 95 to call the church to continue in the faith (Heb 3:7–4:13). Do not harden your heart. Hear the Gospel. Believe the Gospel. Trust in Christ.

Acting on the Promises

After preaching the gospel to yourself, go act. That is the picture in the next scene, which we will look at in the next passage. Moses and Aaron did not make excuses. Rather, the text says, they "did just as the LORD had commanded" (Exod 7:10). What a picture for us! Are you discouraged? Preach this gospel to yourself and go act by faith in our great God. God is in control. God keeps His covenant. God liberates, redeems, and adopts sinners. He gives them an inheritance and makes them objects of His mercy. Now sing the gospel, pray the gospel, meditate on the gospel, and hear the gospel. Fill your mind with it, work it down deep, and act courageously for the glory of God!

Reflect and Discuss

1. When have you been tempted to think that *not* following God would be easier or better?

2. How should our relationship to God through Jesus and the Holy Spirit make us bold in our witness and mission?

3. Have you ever seen someone who is suffering become bitter, turn against the church and its leaders, and appeal to other sources for relief? How can you encourage such a person to remain true to God?

4. Compare (1) questioning God, (2) doubt, and (3) unbelief. What has been your attitude when you approach God?

5. How have you seen God's sovereignty demonstrated in the past? Which is more encouraging for you, remembering such events or reading the promises in the Bible?

6. Which aspect of salvation—liberation, redemption, adoption, or inheritance—is the most dear to you? Why?

7. How would you respond to a non-Christian who said, "I'm barely getting by in this life—how can I even think about the afterlife?"

8. How is it encouraging to see that God's choice of Aaron and Moses was not based on who they were or what they had done?
9. What did the king of Israel (2 Kgs 6:18-23), Jonah (Jonah 3:10–4:1), and James and John (Luke 9:54) need to learn about the judgment and mercy of God?
10. How do you go about preaching the gospel to yourself—in songs, prayer, meditation, Bible reading, or conversation with other Christians?

That They May Know That I Am Yahweh

EXODUS 7:6–11:10

Main Idea: Yahweh wants everyone to know that He is God and there is no other.

I. **No Other Gods: One Dominant Theme (7:14–11:10)**
II. **Four Recurring Emphases: The Preview (7:8-13)**
  A. Emphasis #1: Obedience (7:8-10)
  B. Emphasis #2: God's superior power over Egypt's gods (7:8-12)
  C. Emphasis #3: Counterfeit signs (7:11-12)
  D. Emphasis #4: Perpetual hardening of Pharaoh's heart (7:13)
III. **Four Recurring Emphases: The Plagues (7:14–11:10)**
  A. First cycle of plagues (7:14–8:19)
  B. Second cycle of plagues (8:20–9:12)
  C. Third cycle of plagues (9:13–10:29)
  D. The tenth plague threatened (11:1-10)
IV. **One Dominant Question: Who Is Your God?**

Who is your God? That is the most important question you will ever answer. The book of Exodus is a story that shows us who the real God is. In this section of Exodus, we are looking at the "plagues." Now, I suppose the modern person may look at these plagues and say, "Are you kidding me? This scene is bizarre! Is God a cosmic jerk? Is He trying to annoy the Egyptians?" Or, "This is silly and hard to believe."

It is indeed strange and severe, but you must understand that there is something bigger going on with the ten plagues than what you see at first glance. God was judging not only the Egyptians but also the *gods* of Egypt. In Exodus 12:12 God said that He was going to perform the last sign, the death of the firstborn, and in so doing He was executing "judgments against all the gods of Egypt." This was also repeated in Numbers: "The LORD had executed judgment against their gods" (33:4).

The plagues fell on all the areas of life that were supposed to have been protected by Egypt's gods. James Boyce said,

> There were about eighty major deities in Egypt, all clustered about three great natural forces of Egyptian life: the Nile

River, the land, and the sky. . . . The first two plagues were
against the gods of the Nile. The next four were against the
land gods. The final four plagues were against the gods of the
sky, culminating the death of the firstborn. (Ryken, *Exodus,*
216)

God put His glory on display by judging these false gods. He is the Almighty.

No Other Gods: One Dominant Theme
EXODUS 7:8-13

God wants everyone to know that He is God and there is no other. This
theme echoes throughout the Bible. Later in Exodus, the first commandment says, "Do not have other gods besides Me" (Exod 20:3).
Luther said that there is only really one commandment, the first,
because if you keep it, you'll keep the others! This points us again to
the question, "Who is your God?" It is the most important question you
need to answer.

The Bible describes the God of Moses in so many ways. In
Deuteronomy 4 Scripture says,

> *Or has a god attempted to go and take a nation as his own out of*
> *another nation, by trials, signs, wonders, and war, by a strong hand*
> *and an outstretched arm, by great terrors, as the LORD your God did*
> *for you in Egypt before your eyes? You were shown these things so that*
> *you would know that the LORD is God; there is no other besides Him.*
> (Deut 4:34-35)

Later, in Joshua, we see that Israel also worshiped the gods of Egypt previously and were told by their leader to worship the real God: "Therefore,
fear the LORD and worship Him in sincerity and truth. Get rid of the
gods your fathers worshiped beyond the Euphrates River and in Egypt,
and worship Yahweh" (Josh 24:14). In Isaiah God says, "I am Yahweh,
that is My name; I will not give My glory to another" (Isa 42:8).

In the New Testament we find similar language. We have already
mentioned that Jesus refers to Himself as "I am" (e.g., John 8:58). The
second person of the triune God tells us, "This is eternal life: that they
may know You, the only true God, and the One You have sent" (John
17:3). There is one God, and you need to embrace Him through Jesus
Christ, very God of very God. In 1 Thessalonians 1:9-10 Paul said conversion is about turning from idols to *the living God.*

In 7:5–11:10, we see this overarching message: "that they may know that I am Yahweh." It appears throughout Exodus, especially in these five chapters. In 7:8-13 Moses and Aaron performed an initial sign, or what you might call a "preview of the plagues." There is a pattern set forth showing some common emphases in the ten plagues. That pattern includes four parts (Ryken, *Exodus*, 203):

- The Obedience of Moses and Aaron
- God's superior power over Egypt's gods
- Satan's counterfeits
- The perpetual hardening of Pharaoh's heart

Let's first take a look at this one dominant theme and then look at these other four recurring ideas that are previewed in 7:8-13.

One Dominant Theme (7:14–11:10)

We have alluded to this theme already in the book. God told Israel that He was going to redeem them and give them a land and make them His people so that "You will know that I am Yahweh your God" (6:7); He also said He was going to lay His hand of judgment on the Egyptians for the same reason: "The Egyptians will know that I am Yahweh" (7:5). God's judgment is always mingled with mercy. Do not forget that.

Many people may protest against God's judgment and wrath. This should not surprise us. Whenever people protest against God's judgment, it is a sign that they have minimized their sin and God's blazing holiness. R. C. Sproul says, "Sin is cosmic treason" (*Holiness*, 115-16). These protestors are also minimizing God's sovereignty. God is totally free to do as He pleases. In fact, Paul drew on Exodus in Romans 9 when he said, "I will show mercy to whom I will show mercy, and I will have compassion on whom I will have compassion" (Rom 9:15). Remember also that Israel was not better than the Egyptians. They did not merit salvation. They were saved the same way we are saved: "by grace through faith." They saw the signs and believed. Egypt (at least most of them it seems) did not believe.

There are a number of issues one could study when it comes to the plagues, but I do not want you to miss the forest for the trees. This chart illustrates *God's passion to be known and worshiped.*

Plague	Reference
1. Nile	This is what Yahweh says: Here is how *you will know that I am Yahweh*. Watch. I will strike the water in the Nile with the staff in my hand, and it will turn to blood. (Exod 7:17)
2. Frogs	"Tomorrow," he answered. Moses replied, "As you have said, *so you may know there is no one like Yahweh our God.*" (Exod 8:10)
3. Gnats	Not mentioned
4. Flies	But on that day I will give special treatment to the land of Goshen, where My people are living; no flies will be there. *This way you will know that I, Yahweh, am in the land.* (Exod 8:22)
5. Livestock	Not mentioned
6. Boils	Not mentioned
7. Hail	Otherwise, I am going to send all My plagues against you, your officials, and your people. *Then you will know there is no one like Me in all the earth.* . . . However, I have let you live for this purpose: to show you My power and *to make My name known in all the earth.* . . . Moses said to him, "When I have left the city, I will extend my hands to Yahweh. The thunder will cease, and there will be no more hail, *so that you may know the earth belongs to Yahweh.* (Exod 9:14,16,29)
8. Locusts	and so that you may tell your son and grandson how severely I dealt with the Egyptians and performed miraculous signs among them, *and you will know that I am Yahweh.* (Exod 10:2)
9. Darkness	Not mentioned
10. Final Plague Threatened	The LORD said to Moses, "Pharaoh will not listen to you, *so that My wonders may be multiplied in the land of Egypt.*" (Exod 11:9)

The phrase "I am Yahweh" extends beyond the plagues in Exodus, as well. The phrase recurs in 14:4,18; 16:12; and 29:46. We see here God's great purpose: the glory of His great name. Our greatest happiness will come when we pursue His glory, delight in His glory, and rejoice in His glory.

Four Recurring Emphases: The Preview
EXODUS 7:8-13

Let me show you four recurring emphases that appear in this episode and throughout the plagues. This is sort of like a Western, in which the good guys and bad guys square off for a bit of a scuffle, only to reserve the real battle for later. This is sort of the bar scene in Tombstone, when Doc Holiday twirls his little cup, but later the shootout will happen. There will be utter domination.

Emphasis #1: Obedience (7:8-10)

First, Moses and Aaron were told to take the staff. The staff signified God as the One who was working signs and wonders. It continued throughout Israel's journey as representative of God's presence and power. Then notice: they "did just as the LORD had commanded" (v. 10). This statement shows us growth in Moses' life. Before, when God commissioned him, Moses wanted to argue and make excuses. But now it says they did exactly what He told them to do. This should be everyone's response to God's Word—*immediate, instinctive, loving obedience.*

Emphasis #2: God's Superior Power over Egypt's Gods (7:8-12)

This initial sign has to do with a snake. The word used here signifies a large, deadly, venomous snake, which would likely have been a *cobra*. Again, God was taking on the gods of Egypt, not just Pharaoh. Snakes captivated the Egyptians. Pharaoh wore one on his head as a symbol of his authority. He was to be feared, like snakes were feared. The Egyptians were so awestruck by snakes that it led them to serpent worship. They reportedly built a temple in honor or the snake goddess Wadjet, who was represented by a cobra (Ryken, *Exodus,* 206).

So here is the pattern: Yahweh took on the gods of Egypt. The only true and living God would perform signs that were so astonishing that there would be no doubt that He is superior. So it was not just going to be a frog or two, a few bugs, a little red water, a little hailstorm, a few people with boils, or a cloudy day. No, the plagues were horrific signs of God's judgment and sovereign power. God was making sure people know that He was doing it and that He alone is God.

Emphasis #3: Counterfeit Signs (7:11-12)

The text mentions three groups who try to respond to this sign with their own miracle: wise men, sorcerers, and magicians. The word translated "magicians" is like the Egyptian title for a *priest*. They acted in the service of Egypt's gods. There are numerous Egyptian texts that speak of extraordinary acts performed by these priests.

You may wonder what exactly "occult practices" means. There are a few options. Some think the magicians were like illusionists, who could put on a magic show. Others think they were snake charmers. There is of course a long history of snake charming along the Nile. Some report that these tricks are still done today, in which an Egyptian cobra is paralyzed and made to look like a cane. But I believe that the best way to understand their work is as a wonder performed by the power of Satan. Egypt is clearly in touch with dark power.

We too are in a spiritual war. Paul said, "For our battle is not against flesh and blood, but against the rulers, against the authorities, against the world powers of this darkness, against the spiritual forces of evil in the heavens" (Eph 6:12). Therefore, we must be alert and rely on the Lord's strength as we encounter evil influence. Exodus shows us that while the evil one may have real influence, he is no match for God; Satan is a counterfeiter. Paul said the activity of the "lawless one" is the activity of Satan, who practices "false miracles, signs, and wonders" (2 Thess 2:8-9). Jesus, however, will "destroy him with the breath of His mouth" (2 Thess 2:8).

After the countersign done by Pharaoh's court, Aaron's staff swallowed up their staffs. This was a clear sign that God is superior. God was not doing a magic trick; He was performing a miracle.

Let me point out one more portent in the preview to the plagues. Notice this word, "swallowed." This same word is used later in Exodus 15:12 to describe the drowning of the Egyptians in the sea. God will swallow Israel's enemies, and later God will swallow our great enemy, death (1 Cor 15:54).

Emphasis #4: Perpetual Hardening of Pharaoh's Heart (7:13)

Despite the miracle, Pharaoh remained insensitive. He was not interested in listening to God. He had no feeling for God. He had a heavy, cold, hard heart. This, however, should not have been a surprise: God predicted it would happen (7:3-4).

Pharaoh stands as a warning to everyone. Do not harden your heart to God. He saw some awesome signs and wonders and still refused to listen. Some say they would believe if they saw more miracles. But Pharaoh's issue was not with evidence; his problem was his stubborn heart (cf. Luke 16:30-31). Jesus has given us the final sign, the *empty tomb*. There is plenty enough evidence for a person to believe.

The Israelites saw the same thing as Pharaoh and they believed. The passage previously mentioned in 2 Thessalonians goes on to say that those who are under the influence of the evil one will perish because "they did not accept the love of the truth in order to be saved" (2:10). That is exactly what Pharaoh did; he refused to love the truth and be saved.

Four Recurring Emphases: The Plagues
EXODUS 7:14–11:10

Remember, we have seen that there are four emphases in this section: obedience, God's superior power, counterfeits, and hardening. Let us explore each of these as they are found in the plagues. Because there appear to be *three cycles of three plagues*, we will look at them in three groups. Also worth noting is that plagues three, six, and nine are similar in their brevity and style.

It is also important to address the matter of God's judgment on *Egypt's gods* because He is making the critical point that He alone is God. This point has great application for us as we face the temptation to bow to our own idols. The plagues should serve as a warning not only for those who refuse to believe the gospel but for believers who are tempted to love, serve, and trust anything except the living God.

First Cycle of Plagues (7:14–8:19)

Recurring Emphases	1. Nile to Blood	2. Frogs	3. Gnats
Obedience	7:20-21	8:5-6	8:16-17
God's Power over Egypt's Gods	7:21b	8:6b	8:17b
Counterfeits	7:22a	8:7	8:18 (unable to replicate)
Hardening of Heart	7:22b-23	8:15	8:19

1. Nile River to Blood. God's first display of superior power is appropriate: a miracle on the Nile River (7:14-25). The Nile was the lifeblood of Egypt. Essentially, there is no Egypt without the Nile. It was responsible for transportation, irrigation, drinking water, food, and the setting of the calendar. This type of catastrophe would be similar to cutting off all oil supplies, the stock market collapsing, drinking water being contaminated, and having no food in the grocery store. It would be total chaos. It is no surprise that the Egyptians worshiped the Nile as their creator and sustainer. At least three deities were associated with the Nile: Osiris, Nu, and Hapi (Ryken, *Exodus,* 220). God totally humiliated these gods when He turned it into blood.

Some do not think this was real blood. They claim it was red soil that washed into the Nile. But the biblical record says it is blood (Pss 78:44; 105:29). Moses struck it and it turned into blood. Further, the fish were dying. The spirit of this text is that this was no natural occurrence but a supernatural miracle. It is interesting that in Revelation 16:3-7 water is turned into blood in the great judgment.

The magicians countered the miracle, but the fact that the people were digging for water shows that while they repeated the sign, they could not cleanse the blood from the Nile. Pharaoh refuses to "even take this to heart" (7:23).

To whom are you looking to provide for your needs? While you may have never heard of these Egyptian river gods, people are still tempted to trust in other things to provide for them, instead of God alone. Many place their final hope in the stock market, economic growth, a new president, or something else. All of these will pass away.

2. Frogs. With the second plague, we find frogs are coming up into the house, bedroom, and beds, into the ovens and kneading bowls, and on all the inhabitants of Egypt (8:1-15). This was a humorous miracle when you think about it. Frogs are not that scary or creepy, but when you have them everywhere, then that is scary and creepy, not to mention annoying! Imagine mothers seeing frogs come out of their bread bowl and children having frogs leap out of their oatmeal! The frogs even came into Pharaoh's court!

Think also about the frog deities that God was opposing. One goddess named Heqet was pictured with head and sometimes the body of a frog. Apparently, this goddess controlled the frog population and also assisted women in childbirth. Frogs were so sacred that the Egyptians could not kill them. The Nile and the frogs were symbols of fertility.

Today, frogs are symbols of fertility and life. Those of you who grew up around a body of water like a lake know that if you hear or see frogs, you know life is present. When I was younger, we used to go frog gigging. We would catch frogs, take them home, clean them, and eat the legs. Where there are frogs, there are other forms of life (so we had to watch for snakes when gigging!). Egypt was powerful because this Nile River had life. Now God said, "You like frogs; I'll give you frogs." They, however, could not gig all of these frogs! Because the deities supposedly controlled the frog population, this invasion of frogs was intended to humiliate them.

Next, we find a couple of responses. First, the magicians duplicated the act and brought more frogs, but that actually made things worse. They could do nothing to remove the frogs. Second, Pharaoh offered some false repentance (v. 8). We must remember that a false promise of faith and obedience will not bring salvation. Then Moses began this ministry of intercession. Because of Pharaoh's false confession, another plague was set to arrive. A third response was from the land itself: "a terrible odor in the land" (v. 14). In Exodus 5:21 the foremen said the Hebrews had become odious. Now Egypt reeks.

3. Gnats. In 8:16-19 we find the next plague, which comes unannounced: gnats. Scholars have various ideas over what kind of insect this actually was. They could have been "lice" (KJV) or mosquitoes. Whatever they were, they were touching the people. They were swarming everywhere in Egypt, affecting everyone.

Which god was God striking in this plague? It is hard to pinpoint a particular god in each plague since they were not mentioned specifically. Perhaps it was the earth-god, Geb. This possibility is drawn from God's turning the dust into bugs. God was challenging their trust in the soil and the god of the ground.

Notice that the magicians were now unable to replicate the signs (v. 18). Not only could they not replicate it, they were probably covered with them as well! These magician/priests did not touch insects and they bathed religiously. This is humiliation. The magicians were beginning to see who the real God was. Describing the plague, they said, "This is the finger of God" (v. 19). This does not mean they were converted, but it was a positive step. Still, Pharaoh would not listen.

Second Cycle of Plagues (8:20–9:12)

Recurring Emphases	4. Flies	5. Death of Livestock	6. Boils
Obedience	8:20-24a (implied)	9:1-6a (implied)	9:8-10
God's Power over Egypt's Gods	8:24	9:6b-7a	9:11
Counterfeits	None	None	None (affected personally)
Hardening of Heart	8:32	9:7b	9:12

4. Flies. We are not told when the gnat problem ended, or if it remained. But here we have more little creatures doing God's bidding: flies (8:20-32). Again, we do not know what kind of flies these were, but they were everywhere (v. 24). Most of us hate flies, gnats, and mosquitoes. But can you imagine this?

For the first time a distinction was made between the effects of the plagues on Egypt and on Israel. This is a picture of salvation and judgment. God's people were protected from His wrath. Theologically, we know when we are in Christ we will not face God's wrath; we are hidden with Christ.

These plagues are what some call "de-creation," a reversal of the created order. Instead of order being created out of chaos there is disorder produced from order. The Egyptians believed Pharaoh had the power to maintain order in the cosmos, what they called the *ma'at.* But we know as believers only One can create and sustain the cosmos, and that is our great God. Paul said in Colossians that Jesus holds our lives and the cosmos together. He is our sustainer. Some who want to protest this section, saying that these plagues are impossible, really have one question: "Is there a God or not?" If God created the world, surely He could do a "de-creation" as well. Despite the ruin and disorder, Pharaoh acted the same way: hardening his heart. Notice there is a new pattern: no counterfeits are produced.

What god was being targeted here? We cannot know for sure, but it could be "the god of the resurrection"—Kepher—who was depicted as a beetle. Some argue that these flies were flying beetles, known as scarabs. Scarabs are found on monuments in Egypt.

To whom are you looking for eternal life? Kepher cannot raise the dead. A denomination cannot raise the dead. A political party cannot raise the dead. Only God can raise the dead. People are fascinated with eternal life in culture. We see traces in Peter Pan, the Fountain of Youth, and more. But Jesus said that if you believe in Him, though you die, you will live (John 11:25-26). Another question related to de-creation is, In whom are you trusting for sustaining power? Look to the One who brings order out of chaos.

5. *Death of Livestock.* In the fifth plague, the livestock died (9:1-7). Can you imagine all these huge creatures lying everywhere? (I once hit a cow on the interstate in what was one of the scariest moments of my life! They are huge creatures!) The stench would be horrendous and the cleanup would be exhausting. Again there was a distinction made between God's people and the Egyptians: nothing that belonged to Israel died (v. 4).

The Egyptians had all kinds of sacred cows. Many of their gods were depicted as livestock. Many worshiped a bull (prompting the golden calf worship later?), which they viewed as a fertility figure. At the temple in Memphis there was a sacred place that featured a live bull said to be the incarnation of the god Apis. There were also goddesses that were symbols of love and beauty and motherhood: Hathor and Isis.

6. *Boils.* The plague of the boils (9:8-12) was initiated in the face of the magicians who apparently performed their miracles through this sort of act. It was customary for these "priests" to throw these ashes into the air as a sign of blessing (Ryken, *Exodus*, 273). It might have also been a display of justice since the soot might have come from the brick-making furnace.

As the plagues continue, you may notice an increase in intensity. This sign was directly impacting the inhabitants. In a time when the magicians needed to be able to counter the plague, they could not. Instead, they were affected personally (v. 11). The Egyptians also looked to their false gods for healing. This included Amon Re, Thoth, Imhotep, and Sekhmet. The plague was an attack on all the false gods the Egyptians trusted for healing. In our day, medicine is a wonderful tool, but it is not God.

Third Cycle of Plagues (9:13–10:29)

Recurring Emphases	7. Hail	8. Locusts	9. Darkness
Obedience	9:13-23	10:3	10:21-22
God's Power over Egypt's Gods	9:24-26	10:4-6,14-15	10:22b-23
Counterfeits	None	None	None
Hardening of Heart	9:34-35	10:1,20	10:27-29

7. *Hail.* The seventh plague provides us a record of the worst hail-storm in history (9:13-35). This plague was intense. In verses 14-17 the Lord explained His purposes. They included (1) to display His unique-ness ("no one like Me," 14); (2) to show His power (v. 16a); and (3) for His name to be proclaimed in all the earth (v. 16b).

Have you ever been afraid in a storm? Think of being in the worst storm in history! The severity of the plague caused some of the people of Egypt to respond to God's word. While it is unclear if they were con-verted, we know some responded to God's gracious word by faith and others did not. All the while, the Israelites were safe from the storm.

The salvation of all peoples was on the mind of God. Ryken says, "Even when [God] was judging Pharaoh for his sins, God had a plan for Egypt's salvation" (Ryken, *Exodus*, 283). Of course, God's saving plan for Egypt is sprinkled throughout the Old Testament (Jer 46:26; Isa 19), and we read about how Egyptians were there on the day the church was born on the Day of Pentecost (Acts 2:5-11). God loves the nations, despite Pharaoh's and most of the Egyptians' refusal to heed His word. But this incident shows that perhaps some of them believed. Again, the problem was not with the "nation" but with their idolatry and their refusal to heed God's word.

Once again, Pharaoh practiced false repentance in 9:27-35. Just mouthing off religious words is not sufficient for salvation. We have noted that God hears the genuine prayer of repentance and the cry for the Lord's mercy, but He can see through false repentance. What was wrong with Pharaoh's confession? He did not confess his sin to God. Even when he did confess, he minimized his sin by saying "this time," as if his sins before were minor or had been forgiven. Pharaoh did not turn away from his sin. There is a difference in remorse and repentance. Repentance is a turning away from sin. Beware of practicing false repentance.

In regard to the Egyptian gods, we are unsure which god was being confronted here. They had plenty to choose from. They had gods over all the elements—atmosphere god, sky goddess, goddess of moisture, and gods present in the earth and wind. However we know, as the psalmist said, "lightning and hail, snow and cloud, powerful wind . . . executes His command" (Ps 148:8). There are not a number of gods over different parts of creation; there is one God, who is our Creator and Redeemer.

Where do you go for refuge, shelter, and peace? Go only to God.

8. Locusts. The scene is getting darker and darker and the music is changing to something akin to the music in the film *Gladiator* (10:1-20). This scene starts off by announcing the Lord's hardening of Pharaoh's heart. Hereafter in the plagues it is usually the Lord who is referred to as the hardener of Pharaoh's heart.

God told Moses that the plagues were not just for Egypt but also for Israel, and they were to tell their sons about their God. The Exodus was the story of Israel. It was the story that shaped them as a people, and it was to be retold. We are part of that grand story that continued to the New Testament with the coming of Jesus. We are to keep telling this story.

This scene is horrific. This intense episode points forward to the ultimate sign of judgment in the final plague. Nothing like this was ever known in Egypt. It had become so bad that Pharaoh's servants said, "Let [them] go" (v. 7). It seems like Pharaoh was going to listen, but it was not the case. He responded with qualified obedience (v. 10). He only was willing to send the men away, not the women and children. But that was not the plan of God. Moses told him everyone would be going (v. 9). In his anger and pride, Pharaoh threw Moses out (v. 11).

As a result, the locusts came over the land and not a green thing remained—neither tree nor field plant (v. 15). But Pharaoh still minimized his sin. He basically said, "Forgive me this one time." He was not practicing biblical repentance. He failed to see the nature of his sinful actions and the gravity of these plagues.

God was continuing to humiliate the Egyptian gods. This time it was an assault on the gods of the fields. Many Egyptians depended on Min, the patron god of crops; Isis, the goddess of life (who prepared flax for clothes); Nepri, the god of grain; Anubis, the guardian of the fields; and Senehem, the protector against pests. These gods failed miserably.

9. Darkness. Nothing says judgment like darkness (10:21-29) and death (11:1-10). That is what signs nine and ten were about. The darkness was to be "felt" (10:21). God intended for this warning to immobilize the Egyptians, to stun them. Few of us have probably ever been in true darkness. In complete darkness, you cannot even see someone standing in front of you. Travel in the ancient world was done in the day. It was not like the modern day in which we travel at night because we have lights. And this was pure darkness all day long. Three days of darkness! Imagine this! This prefigured the death to come. Darkness was the realm of the dead, and the final plague would come at midnight.

Once again, Pharaoh offered a qualification to what the Lord asked. This time he said, "only your flocks and herds must stay behind" (v. 24). When Moses rejected his offer, Pharaoh was so angered that he no longer wanted to see Moses' face (v. 28). Soon, he would not see it ever again.

Darkness would have been terrifying to the Egyptians because they also worshiped the sun. "Every morning the rising of the sun in the east reaffirmed the life-giving power of Amon-Re" (Ryken, *Exodus*, 304). The sunset represented death, but the sunrise offered them the hope of the resurrection. Moreover, the Pharaoh was known as the son of Re, the incarnation of Amon-Re. Amon-Re for most was the king of all Egypt's gods. But Amon-Re, the biggest of all of Egypt's gods, could not help them!

Who is your Savior? Do you look to Jesus every day and find your identity, salvation, and hope in Him? He alone is incarnate God. He crushed our greatest enemy, and to use the language of the preview to the plagues, He swallowed up death, conquering sin and death, giving us eternal life. Paul said, "Death has been swallowed up in victory. Death, where is your victory? Death, where is your sting?" (1 Cor 15:54-55).

The Tenth Plague Threatened (11:1-10)

Recurring Emphases	10. Final Plague Threatened
Obedience	11:1-4
God's Power Over Egypt's gods	11:5-9
Counterfeits	None
Hardening of Heart	11:10

As the final plague approached, the Lord prepared Israel to go out of Egypt. Israel was told to ask for silver and gold. This is the fulfillment of the account in Exodus 3:21-22. They were simply to ask for it. There were no gimmicks here. The Lord was fighting their battle for them. Moreover, "Moses was highly regarded in the land of Egypt" (11:3). This too was a fulfillment of his call. God promised to be "with him," and that is what made him effective.

In verses 4-8 Pharaoh was warned of the final plague. In this plague there was no word about asking Pharaoh to "let them go," there was only a statement of what was coming. This is showing us the finality of the plagues. Moses foretold that the "firstborn" of both man and animals would be killed. This language is not new to us, for previously God had referred to Israel as His firstborn (4:22) and indicated that Pharaoh would pay with his firstborn (4:22-23). It was too late for Pharaoh now. There was no further request for his cooperation.

Moses was furious for some reason (v. 8). We do not know why, but one can guess that Pharaoh's pride was angering him. But he understood, as he had been speaking for God, that God was going to make Himself known. The worst of all the ten plagues was coming next: the death of the firstborn. Pharaoh would experience this firsthand.

One Dominant Question: Who Is Your God?

In this section of Scripture we meet the real God. This God is Almighty. He rules over creation alone. He is sovereign. He is the jealous God. He will not share His glory with another. He will punish people according to their sins. He is merciful. He will save all who cry out to Him in humility and genuine repentance.

As we said, mercy and justice are always mingled, and the most important, glorious act of mercy and justice happened when God put forth His Son on the cross. God passed over us and punished Jesus in our place. Jesus Christ, the Righteous One, was punished *in place of us*. He was crucified *instead of us*. He took God's wrath *on behalf of us*. Everyone will be judged. Either Jesus took your judgment at the cross, or something worse than the plagues is coming your way as you face the judgment. For believers, we rejoice because through Christ there is no condemnation. Jesus took our curse. He experienced darkness—the darkness that happened at the cross and the darkness of the tomb. By His death and resurrection, we who deserve death have nothing but mercy forever.

Know Christ as your Savior, or fear Him as your Judge. Do not harden your heart against Him.

Reflect and Discuss

1. How is the first commandment, "Do not have other gods besides Me," related to what Jesus called the greatest command (Matt 22:37-38)?
2. How does it change your understanding of the plagues to know that they were not directed primarily at the people of Egypt but at their gods?
3. How does God's purpose in the plagues—that people would know that He is Yahweh—represent the opportunity for Egypt to experience mercy? Why did most of Egypt experience judgment instead?
4. Do you find it frightening that the Egyptian magicians were able to do miracles similar to the plagues? How was their magic inferior to God's miracles? How does God's display of superiority in Exodus encourage you when you engage in spiritual warfare?
5. What serves some people as gods of provision and prosperity today? As gods of agricultural success? As gods of security and peace?
6. How can something harmless, such as frogs or flies, become a horrifying plague? How have such things been portrayed in movies?
7. How was Pharaoh's false repentance, prompted by the horror of the plagues, different from genuine repentance? What are some characteristics of false conversion to Christianity?
8. How would you respond to someone who points out that some aspects of the plagues could have arisen naturally? Which aspects of the plagues show undeniable evidence of supernatural origins?
9. Why is the story of the exodus out of Egypt important for Christians to tell to their children? How is our telling of the story different from Israel's?
10. How do we sometimes qualify our repentance and submission to God? Which of these reservations persist for many years after our conversion? How do we move toward complete submission?

The Passover

EXODUS 12:1–13:16

Main Idea: In the story of the Passover, we remember God's saving power and grace from generation to generation.

I.   Remember the Substitute (12:1-28).
II. Remember the Severity and Mercy of God (12:29-32).
III. Remember God's Deliverance (12:33-42).
IV. Remember the Strong Hand of the Lord (13:1-16).
V. Worthy Is the Lamb.

Stories and experiences shape our lives. Think about your own life. Have you had any experiences that you will never forget? What events in the past continue to have ongoing consequences? Perhaps these events include moving to a new location, proposing to your wife, beginning your first day of college, or having your first child. As we continue our journey through Exodus, we find a story that was life changing for the people of Israel: the Passover. In the story of the Passover we see God's redemptive power, mercy, and justice displayed and His promises kept. In the institution of the Passover celebration (or Festival of Unleavened Bread), we see the need to *remember* God's saving power from generation to generation (Exod 13:3).

This idea of *remembering God's grace* is an important practice for Christians. We are a forgetful people. The Scriptures urge us to "Remember the great and awe-inspiring LORD" (Neh 4:14); "Remember your Creator in the days of your youth" (Eccl 12:1); "Remember the wonderful works He has done" (Ps 105:5); and "Remember Jesus Christ, risen from the dead" (2 Tim 2:8 ESV). New Testament writers often remind their readers of essential gospel truths (2 Tim 2:14; Rom 15:15; Phil 3:1; Jude 5; 2 Pet 1:12-15; 3:1-2). When Jesus instituted the Lord's Supper (which is of course linked to Passover), He said, "Do this in remembrance of Me" (Luke 22:19). It is important that we remind ourselves, and others, of all that God has done for us.

In the passage before us, God wanted His people to remember the exodus from Egypt, so He gave them a multi-sensory way to remember it: Passover. The Israelites observed the first Passover in Egypt. They celebrated it for 40 years in the wilderness (Num 9:1-5). When they entered the promised land, they kept it as well (Exod 12:15; Josh 5:10-11). I have outlined this section with four "remembers" to help us apply the Passover event.

Remember the Substitute
EXODUS 12:1-28

In the United States, significant events can result in scheduled holidays. We take time each year to celebrate Memorial Day, Independence Day, Labor Day, Veterans Day, and many more. These days are a time to remember what has happened in the past. They tell of where we have been and where we are going. In Exodus 12, we find God doing something on a much grander scale. God changed the calendar of the Israelites so that they would celebrate the Passover. He told Moses and Aaron that there would be a new calendar and it would be a sign of a new beginning. This tells us of the importance of the event.

God established their calendar based on theology. At the beginning of each year, they would remember God's great salvation. God came first in their lives and was central to all that they did. This change in their calendar to focus on theology points us to transformation. God calls us to keep Him at the center of our lives. Because of this, we are continually going through a transformation process for God's glory and our sanctification.

The instructions for the Passover were given twice in chapter 12 (vv. 1-13,21-23), separated by instructions regarding the Festival of Unleavened Bread (vv. 14-20). Verses 1-13 include the Lord's instructions to Moses. Then in verses 21-23 Moses relayed the instructions to the elders.

They were to take a lamb on the tenth day of this month for each household or for the number of people who could eat a lamb (v. 4). The lamb served as a substitute. However, the lamb was only acceptable if it was a one-year old male without blemish (v. 5). It was selected on the tenth day and kept until the fourteenth day. These qualifications were very important. In Deuteronomy 17:1 God said that a blemished animal used for a sacrifice was an abomination. Israel needed a perfect substitute, a perfect sacrifice.

This need for a perfect sacrifice reminds us of our own state. We, being corrupted by our sin, cannot save ourselves. Our good works are like the blemished lamb—unworthy before a holy God. We need One who serves as a substitute on our behalf. Jesus is the lamb for the household of God. Only through faith in Him are our sins covered. He alone is our hope.

In verses 6-7 we see what was to happen to this unblemished lamb. It was killed at twilight. The slain lamb vividly reminded everyone that all deserve judgment (cf. Rom 3:23). Consequently, a blameless life had to be sacrificed in the place of the guilty who needed salvation. The blood of the lamb was applied to the doorposts (v. 7). The obedience of placing the blood on the doorposts showed that a person believed God would keep His word and pass over him, sparing him from judgment. So Israel escaped judgment through this sacrifice, and salvation was accomplished by faith in the substitute.

In verses 8-11 God also provided instructions on how to serve and eat the lamb. It would be eaten with unleavened bread. The use of unleavened bread and the instruction to wear their clothes in a certain manner revealed that they needed to be prepared at any moment to depart. It was a reminder that they must be ready to follow God at a moment's notice. In addition, they ate bitter herbs as a reminder of the bitterness they experienced in Egypt. The Passover would serve as a reminder of their time and escape from Egypt.

We likewise should remember the bitterness from which God has saved us. We were in a bitter bondage to our own sins, yet through Christ, our perfect Passover Lamb, we were delivered from the wrath of God and given new life (see 1 Cor 5:7; Heb 9:14). Many do not praise the God of grace with passion because they have a low view of sin. Thomas Watson said, "Till sin be bitter, Christ will not be sweet." Remember what God has done for you in delivering you from bondage and giving you life.

Next we see a transition to the Lord's response to the blood that is placed on the doorposts (vv. 12-13). God would now act decisively against the powerless gods of the Egyptians. While some had already been judged, all would now be judged. In His mighty judgment, God signaled that the real King is present. Yahweh was to be feared, not Pharaoh! Only the Lord is the true, righteous judge, and He would make Himself known. The events of Passover are an awesome demonstration of God's holy judgment on Egypt and their false gods.

It is also important to recognize the sign imagery of verse 13. The blood on their doors served as a sign that judgment had already fallen at that house. Just as the plagues were a sign to Egypt of God's justice and judgment, now the Passover was a sign of God's mercy to Israel! God continued to keep the promise of Genesis 3:15 and the Abrahamic covenant. In the midst of looming judgment, God provided for the seed of woman. He protected Israel from slavery and death for future salvation. In accomplishing this, He said, "when I see the blood, I will pass over you. No plague will be among you to destroy you when I strike the land of Egypt." God accepted the blood of the sacrifice and passed over their sin. Similarly, those who have been born again have Christ's blood covering them. God sees Christ's blood on us and passes over our sin. He forgives our trespasses and sees Christ's righteousness as our own. What a merciful God!

God would make a distinction with Israel, but this was not to say that Israel was innocent. Israel was not innocent here based on their bloodline. They were found innocent because of the applied blood of the substitute. God judged Egypt, but He also judged Israel. The Passover demonstrated that apart from blood of the lamb, Israel would be found guilty. Why? Because God is holy. All are sinners and deserve to be cut off from God. We are all like Pharaoh, even if we do not have the title. But God in His grace provides a way of salvation through the blood of a substitute.

Though the Israelites had been protected from previous plagues, they now had to act faithfully in order to appropriate the means by which the Lord would "pass over" them. The author of Hebrews reflected on this event: "By faith he instituted the Passover and the sprinkling of the blood, so that the destroyer of the firstborn might not touch the Israelites" (Heb 11:28). Blood represents life. Without it, we die. Righteousness is the lifeblood we need in order to be in relationship with God. Because we do not have this in ourselves, we need another's righteousness. Where does your righteousness come from? You need Christ's righteousness, His blood, His life.

In verses 14-20 God focused on the future of this event and what Israel would do in the promised land. For seven days, they would eat unleavened bread. The Festival of Unleavened Bread was initiated by Passover and observed for seven days. These were not two separate holidays but one weeklong celebration. Why bread without yeast? It was because the Israelites ate it before it could rise. It was symbolic of their hasty departure (12:11,39).

Some argue that the organization of this passage is intended to teach an additional truth; namely that "we are saved in order to be sanctified" (Ryken, *Exodus*, 338). Ryken says,

> Passover is about getting saved. It reminds us that we have been delivered from death by a perfect substitute whose blood was shed as a sacrifice for our sins. The Feast of Unleavened Bread reminds us what God wants us to do once we've been saved, and that is to live a sanctified life, becoming more and more free from sin. (ibid.)

Whether the Holy Spirit intended Moses to make this point is debated, but it makes sense theologically. We have been redeemed in order to live holy lives (1 Pet 1:15-21).

Of course, theologians have often seen yeast as a symbol for sin. And Jesus Himself used this image, saying, "Be on your guard against the yeast of the Pharisees, which is hypocrisy" (Luke 12:1). Even more tied to Exodus is Paul's use of this image (along with the Passover Lamb image) when talking about the need to purify the church in Corinth:

> *Your boasting is not good. Don't you know that a little yeast permeates the whole batch of dough? Clean out the old yeast so that you may be a new batch. You are indeed unleavened, for Christ our Passover has been sacrificed. Therefore, let us observe the feast, not with old yeast or with the yeast of malice and evil but with the unleavened bread of sincerity and truth.* (1 Cor 5:6-8)

Peter Enns reminds us that Paul's charge for purity here was not an appeal to mere moralism; that is, for the Corinthians to "just do their best." Instead Paul was urging them to live holy lives in light of Christ's sacrifice and in light of their new identity as the redeemed. He says,

> [T]he basis for their [the church in Corinth] morality is twofold: Christ's death has atoned for their sin and, perhaps more important, in Christ, the people are *already* a new batch without yeast. *They are to act like what they are*, which is not the result of their own efforts but the results of Christ's efforts. (Enns, *Exodus*, 265; latter emphasis added)

We too are to remember the substitute. We are "a new batch" because of what He has achieved on our behalf. Now, by God's grace, let us remove the leaven and become what we are.

In verses 24-27a we see that the Passover observance was not only a way to reflect on God's grace but also an important means of teaching the younger generation of God's mighty salvation (cf. 10:2). The necessity of training children in sound doctrine repeatedly appears in the Passover account (see notes at 13:8-9,14-15).

Notice the people's reaction in verses 27b-28 to these instructions: worship and obedience. They "bowed down and worshiped" (v. 27b), and "they did just as the Lord had commanded Moses and Aaron" (v. 28). This theme of worship and obedience runs right through Exodus. By remembering who God is and what He had done, they gave God praise and obedience. May we do the same.

Remember the Severity and Mercy of God
EXODUS 12:29-32

The firstborn child in the time of Moses held much responsibility and had wonderful privileges. We can understand the tragedy to lose any child, but it was especially devastating to lose the firstborn in those days. With this in mind, God's judgment on Egypt—killing the firstborn— tells of the seriousness of their transgressions. In this passage on the death of the firstborn, we see God's redeeming power displayed in a "great reversal." God began by striking down the firstborns of Egypt. He would end the negotiations with one cataclysmic sign. He judged all of Egypt without distinction, from the rich to the poor, the good and the bad. The cries in the land extended to all people. The destroyer was going to go through the mightiest nation in the world like a knife through butter.

Earlier we read God's word to Moses: "Then you will say to Pharaoh: This is what Yahweh says: Israel is My firstborn son. I told you: Let My son go so that he may worship Me, but you refused to let him go. Now I will kill your firstborn son!" (4:22-23). Here we see that God kept His word. By means of the tenth plague, God turned turn evil on its head. Pharaoh had enacted an unrighteous judgment on the Hebrew boys by throwing them in the Nile, now God enacted a righteous judgment on Egypt's sons. Pharaoh's judgment came back on his head. In addition, by striking down the "gods" of Egypt, in particular Pharaoh's son, God told Pharaoh that he is not God and neither is his son. There is only one true God! This blow hurt Egypt not only personally through the loss of the son of succession but also theologically as God's power over their gods was displayed.

We should remember the severity and mercy of God. We are all like Pharaoh. We all deserve this kind of judgment. Some think they will never be judged. They think that they can spend their life as a little Pharaoh, piling up pyramids full of stuff, chasing fame, and refusing to bow down to the true God. Sadly, they will end up much like Pharaoh unless they look to God alone for mercy. Are you turning to the Substitute, Jesus Christ, that you might receive His mercy?

There were great cries in Egypt, since "there wasn't a house without someone dead" (12:30). Pharaoh then relented and released Israel. Notice the pathetic nature of this cataclysmic reversal. As Pharaoh was humiliated, he was now begging another to bless him (v. 32)!

This great reversal led to great liberation: Israel was freed from slavery. The promises of Genesis 3:15 were secured. And in the midst of what seems like a harsh judgment, we should remember John 3:16: God loved the world by protecting His coming Son, the seed of the woman, so that everyone who would believe in Him might not perish but have everlasting life.

Remember God's Deliverance
EXODUS 12:33-42

John Newton spent much of his life on ships. He was involved in slave trade and was caught up in numerous sins. God spared Newton's life a number of times at sea, yet Newton did not recognize the providence of God. Shortly before he was born again, Newton and his crew were delivered from a storm that would have swallowed their ship had they not reached land. As God had been working in his life, Newton began to see God's providence and deliverance time and time again through the years. He saw the coming of deliverance (Newton, 73–80).

The Israelites, likewise, would see the coming of God's deliverance. Here the exodus event was taking place. The Lord told the Israelites to be ready, and they were. The time finally came for them to leave Egypt. As the Israelites left the land, they pillaged the Egyptians as God commanded, receiving their gold and silver (v. 35). This was a sign of God's faithfulness to keep His word. Through Israel's many hardships and struggles, God had remained faithful. Deliverance had arrived, and He had provided for His people. This points us to the greater exodus we have in the gospel. We have a King who vacated a grave and gave gifts to men (Eph 4:7-10). He gives us the spoils of His ultimate victory.

There are three promises in particular that are fulfilled in Israel's getting out of Egypt. First, we see the fulfillment of Genesis 15:14. God promised that the people would be rich upon leaving the land. This promise was fulfilled, and that only by God's grace, for He gave them favor in sight of Egyptians.

Second, the promise that they would be a great, multiplying nation had been fulfilled (Gen 12:2). They were no longer the original family of 70 sojourners who had first arrived in Egypt. Instead, there were six hundred thousand men, not including women and children (Exod 12:37). I think of the enormous amount of people who cram into Times Square on New Year's Eve to celebrate the New Year. As I see these people on television, it seems as if hardly anyone can move. Imagine this massive amount of people fleeing Egypt. What an immense migration!

Third, the nations were being blessed through the seed of Abraham (Gen 12:2). In Exod 12:38 the text says, "An ethnically diverse crowd also went up with them." This means that many who were not descendants from Abraham or Israel joined the Israelites as they left Egypt (Stuart, *Exodus*, 303). They saw the signs and believed! Stuart says, "In this regard they were predecessors to Ruth who declared to Naomi, 'Your people will be my people and your God my God' (Ruth 1:16)" (ibid.). In Exodus we see the beginning of the fulfillment of this promise that the nations would be blessed through the seed of Abraham. Ultimately, this was fulfilled through the coming of Christ (Gal 3:16). By faith in Christ the nations are made "sons of Abraham" (Gal 3:7-9). As Christians we must share in this passion to see the nations worship the true God, making disciples of all nations (Matt 28:16-20).

Israel was in Egypt 430 years, but God delivered them. Our God keeps His promises. Believe God's promises. Do not resort to being a practical atheist. Instead, be strengthened by the word of the Lord.

As Israel departed, God provided additional future instructions for Passover observance (Exod 12:43-51). This is likely made necessary because the large number of people leaving Egypt included those Egyptians who had believed in the God of Moses. God said that they were not to break the lamb's bones (v. 46). This was probably one of the texts John has in mind as being fulfilled in the death of Jesus on Passover (John 19:36; cf. Ps 34:20).

Also, He specified that the Passover meal was only for the covenant community. The main emphasis in these verses (vv. 43-51) was circumcision. This act was the sign that one belonged to the community of faith, and it qualified one to participate in the Passover meal. "Outsiders" or "foreigners" were not allowed to eat the meal, not because of their ethnic status or social status but because of faith and practice status. Concerning ethnicity, already noted is the fact that many non-Israelites came out of Egypt with Israel and became part of the covenant community by faith. Concerning social status, the text says that "slaves" could also participate in the meal (v. 44). Everyone was welcome to the table as long as they were circumcised—trusting and worshiping only the living God.

Remember the Strong Hand of the Lord
EXODUS 13:1-16

We all have at times set things aside—whether it be money or time or a number of other things—for some greater purpose. In chapter 13 God called for the Israelites to set aside their firstborns to Himself (vv. 1-2,11-16). This act was connected to the tenth plague and the fact that God had distinguished Israel as His firstborn. The firstborn represented the whole family. By dedicating the firstborn to God, they were saying, "our family belongs to you, Lord."

Notice that God commanded the Israelites to "redeem" their firstborn sons (not sacrifice them; 13b). This required a payment, and if it was the same offering made for donkeys, it would have been a lamb (v. 13a). Again, the image of salvation by substitution is made clear.

We see an example of the consecration of the firstborn with Mary and Joseph taking Jesus to Jerusalem (Luke 2:22-24). Luke quotes Exodus 13:1. Of course Jesus did not need to be "redeemed" (v. 13), but it was necessary for Him to fulfill all righteousness. Mary and Joseph offered up "a pair of turtledoves or two young pigeons," perhaps because they were too poor to afford a lamb. (They were actually holding the Lamb!) Further, Jesus, the ultimate firstborn (Rom 8:29; Col 1:15; Heb 12:23), consecrated His whole life to serving the Father. (Jesus as "the firstborn" does not mean that Jesus was not eternal, but it speaks of

His supremacy.) Ryken says, "How proper it was, then, for his earthly parents to give him over to his heavenly Father at the time of his birth" (*Exodus*, 373). Amazingly, in order to redeem us, God offered up His own firstborn Son (Rom 8:32). Now we no longer belong to ourselves but to God (1 Pet 1:18-19; 1 Cor 6:19-20).

In Exodus 13:3-10 we see a reiteration and expansion of the regulations for the Festival of Unleavened Bread. It was to be observed in detail and then taught to the children. Notice the phrase "for the LORD brought you out of Egypt with a strong hand" (13:9). It was used already in verse 3 and is repeated in verses 14 and 16. This phrase frames this whole section; it provides a picture of God's mighty salvation. The meal caused them to remember that God delivered them from bondage by His mighty hand.

Food has a natural way of bringing back memories. When my wife and I were in Ukraine for 40 days adopting children, we did not have a lot of access to various restaurants. But we did have a McDonalds, so we ate there a lot. Now every time I smell McDonalds or walk into a McDonalds, I think about our adoption journey. In a similar but more dramatic and important way, the Passover and Festival of Unleavened Bread brought back essential memories of God's strong hand of salvation.

We are called to remember Christ's work on our behalf through the Lord's Supper. This meal signifies our great deliverance. In it, we taste and see Jesus' work on our behalf. Just as Israel looked back to the Passover, we look back to God's work on the cross for us and ahead to our glorious future with our King.

In verse 8 God again gives us a model for parenting (cf. vv. 14-16; 12:26-27). Here the child was being told of the great deliverance that God had provided. This is also something we should implement. Children ask all kinds of questions, especially "Why?" Some questions are very silly, but others are quite serious. When they ask you about the Lord's Supper or other questions regarding salvation, are you ready to answer? This is a great time to share the gospel with your own child. We were slaves, but God rescued us. We deserved the death angel, but God passed over us. Then tell them of the marriage supper in the future (Rev 19). One day we will sit down at a banquet table with our King! Tell them it is "by the strong hand of God" that the captives are free. As parents, we have a holy responsibility of catechizing our kids, pointing them to Jesus.

Worthy Is the Lamb

How can we conclude this amazing section of Exodus? Let us remember that true freedom comes in Jesus Christ, the Lamb of God who takes away the sin of the world (John 1:29). He is the lamb who provides us with total perfection and protection from God's judgment (1 John 2:2; 3:10). He was the spotless, unblemished lamb, chosen before the foundation of the world (1 Pet 1:19-20). He was the lamb whose bones were not broken (John 19:33-36); the ultimate lamb, crucified during Passover (Matt 26:26-32). This lamb will apply His blood to our account (2 Cor 5:21). Will you recognize this today?

If you are wondering, "How can a sinner come into the presence of a holy God?" Look to the Lamb! Russell Moore says,

> Does it remind you that the death angel is coming for us too? . . . If the Lord waits . . . we will all be placed in the ground. We aren't gods! But what the gospel reminds us of is that we're passed over . . . so even as we eat and drink in this life, we keep our shoes on, we recognize the people we belong to, and when we finally stand in judgment we don't come cowering in fear, we come marching triumphantly to Zion right through that door, that narrow little door that everybody great or small must pass through if we would be redeemed. And it's the one with blood all over it—that's the Gospel! ("The Blood-Splattered Welcome Mat")

We can come into the presence of a holy God through an unblemished substitute. Salvation only comes through this Jesus who lived the life you could not live and died the death you should have died. In a famous sermon, R. G. Lee put it like this:

> And the only way I know for any man . . . to escape the sinner's payday . . . is through Christ Jesus, who took the sinner's place upon the Cross, becoming for all sinners all that God must judge, that sinners through faith in Christ Jesus might become all that God cannot judge. ("Pay Day Someday")

Praise God we have a substitute: Christ Jesus, our Passover Lamb! If you have come to Him by faith, you can sing the song of the redeemed:

> *Then I looked and heard the voice of many angels around the throne, and also of the living creatures and of the elders. Their number was*

*countless thousands, plus thousands of thousands. They said with a
loud voice:*

*The Lamb who was slaughtered is worthy to receive power and
riches and wisdom and strength and honor and glory and blessing!*

*I heard every creature in heaven, on earth, under the earth, on the
sea, and everything in them say:*

*Blessing and honor and glory and dominion to the One seated on
the throne, and to the Lamb, forever and ever!*

*The four living creatures said, "Amen," and the elders fell down
and worshiped.* (Rev 5:11-14)

Reflect and Discuss

1. Which of your country's holidays call for somber reflection? Which
   ones call for joyful celebration? Which holiday do you find the most
   meaningful?
2. How do traditional symbols and activities help us celebrate holidays? Which ones do you find the most meaningful?
3. How do symbols and activities help to teach children important
   truths? How do they help adults remember?
4. How did faith and deeds both play a part in the Passover? How do
   they play a part in the salvation of a Christian?
5. What part does obedience play in obtaining deliverance? What part
   does obedience play after salvation?
6. Which aspects of the Passover story have parallels in Jesus' substitu-
   tionary atonement? Why are the perfect lamb, bitter herbs, blood,
   and unleavened bread important?
7. Why was Israel granted grace? Was it their ancestry or their goodness? Why are Christians granted grace?
8. In what way is every person like Pharaoh?
9. How is a firstborn regarded differently from other offspring, both
   technically and psychologically? What other places in the Bible deal
   with a firstborn or firstfruits?
10. What are the similarities between Passover and the Lord's Supper?
    How can familiarity with Passover make celebrating the Lord's
    Supper more meaningful?

Who Is Like You, O Lord?

EXODUS 13:17–15:21

Main Idea: We should praise Yahweh because there is no one like Him in majesty and mercy.

I. **The Lord Is Faithful (13:17-22).**
   A. Trust in His wisdom (13:17-18).
   B. Rest in His promises (13:19).
   C. Journey by His presence (13:20-22).
II. **The Lord Is Passionate about His Glory (14:1-9).**
III. **The Lord Saves Sinners (14:10-31).**
   A. What we are saved from: bondage
   B. How we are saved: crossing over by grace
   C. Why we can be saved: a mediator
IV. **The Lord Is Worthy of Praise (15:1-21).**
   A. Everyone should sing to the Lord (15:1,20-21).
   B. Sing about Him and to Him (15:1-18).
   C. Sing of His glory and His salvation (15:1-18).

The book of Exodus magnifies the greatness of God. We have seen and will continue to see that there is none like Him. He is God, and there is no other. In this section of Scripture, the greatness of God is majestically and mercifully displayed. A powerful summary statement of Yahweh's uniqueness is in Exodus 15:11-13:

> LORD, who is like You among the gods? Who is like You, glorious in holiness, revered with praises, performing wonders? You stretched out Your right hand, and the earth swallowed them. You will lead the people You have redeemed with Your faithful love; You will guide them to Your holy dwelling with Your strength.

As we continue, we will see four truths about our incomparable God: (1) the Lord is faithful; (2) the Lord is passionate about His glory; (3) the Lord saves sinners; and (4) the Lord is worthy of praise.

The Lord Is Faithful
EXODUS 13:17-22

Trust in His Wisdom (13:17-18)

The "way of the sea" was the quickest way for Israel to leave Egypt. They would have arrived in less than two weeks instead of 40 years! That was the shortest way, but not the best way. There were enemies in that direction, and Israel was not ready for battle: "The people will change their minds and return to Egypt if they face war" (v. 17). They would have turned back to Pharaoh at the first sign of trouble. Even though they left "in battle formation" (v. 18), this does not mean they were ready to fight. Later in their journey, once they reached Canaan and saw how big their enemies were, they said, "Let's appoint a leader and go back to Egypt" (Num 14:4).

God's route was not an easy route, however. Soon they would be hemmed in between the Red Sea and Pharaoh's army. God teaches them many things on this journey. God has other purposes in mind, involving much more than moving them from point A to point B. The Israelites will later doubt God, like we are tempted to do as we journey in this life. But we must trust in the wisdom of God.

Remember Genesis 50:20. This is the "Romans 8:28" of the Old Testament. Joseph said that the evil act of selling him into slavery turned into a good thing. He said, "You planned evil against me; God planned it for good to bring about the present result—the survival of many people." So what looked bad was actually good. We do not always understand (or like!) what God is doing, but we can trust that for those who love God and are called according to His purpose, He is working all things for their good; and according to Romans 8:29, that ultimate good is conformity to Jesus Christ. In many of life's circumstances we do not know what is going on, but we must trust in the wisdom of God, knowing that God is good and He is working out His sovereign purposes.

Here is an example of this in my own life: I wanted to plant a church when I was about 25 years old, but it took ten years to finally fulfill this desire. However, I know that God does not waste anything. Perhaps this ten-year season was intended to get me to a place where I could not just plant a church but also teach at a seminary. I also know that I was not ready to plant a church at age 25. Looking back, I can see how God had a lot of other important ministries for me to do over those ten years. We cannot comprehend the vast knowledge of our Lord, but we can trust Him!

It is hard to make sense of things in our minds because we are not God. Our minds cannot grasp the big picture. God knows what He is doing. We may not know the way we are going, but we know our Guide. We can say like Paul in Romans 11:33-34,

> *Oh, the depth of the riches both of the wisdom and the knowledge of God! How unsearchable His judgments and untraceable His ways! For who has known the mind of the Lord? Or who has been His counselor? Or who has ever first given to Him, and has to be repaid? For from Him and through Him and to Him are all things. To Him be the glory forever. Amen.*

Rest in His Promises (13:19)

We have mentioned that when Israel left Egypt they took some of the Egyptians' riches. Now we see that they took something else—actually someone else: Joseph! Well, it was not really Joseph, but it was his bones. The Israelites carried out the last wishes of Joseph (see Gen 50:24-26; Heb 11:22). This simple act demonstrated that God was fulfilling His promises. Joseph believed God was faithful and that He would make good on His promise to Abraham. And he said, when you go, take me with you.

Like Joseph, we have been given so many amazing promises. Already in Exodus we see God's promises coming true. God is still in the promise-keeping business. Like Joseph, we are looking for something else. In your daily Bible reading one thing you should do is look to see God. Where is God, what is He like, and what is He doing? Where is Jesus? You should ask these questions and then ask, "What promise is here that I can rest in today?" Through the Scriptures we are promised many wonderful things, such as an eternal rest in the new heavens and new earth. "For we do not have an enduring city here; instead, we seek the one to come" (Heb 13:14). Put your trust in God, who has promised us something better to come.

Journey by His Presence (13:20-22)

In these verses, we see the wonderful provision of God to guide Israel by day or night. They had a cloud in the day and fire at night. Once again, fire is a picture of God's presence. Many scholars have tried to deny this miracle, claiming it was just a natural rain cloud. The problem with that claim is that the pillar of cloud traveled with them in the arid desert for 40 years!

Likewise, God never leaves us; He guides us. I can imagine one saying, "Well, I sure would like to have a cloud!" "I would like to order up a cloud to hover over the guy I should marry!" Or "I would like to have a cloud lead me to my college destination!" Actually, in the new covenant, after Christ's earthly ministry and ascension, we now have something better; namely, the Holy Spirit indwelling individuals. Paul referred to the indwelling of believers in numerous places. In Colossians, he described the new covenant and said, "Christ in you, the hope of glory" (Col 1:27). Christ by the Spirit is in individuals (Jew and Gentile)—not in a tabernacle or in the temple, but in believers who are the dwelling place of God.

I am convinced Old Testament believers were empowered to *believe*; that is, they were regenerated. And God was *with His people* (as exemplified with the cloud) but not *in His people* (with the exceptional case of the mediators). That all changed in the new covenant. Jesus, referring to the time after His ascension and the sending of the Spirit, said, "He remains with you and will be *in you*" (John 14:17; emphasis added; cf. John 7:37-39). In James Hamilton's *God's Indwelling Presence*, he summarizes this view. Commenting on John 14:17, he says,

> Here Jesus encapsulates the Bible's teaching on God's
> dwelling in relation to believers in the old and new covenants.
> In the old covenant God faithfully remained *with* His people,
> accompanying them in the tabernacle and the temple. Under
> the new covenant, the only temple is the believing community
> itself, and God dwells not only among the community
> corporately (Matt 18:20; 1 Cor 3:16; 2 Cor 6:16), but also *in*
> each member individually (John 14:17; Rom 8:9-11; 1 Cor
> 6:19). (Hamilton, *Presence*, 3)

Then he adds,

> This does not exclude an interior ministry of the Spirit to
> individuals under the old covenant. Whereas God may not
> have been continually in his people, He could operate upon
> their hearts through other means. (ibid., 25)

Thus, God was with His people by the Spirit in the old covenant, actively at work, though not indwelling individuals.

To reinforce this idea of the Spirit's work among the people in this particular portion of Exodus, consider Isaiah 63:7-14. Isaiah was reflecting on the deliverance of Israel from Egypt and the parting of the Red Sea. He said that when God delivered Israel at the Red Sea, He put His Spirit "among the flock." Hamilton says, "[A] case can be made that the Holy Spirit may be the same as the pillar of fire and the cloud" (ibid., 39).

As you make your journey in this life, know you are not alone if you are a believer. We are not left as orphans (John 14:18). We have God not only among us, *but in us*! So, no, you do not have a cloud. Instead, you have the Spirit Himself, guiding you into all truth. Will you journey by His presence?

The Lord Is Passionate about His Glory
EXODUS 14:1-9

The strategy described in the first three verses was crazy unless God was in charge. Israel was on their way out when God told them to go back and camp between the sea and the desert. The precise location is debated, but we know the sea refers to the Red Sea. It seems likely that they crossed the northern part of it. Upon traveling to this location, Israel had become vulnerable. It seems that if Pharaoh approached, they would be trapped.

God used unusual strategies throughout the Bible. Remember Abraham and Sarah's age when they had a child (Gen 21:5)? Have you heard the story of Gideon and his little army (Judg 6–8)? What about Jehoshaphat's battle with the Ammonites and Moabites (2 Chr 20)? What about the demoniac and the pigs (Mark 5)? Ultimately, God used an unusual strategy with Jesus Christ going to the cross. Satan, like Pharaoh, must have thought that he had Jesus trapped, that He was about to die. Yet in His unusual strategy, God brought deliverance for us and glorified Himself.

Verse four tells us that God does what He does *for His own glory*. He said, "I will receive glory by means of Pharaoh and all his army, and the Egyptians will know that I am Yahweh." This is central in Exodus. Know that He is God and that He gives His glory to no other. God is passionate about His glory. "For from Him and through Him and to Him are all things. To Him be the glory forever. Amen" (Rom 11:36).

As the story continues, Pharaoh pursued God's people just as God said that he would (Exod 14:5-9). Pharaoh thought he had a good military strategy, but what he was actually doing was fulfilling the purposes of God and bringing Him glory (Rom 9:17). As he pursued Israel, he would have used the best of chariots while Israel fled on foot. Egypt had all the modern military advantages. Surely they thought the Israelites would be defeated. Pharaoh was singing victory songs before the battle had begun. However, he had another thing coming.

We see Pharaoh's hardness of heart throughout this story: (1) he initially refused to do what God wanted, (2) he negotiated, (3) he asked for prayer for blessing, and (4) when he finally let Israel go, he changed his mind. Pharaoh stands as a warning for us today. God's patience will eventually turn to wrath. Do not be swallowed up. Heed God's word and turn to Jesus. There are two ways God can be glorified in someone's life: in His just judgment or in His saving mercy. Which way will you glorify Him?

The Lord Saves Sinners
EXODUS 14:10-31

From verse 10 to the end of the chapter, we find one of the most important stories in the Bible: crossing the Red Sea. God is going to get His people out of Egypt through the miracle of the sea, and He is going to judge the Egyptians by swallowing them up in the sea. I want to walk through these verses and then point out some truths about the Lord's salvation that we see here.

In verse 10 God's people saw the Egyptians, and they were afraid! The Egyptians were superior soldiers. They had "weapons of mass destruction," so to speak. But what is the real problem? Israel was forgetting that it was God who brought them to this place. They needed only to fear God and trust in His love (cf. Ps 106:1-10).

Then, in verses 11-12, the Israelites began to complain to Moses. This will become an ongoing challenge that we will talk about later.

Moses told them, "Don't be afraid. Stand firm and see the LORD's salvation He will provide for you today; for the Egyptians you see today, you will never see again. The LORD will fight for you; you must be quiet" (vv. 13-14). What kind of strategy is this? Stand there quietly? "The LORD will fight for you"? Yes. That is the right strategy. Later, this same promise is used again. Think of Jehoshaphat: the musician Jahaziel stepped up, by the power of the Spirit, and said,

*Listen carefully, all Judah and you inhabitants of Jerusalem, and
King Jehoshaphat. This is what the Lord says: "Do not be afraid or
discouraged because of this vast number, for the battle is not yours,
but God's. . . . You do not have to fight this battle. Position yourselves,
stand still, and see the salvation of the Lord. He is with you, Judah
and Jerusalem. Do not be afraid or discouraged. Tomorrow, go out to
face them, for Yahweh is with you."* (2 Chr 20:15,17)

Do you see this theme? Do not be afraid. The battle is not yours. Stand
still, and see the salvation of the Lord.

In Exod 14:15-18 notice how God singled out Moses. God gave
Moses instructions to divide the sea. Imagine what Moses' human reaction might have been to these instructions! Those of us who have heard
this story miss the shocking nature of it. Pharaoh is coming, the people
are complaining, and God says, "Hold out your stick, and I will part the
waters!" Why? Once again the theme of God's glory is repeated: there is
no one like Him (vv. 17-18).

After these instructions, "the Angel of God" enters the scene (v. 19).
There is a lot of mystery about this Angel. The Angel and the cloud
move behind the Israelites. Are these two distinct entities or the same?
In chapter 3, "the Angel of the Lord" spoke from the bush, and perhaps
this is the same type of theophany, where the Angel and the physical
manifestation are the same. I am not sure. Whatever we make of this, we
know that God is present to both guard and guide His people. Here the
cloud keeps the Egyptians from getting near the Israelites. Thus, God
continues to keep His promises.

God's deliverance manifested itself through the parting of the
waters (v. 21). By this means, the Israelites walked through to safety
(v. 22). Can you imagine this? The water is pulled back to be a wall. The
idea of a "wall" carries the idea of a "city wall." Stuart says, "A city-wall
sized wall of water on either side of them implies the division of a deep
body of water, not merely the drying out of a shallow one or the drying
out of wet terrain" (Stuart, *Exodus*, 342). When I read this, I think of
Niagara Falls. It is massive. This parting of the waters of the Red Sea is
not too hard for the Lord of all creation.

This is not the only time God will part waters. If you struggle with
this, you will struggle to believe other events in the Bible. Regarding
the Jordan River crossing, Joshua said, "The water flowing downstream
will stand up in a mass" (Josh 3:13). God also parted the Jordan for

Elijah and Elisha (2 Kgs 2:8,14). For the living God, parting water is no problem.

As the Egyptians pursued the Israelites, "the LORD looked down," majestically exalted above all (Exod 14:24). He threw the Egyptians into a panic and clogged the wheels of their state-of-the-art chariots (vv. 24-25). They should have fled, but they did not. After Israel's crossing of the sea, Moses stretched out his staff so that the waters might come down on the Egyptians and everything with them (v. 26). This was total elimination. At daybreak, the Israelites could see God's victory, for the Egyptians were swallowed up when the water went back into the gap (vv. 27-28). Verse 29 provides a summary statement: Israel had walked on dry ground to safety.

The reality of judgment and salvation are clear in verses 30 and 31. Imagine this scene: Bodies are washing up on the shore. Here is the dreadful picture of unrepentant sinners. The waters of judgment came down on those who refused to believe. Pharaoh reaped what he sowed. In contrast, we see the happy picture of believers who have been saved from the waters of judgment. They were delivered to the other side by grace through faith.

At the Red Sea, the same body of water is a place of both judgment and salvation. Paul said the Israelites were baptized into Moses (1 Cor 10:1-4) as we are baptized into Jesus (Rom 6:3; Gal 3:23). They were identified with him, as we are identified with Christ. As Moses led his people through the waters of judgment to the other side, those who are in Christ will pass through the waters of death to the other side safely because of His mighty resurrection. That is exactly what the ordinance of baptism represents: passing from death to life. I like to keep candidates under longer to get the full effect! Sometimes people say, "I'm scared to death of water." Great! That's even better! In baptism, we are saying, "I have died with Christ, I have been buried with Him, and I have been raised with Him!" (see Rom 6:1-4).

The story of the exodus is a picture of what has happened to us in salvation and in the Christian life. There are three parts to their *getting out* that we identify with as believers in Jesus.

What We Are Saved from: Bondage

The Israelites were delivered from their enslavement. This is a picture of salvation. They were now free. But there was a problem (vv. 11-12).

They got out of Egypt physically, but Egypt had not gotten out of their hearts (cf. Acts 7:39). Later some would contend that they would have been better off if they were still in Egypt (16:3).

How does this relate to us? God redeems us from bondage, also. But our bondage has many "layers" (Keller, "Getting Out"). Objectively, we are free from condemnation through Jesus. We have positional freedom. The penalty of sin is gone. There was an objective guilt on us, but through Jesus we are freed. We can say, "no condemnation now exists for those in Christ Jesus" (Rom 8:1). Subjectively, however, we still struggle with going back to Egypt, to our old way of life. We are not slaves, but we tend to live like slaves.

We can recognize three ways this slavishness of the heart may be explained. First, we can fall back into the slavishness of sin (Rom 6:1-23). We are free from the law and live under grace, but Paul said, "do not let sin reign in your mortal body" (6:12). Every day we must put sin to death. Second, we can revert to works righteousness. An example of this would be the Galatians. They wanted to go back to a works-based system of salvation. Our hearts want to create a performance-based Christianity. We have to fight every day to believe our salvation is in Christ alone. Third, we still deal with our old idols. We fight the temptation to yield to our old masters that say, "Serve me or die" (Keller, "Getting Out").

Therefore, on the one hand we can say, "I'm free," but on the other hand we wrestle in this body of flesh. What we call objective and subjective issues in theology are justification and sanctification and glorification. We have been saved from the penalty of sin (justification). We are being saved from the power of sin (sanctification). We will one day be saved from the presence of sin (glorification). Exodus gives us a story to see these things.

How We Are Saved: Crossing Over by Grace

In verses 13 and 14 Moses told the Israelites to stand quietly and "see the Lord's salvation He will provide for you today" (v. 13). He said, "The Lord will fight for you" (v. 14). The principle of grace could not be clearer here. Salvation is not about what we do but about what God has done for us in Jesus. God saves sinners by grace through faith, not by human works. Paul said,

> For what does the Scripture say? Abraham believed God, and it was credited to him for righteousness. Now to the one who works, pay is not

considered as a gift, but as something owed. But to the one who does not work, but believes on Him who declares the ungodly to be righteous, his faith is credited for righteousness. Likewise, David also speaks of the blessing of the man God credits righteousness to apart from works: How joyful are those whose lawless acts are forgiven and whose sins are covered! How joyful is the man the Lord will never charge with sin! (Rom 4:3-8)

Notice how the Old Testament teaches the same gospel. Do you know this blessing of having your sins forgiven by the God of all grace?

The Israelites crossing over the Red Sea is another great picture of salvation. The minute they crossed over the sea, they crossed over from death to life. This reminds me of Jesus' words about eternal life: "I assure you: Anyone who hears My word and believes Him who sent Me has eternal life and will not come under judgment but has passed from death to life" (John 5:24). John also spoke of crossing over from death to life: "We know that we have passed from death to life because we love our brothers. The one who does not love remains in death" (1 John 3:14).

This idea makes Christianity different from every other religion. In other systems of belief, everyone is trying to get to the other side, but they must work at it. They give alms, pray five times a day, make a holy pilgrimage, and more. But this is not the case with biblical Christianity. God does the work. You embrace Him, and boom! you cross over. Everything changes.

Everyone is either justified or condemned. You either are adopted or you are not adopted (Keller, "Getting Out"). Have you crossed over? Are you a Christian? If your answer is something like "I'm trying," then you do not understand what Scripture is saying. You cannot earn it with good works or religious efforts; you simply receive salvation by grace through faith.

Think about the power of this. Consider Paul: he persecuted people before he came to Christ. Yet he could later write that there is no condemnation (Rom 8). He did not say, "Now I need to pay God back." No. He crossed over. He still had room to change on the inside, as we talked about with the subjective nature of sin, but Paul knew that he was free and forgiven.

Tim Keller points out that the *quality of the faith* of those who crossed over really is not mentioned ("Getting Out"). One might imagine that some went through the Red Sea scared to death but believing while others went through confidently. Keller reminds us that we are saved by the *object* of our faith, not the quality of our faith. Do you have faith in this Savior? If you are a Christian, you have crossed over. Your greatest enemy has been defeated.

Why We Can Be Saved: A Mediator

It is important to consider why the Israelites did not drown in this event (what some call "The Eleventh Plague"). We have already recognized God's grace as the basis for their salvation. Without grace, they too would have been swallowed up. They were not saved because of their goodness but because of God's mercy. But we can go a step further. Why did the Israelites not get crushed? They had a mediator.

Consider Moses' role. On the one hand he was identified with the Israelites, and on the other he was identified with God. You have one man so identified with the Israelites that their guilt was on him. He got rebuked for the Israelites' sin in verse 15. God said, "Why are you crying out to Me?" There is no indication that Moses himself was crying, but he got rebuked anyway. He was also so identified with God that God's power was working through him (vv. 21,26). That is a mediator. He is the man in the middle. But there is another mediator, a better one, Jesus Christ. He was not just rebuked for one sin in one verse, but this mediator took God's wrath for all our sin. And this mediator was God (John 1:1). Jesus is the only way we cross over. He is our mediator.

The Lord Is Worthy of Praise
EXODUS 15:1-21

This song of praise is magnificent! It is the first song in the Bible. Apparently Moses penned it right after the deliverance. Notice just a few truths about it.

Everyone Should Sing to the Lord (15:1,20-21)

Moses and all the people sang of the Lord's triumph. Miriam went out with all the women and sang of His glorious triumph with dancing and a tambourine (vv. 20-21)! Everyone was singing because everyone had been rescued.

Every believer should sing to the Lord, not because they have a good voice, but because of what God has done for them! Praise is the natural response from those who have experienced God's grace. The exodus was the most important event in the Bible until the cross. What did they do after it? Sing! That is what saved people do. This pattern continues throughout the Bible all the way to Revelation 5, where we see everyone worshiping the Lamb who redeemed a people with His blood. The Song of Moses is similar to other songs or psalms in both the Old Testament and New Testament. Examples include

- Deborah and Barak's song in response to victory over Sisera and Jabin of Canaan (Judg 5:1-31);
- Hannah's song at the birth of Samuel (1 Sam 2:1-10);
- Mary's response to the angel's news and Elizabeth's greeting (Luke 1:46-55); and
- Zechariah's prophecy after the birth of John the Baptist (Luke 1:68-79).

The exodus song is rich with lyrics, as are the other songs in the Bible. We have no melody for these songs, but we have the words. That shows us how important the lyrics are in music. Here they were narrating God's work: His mercy and His judgment. This is important. It is not just "mood music." It is a good model for reminding yourself of God's redeeming grace. Songs help us remember. Songs are portable theology. Everyone should sing from their heart to the Savior for the great deliverance they have received.

Sing about Him and to Him (15:1-18)

It is difficult to outline the structure of this song. It has been done various ways by different scholars. One way to look at it is like this: In verses 1-5 and 18 the song is *about God*, and in verses 6-17 the song is sung *to God*. Notice the shift in verse 6 to "You." We sing *about* who God is, and we sing *to* Him, personally, in worship, expressing to Him our love for Him and gratitude for His salvation.

Sing of His Glory and His Salvation (15:1-18)

This song talks about who God is, what He has done, and what He will do as God and Savior.

God's Glory. This song tells of the splendor of God and His attributes. First, we see the *name* of God. "Yahweh is His name" (v. 3). Here there are clear echoes of chapter 3, where God revealed His name to Moses. God is self-existent and self-sufficient.

Second, we see God is the *personal* God. He is "*my* strength and *my* song" and "*my* salvation" (v. 2). You can know this same God. The exact representation of Him is found in Jesus (Heb 1:3).

Third, God is the *covenant-keeping* God. Moses described Him as "my father's God" (v. 2). Just as God demonstrated His power and glory in the past, so He does now.

Fourth, God is a *warrior* (v. 3). God will reign triumphantly over all His enemies, as He did over Pharaoh (vv. 4-10,12,14-16). Throughout the Bible God was opposing the enemies of Israel or, at times, opposing Israel themselves. Then at the cross God was in Christ triumphing over our greatest enemies. In Revelation we see that He will return to triumph over Satan (Rev 20:7-10).

Fifth, God is *unique*. "Who is like You among the gods?" (v. 11) Moses asked. These words are echoed in Psalms 86:8 and 89:6. God is without peer. He is incomparable and utterly unique.

Finally, God is *loving*. "You have redeemed with Your faithful love" (v. 13). In God's great grace and mercy, He rescues and leads us.

God's Salvation. This song also highlights the greatness of God's salvation. He is *sovereign* over salvation. God was not acting arbitrarily in all of this; He was working out His sovereign purposes, leading His people out to His holy abode (v. 13). And all the kings of the nations would be silent when God would bring His people to His sanctuary (v. 17). Notice how they sang in faith about future events as if they had happened already! It would be a hard, complicated journey to Canaan, but they were singing of the Lord's triumph (v. 15).

God also *redeems*. Here again is that wonderful word "redeem" (v. 13). The song's reference to God's redemption points back to 6:6. Redeem *(ga'al)* means to "reacquire" or "get back for oneself" or "buy back" (see 6:6; Ps 74:2; 77:15; 106:10; Isa 41:14; 52:9; 62:12). Christ did not redeem us with money but with His own blood (1 Pet 1:19). He rescued us from our awful situation with the payment of His life. In addition, the text says that Yahweh is going to bring Israel to His "dwelling" (v. 17). Stuart summarizes this verse:

> A grand theme of Scripture appears at this point in the song. Even though God has graciously come at various times and ways—most fully in Christ—to the place where we live, it has always been God's plan that his people should, because of the work of Christ, eventually join him where he lives. The story of ancient Israel mirrors this. God called them out of where

they had been born and had been living (Egypt), bound them to himself in a covenant (at Sinai and again in Deuteronomy), and then led them to his holy dwelling (Israel/Jerusalem/the temple). The same sort of thing happens in Christ, yet on a greater and more lasting scale. God calls those who believe in him out of where they have been born and are living (earth), binds them to himself in a (new) covenant (by believing in Jesus as Savior and Lord), and then leads them to his holy dwelling (heaven) (*Exodus,* 355–56).

The Lord will also reign forever (v. 18). This is an obvious note about the eternal nature of God's salvation. Gloriously, John the apostle heard God's people in heaven singing "the song of God's servant Moses and the song of the Lamb" (Rev 15:3), a song which is new, but is as old as the exodus!

Great and awe-inspiring are Your works,
Lord God, the Almighty;
righteous and true are Your ways,
King of the Nations.
Lord, who will not fear
and glorify Your name?
Because You alone are holy,
for all the nations will come
and worship before You
because Your righteous acts
have been revealed. (Rev 15:3-4)

Indeed, we have experienced the greater exodus. And we shall forever sing His praise. Our souls will forever say, "There is no one like You, O God!"

Reflect and Discuss

1. Looking back, when was God teaching you the most on your life's journey? At the time, did it seem like you were being delayed? How can your past experience help you as you face more delays?
2. Which of God's promises have already been fulfilled in your life? Which promises are you looking forward to receiving?
3. What was the advantage of the pillars of cloud and fire that were *with* Israel? What is the advantage of the Holy Spirit who is *in* Christians?

4. What is the key to theology: the love of God, the glory of God, the salvation of mankind, or something else? How would you describe the "big picture" of theology to an adult Sunday school class?

5. Has God ever put you in an impossible situation and then brought you through? What is the value of this kind of experience for you and for God?

6. When is it appropriate to "stand still" and see God's salvation? When does obedient activity come into play?

7. How would you respond to someone who says that God merely dried up a few inches of water in a marshy area?

8. How is Israel's crossing of the Red Sea similar to Christian baptism?

9. What is your favorite song melody? What are your favorite Christian praise or hymn lyrics? How do good lyrics teach good theology?

10. What is the value of singing songs *about* God? What is the purpose of singing songs *to* God?

Wilderness University

EXODUS 15:22–17:7

Main Idea: On our wilderness journey, we learn to trust God for our provision, just as we trust Christ for eternal life.

I. **Israel in the Wilderness**
    A. Test 1: Bitter water (15:22-27)
    B. Test 2: Bread from heaven (16:1-36)
        1. It was supernatural (16:11-15).
        2. It was sufficient (16:16-30).
        3. It was sacred (16:31-36).
        4. It was sanctifying (Deut 8:3).
    C. Test 3: Water from the rock (Exod 17:1-7)
        1. They demanded God's provision (17:2a).
        2. They questioned God's protection (17:3).
        3. They doubted God's presence (17:7).
II. **Christ in the Wilderness**
    A. Christ passed the test that Israel failed (Matt 4:2-3).
    B. Christ is the bread we need for eternal life (John 6:25-59).
    C. Christ is the rock that was struck for our salvation (1 Cor 10:1-5).
III. **Two Responses to the Wilderness Story**

While I was the first guy in my family to graduate college, the other men in my family are still smarter than I am in most subjects. And they like to remind me of it! From trivia games to skills in building million dollar homes, the men in my family have reminded me that there are some things that I could not learn in the university. But as Christians, there is a school that we all attend. God trains us, disciplines us, and sanctifies us in "Wilderness University." Spurgeon called the wilderness "the Oxford and Cambridge for God's students" ("Marah").

In this chapter we are going to look at Israel's wilderness experience. Ryken says, "Going through the wilderness was not necessary for Israel's salvation, but it was necessary for their sanctification" (*Exodus*, 414). Clement of Rome, an early church father, said about the sanctifying purpose of the wilderness, "After this [Red Sea crossing], Moses, by the command of God, whose providence is over all, led out the people of the Hebrews into the wilderness . . . that [He] might *root out the evils which had clung to them* by a long-continued familiarity with the customs of the Egyptians" (ibid., 434; emphasis added). Yes, God is rooting out the evils that clung to them.

Like Israel, we too are sojourners, who have been redeemed by the blood of the Lamb, who have crossed over to the other side by grace, and who are now on the way to promised land. In this faith journey, in our wilderness, God is sanctifying us and teaching us to trust Him, love Him, and follow Him.

We need to learn some things from Israel's wilderness experience since their story is our story. To do so, let us reflect on this story in two parts. First, let us consider Israel in the wilderness, examining the three tests that they took. Second, let us consider Christ in the wilderness and note three ways His experience was connected to Israel's wilderness experience.

Israel in the Wilderness

Three consecutive stories have to do with food and water. Israel gets hungry and thirsty, and they complain. Their grumbling serves as a warning to us, but it is also not surprising to us. Have you ever been on a road trip and gotten irritable when hungry? One of the biggest parts of the drama of road trips often has to do with food. I remember when I took a group, of 45 people to Israel, and though they were not a grumbling group there were some complaints about food. Many questions before the trip had to do with food, and many during the trip had to do with food. So Israel's grumbling about the Wilderness University meal plan should not surprise us. Yet we are not to follow their example (1 Cor 10:9-10).

Test 1: Bitter Water (15:22-27)

The first test here is sort of like a "pre-test." It includes a bit of a preview of tests to come and a minicovenant that anticipates fuller understanding of God's ways. In verse 22 we find a description of the land. It was a huge, rugged, wilderness region in northern Sinai, stretching from what in modern times is the eastern side of the Suez Canal to the Negev of Israel. It was not exactly a great place for six hundred thousand men—plus women and children—to camp. The problem in the desert is that the water is bitter; as a result, they called it Marah (v. 23). Our most basic physical need is water, so the lack of water troubled the Israelites. They were in a desert and thought they had found water, only to discover it was undrinkable. Have you ever been overseas in a place where you cannot drink the water? In those occasions you live with sort of a fear, always boiling your water, keeping bottles of water, and doing everything to ensure you will not get sick. You can identify a bit with the Israelites here.

The Israelites responded to their need and fear by grumbling against Moses (v. 24). "What are we going to drink?" they asked. Complaining and grumbling are signs of ungratefulness, self-centeredness, immaturity, and insecurity. It is what children do in minivans and in response to homework assignments. We have a "whining and arguing" chart on our refrigerator for our kids. We are trying to teach our kids to be grateful and respectful, contrary to the Israelites here.

By now you would think the Israelites would have learned to cry out to God in prayer rather than complain. Instead, they show their immaturity. However, Moses does cry out to God, and the Lord answers Moses (v. 25a).

Is your first reaction to trouble faith-filled prayer or grumbling and anxiety? Some have called anxiety "functional atheism." When you worry, you do not believe in God.

Moses brought his trouble to the Lord. In response, the Lord told him what to do. Obediently, Moses threw a log into the water and the water became sweet. Some have tried to find a scientific explanation for this. The best way to understand it is to believe it as a miracle. What is amazing here is not just that God can do a miracle, making the water sweet, but that He is willing to do it for these complainers! This is grace. God's grace is sweet.

As we continue, we see that God tested His people (vv. 25b-26). He made a small covenant with them, providing the terms of their relationship. If they kept His word, He would bless them. Heeding His voice and doing what is right included Passover, the Festival of Unleavened Bread, and the consecration of the firstborn. Later, God would reveal more through Moses. However, if they did not follow God's ways, He said that they would experience "diseases" that fell on the Egyptians.

From this we can identify three applications. First, we can apply the pattern of instruction to our lives today. Israel was first rescued and then they began to learn about obedience and following God's word. These requirements were not the basis of their salvation. They were conveyed after they were saved, in order to teach them how to now live for God's glory. This is the same pattern for the Ten Commandments, which we will examine later. God brought them out of Egypt, and then He instructed them on how to live.

Second, we have the same restoring God who was with Israel. He is Yahweh-Rophe', "the God who heals." Here again is a pattern in Exodus. God did wonders so everyone might know that He is the Lord. In the next chapter we will see Him conquer one of Israel's enemies and provide another name for Himself (17:15). Here it is *rophe'*. Ryken says *rophe'* refers to "wellness and soundness, both physically and spiritually" (*Exodus,* 421). The miracle at Marah shows that God can heal the waters and the body. He is the restorer. Then in verse 27 we see a beautiful picture. God brought the people to Elim, "where there were 12 springs of water and 70 date palms." The text says, "They camped there by the waters." Wherever this was located, it was obviously a place of abundance and refreshment. God restores and refreshes.

Third, we have the same God who is able to care for His people by a miracle (healing the water) or by His providence (taking them to a place that has water). Both are gifts, and they should cause us to be grateful for them both.

Test 2: Bread from Heaven (16:1-36)

This is a very important story, referred to in numerous places in different ways elsewhere in Scripture. In verses 1-12 we find Israel complaining against Moses about food after setting out from Elim. In His mercy, the Lord provided both manna and quail.

Over and over we read about Israel's "grumbling" (vv. 2,7,8,11). Complaining is a serious sin, more serious than you might think. (See 1 Cor 10:1-12. Notice the sins mentioned there.) Paul told the church in Philippi, "Do everything without grumbling and arguing" (Phil 2:14).

What did the children of Israel complain about? They grumbled under Pharaoh (Exod 2:23). They grumbled at the Red Sea (14:11-12). They grumbled at Marah (15:23-24). They grumbled about their leaders (16:2-3; 17:3-4; also Num 11). God just did a miracle turning bitter water into sweet water; He showed Israel that He would care for them; yet they still complained. What would you have done if you had brought out the people from Egypt and they began to murmur, "[in Egypt] we sat by pots of meat"? I would have been angry.

I remember coming back from Ukraine with our four newly adopted kids after spending 40 days out of the country. When we landed in Memphis, I took everyone to get barbeque! I was so excited. I like a lot of Ukrainian dishes, but I missed some of my favorite foods, like pulled pork. I asked the kids what they wanted, and they each picked out a barbecue plate. To my shock, when I set it down they complained and said they did not want to eat it. My shock turned to anger. I was so upset because I thought they were ungrateful. I thought they should be excited, considering where they came from and what they used to eat. This was Memphis barbeque! I eventually cooled down. In contrast, God reacted with mercy here to the Israelites. He still provided for them in spite of their ingratitude.

The provision of manna includes a number of important lessons. We will look at the nature of this provision and make some running application. Consider four aspects of God's provision:

It was supernatural (16:11-15). God miraculously provided bread from heaven (16:4,11-13). Now, most people work for bread. That is the way God designed it. Paul told us that a man who is not willing to work should not eat (2 Thess 3:10). Some refuse to work because in a fallen world work is very toilsome. In Genesis 3 God said to Adam that one of the results of the fall for men is that their work would be difficult. He said, "You will eat bread by the sweat of your brow" (3:19). So from the beginning, bread has been a result of man's hard labor. Most of the world has not lived like us in America. We go to the grocery store and we have cinnamon-raisin bread, Texas toast, Italian ciabatta rolls, crusty French baguettes, and more. We purchase it with a debit card and go on our merry way. Yet most people throughout history have had to work diligently to have bread.

However, Israel received bread from heaven! It was a supernatural provision of God. They received bread apart from their labor (except for going to collect it). And God did it for 40 years (v. 35)!

Another sign that this was miraculous is how the Israelites responded to the manna. They called it "manna," which is related by similar sound to the expression "What is it?" (vv. 14-15,31). They were totally mystified by it, showing us that they had never seen anything like it. Verse 31 gives a further description: "It resembled coriander seed, was white, and tasted like wafers made with honey." Apparently, it was very tasty.

Some have tried to give a human explanation of this, saying this was something that was common in the wilderness. That is not the picture here. This was a curious type of wafer with honey. The psalmist says it was "the bread of angels" (Ps 78:25). Further, they also received quail at one particular time, in spite of their grumbling (Exod 16:12-13). These quail flew in and were able to be captured by hand! God provided meat just as He said. The psalmist says, "He rained meat on them like dust, and winged birds like the sand of the seas" (Ps 78:27).

It was sufficient (16:16-30). In verses 16-21 we see that God gave enough for the day. The text says that God gave them manna every day for 40 years. God also said, "Do not try to hoard it." If they were to think, "Hey, this 'crispy crème stuff' is pretty good, I think I'll save some for later in case God doesn't keep His word," then they would learn that God was providing enough for their daily bread only. Each person was to gather as much as they could eat; when they did so, there was no lack among any of them.

Paul cited Exodus 16:18 in 2 Corinthians 8:15, "As it has been written: The person who gathered much did not have too much, and the person who gathered little did not have too little." Paul encouraged Corinthian Christians to give generously to those in need. He reminded them not to hoard the good gifts of God. Paul went on to say more about God's sufficiency and how we should be cheerful givers (2 Cor 9:6-15).

They were told not to leave some until the next morning, but some tried, and it bred worms and stank (Exod 16:20). Once again, they failed to trust God.

God gave enough for the Sabbath (vv. 22-30). God was teaching them about "daily bread" and the Sabbath principle. He was their provider every day. The exception to the day-by-day rule was the sixth day (v. 22). On that day, they were allowed to collect enough for the Sabbath. God was teaching them about the solemn rest they needed. In this case, the bread would not have worms in it (v. 24). Again Israel failed to trust God and listen (vv. 27-30). They went out to find bread on the seventh day, but they found none, and they received God's rebuke.

In the giving of the Ten Commandments, the fourth begins with "Remember the Sabbath day." It assumed that they were familiar with the idea of resting on the seventh day. They knew about it from the manna experience, and of course the Sabbath goes back to creation. The Israelites had a hard time believing that God would provide for them if they kept the Sabbath. It sounds like people today. The Sabbath was a day for rest, and it distinguished the Israelites from the Egyptians and surrounding nations. It was a sign of God's provision, His goodness, and their faith, and it pointed to a future rest.

It was sacred (16:31-36). God told Moses to save a bit of the manna (v. 34). Eventually it was placed in the ark, along with the "testimony," which refers to the two tablets with the Ten Commandments (Heb 9:4). The ark had not been built yet (Exod 25:10-22; 37:1-9). It served as a way of reminding the people about God's mighty salvation and His provision. Throughout the exodus, they were told to do several things to "remember." God did not want His people to forget His blessings. He cared for them with manna throughout the exodus until they entered the promised land. We read in Joshua,

> *And the day after they ate from the produce of the land, the manna*
> *ceased. Since there was no more manna for the Israelites, they ate from*
> *the crops of the land of Canaan that year.* (Josh 5:12)

It was sanctifying (Deut 8:3). In Deuteronomy, Moses reflected on the manna, and he said that the miracle bread was not intended to just sustain them physically. It was also intended to teach them a deeply spiritual lesson:

> *Remember that the LORD your God led you on the entire journey these*
> *40 years in the wilderness, so that He might humble you and test you*
> *to know what was in your heart, whether or not you would keep His*
> *commands. He humbled you by letting you go hungry; then He gave*
> *you manna to eat, which you and your fathers had not known, so that*
> *you might learn that man does not live on bread alone but on every*
> *word that comes from the mouth of the LORD.* (Deut 8:2-3)

God was not just filling their bellies, He was trying to shepherd their hearts. He said that this experience was intended to humble them and teach them to depend on God's word. God was disciplining them, shaping them. We need God's word every day just as the Israelites needed manna every day. The God who was worthy to be trusted for bread is the God who is worth listening to everyday. He sanctifies us through His word (John 17:17).

Test 3: Water from the Rock (17:1-7)

As the Israelites moved on, this time in "Rephidim," they had no water. Instead of trusting God and seeking God, once again they do something else. They "complained to Moses" (v. 2). They demanded water and "grumbled against Moses" (v. 3).

At the end of this event, we read how they were also asking, "Is the LORD among us or not?" (v. 7). This is awful. Therefore, they named the place "Massah and Meribah," which means testing and arguing (see Ps 95). Instead of trusting God, they were testing God. Let us learn from their example and not imitate them. What were they doing? Notice three failures.

They demanded God's provision (17:2a). They demanded water to drink. We do this when we make demands on God at home or in the church, insisting that He work on our terms. There are times we must wait on the Lord patiently.

They questioned God's protection (17:3). They asked why God brought them out of Egypt. Was it to watch them die? We do this when we accuse God of trying to harm us in our trial. We should remember that He has brought us through a greater exodus; He is worthy of total trust.

They doubted God's presence (17:7). They doubted if God was with them as He had promised. We do this when we think God has abandoned us in our wilderness. Yet God always remains faithful.

None of these accusations were true. Israel's great problem was that they refused to remember who God is and what He had done (see Pss 95:9; 106:13). One obvious remedy to our own discontent and unbelief is to remember what God has done for us in Christ.

Then see what God did (Exod 17:4-6). After Moses prayed, God provided water from the rock. God appeared at Horeb where He first met with Moses in the burning bush. Notice the scene described in Psalm 105:41: "He opened a rock, and water gushed out; it flowed like a stream in the desert." The text does not say how God appeared specifically, but God appeared and the people were saved through the miraculous provision of water when Moses struck the rock with his staff. This miracle demonstrated that God did not bring them out to the wilderness to kill them and that He was indeed with them.

Later, Moses was told to speak to a rock, but he instead struck it twice. God was so angry that Moses was prohibited from entering the promised land because of this failure (Num 20:10-12).

Christ in the Wilderness

We can see three connections between Christ's wilderness experience and the Israelites' wilderness experience.

Christ Passed the Test that Israel Failed (Matt 4:2-3)

We desperately needed Jesus because no one could pass the test. We get a picture of Jesus succeeding where Israel failed in Matthew 4 and Luke 4. After Jesus went through the waters of Jordan, He was tested for 40 days in the wilderness, corresponding to Israel's 40 years of testing in the wilderness. His first temptation or test concerned bread. The tempter said, "If You are the Son of God, tell these stones to become bread" (Matt 4:3). What did Jesus quote? He quoted Deuteronomy 8:3: "man does not live on bread alone but on every word that comes from the mouth of the LORD." He went on to quote Deuteronomy 6:16 and 6:13 (Matt 4:7,10). Thus Jesus identified with Israel's wilderness experience, but instead of failing, He did not yield to temptation but triumphed obediently and victoriously.

Often what we think Jesus was doing in the wilderness for 40 days was showing us why we should do Bible memorization. Bible memorization is valuable, but more was happening there. The authors are showing us that there is a truer and better Israel who passed the test in the wilderness triumphantly. And He went on to pass every test, fulfilling God's law perfectly. Unlike Israel and us, Jesus did not yield to temptation and He did not grumble in His obedience. He lived the life we could not live.

Christ Is the Bread We Need for Eternal Life (John 6:25-59)

After Jesus did the miracle of bread in John 6, everyone wanted to follow Him. But Jesus knew their hearts. He said, "Don't work for the food that perishes but for the food that lasts for eternal life, which the Son of Man will give you, because God the Father has set His seal of approval on Him" (v. 27).

The people did not fully understand, and they said, "What sign then are You going to do so we may see and believe You?" (v. 30). Then they brought up manna: "Our fathers ate the manna in the wilderness, just as it is written: He gave them bread from heaven to eat" (v. 31). Jesus had actually already given them a sign. He had fed the multitude. He was the true and better Moses. But what was most important to Jesus was spiritual life. So He turned the discussion:

> Jesus said to them, "I assure you: Moses didn't give you the bread from heaven, but My Father gives you the real bread from heaven. For the bread of God is the One who comes down from heaven and gives life to the world."

> *Then they said, "Sir, give us this bread always!"*
>
> *"I am the bread of life," Jesus told them. "No one who comes to Me will ever be hungry, and no one who believes in Me will ever be thirsty again. But as I told you, you've seen Me, and yet you do not believe."* (John 6:32-36)

Jesus said He could do more than supply bread. We need Him more than bread. He was saying, "I am the bread of life, and without Me you cannot live forever."

Notice what they did in verses 41-42. They did exactly as the Israelites: they grumbled.

> *Therefore the Jews started complaining about Him because He said, "I am the bread that came down from heaven." They were saying, "Isn't this Jesus the son of Joseph, whose father and mother we know? How can He now say, 'I have come down from heaven'?"*

They wanted salvation on their own terms. God has given us salvation in Christ, the bread of life, and people still grumble at the thought of a crucified Savior or at the idea that there's only one way. They should instead fall on their knees and say, "Yes, I will take Christ and live forever."

Jesus went on to say that some would come to Him (v. 37). He said that those who came would come by faith and they would "eat His flesh," meaning they would receive Him by faith.

> *No one can come to Me unless the Father who sent Me draws him, and I will raise him up on the last day. It is written in the Prophets: And they will all be taught by God. Everyone who has listened to and learned from the Father comes to Me—not that anyone has seen the Father except the One who is from God. He has seen the Father. I assure you: Anyone who believes has eternal life. I am the bread of life. Your fathers ate the manna in the wilderness, and they died. This is the bread that comes down from heaven so that anyone may eat of it and not die. I am the living bread that came down from heaven. If anyone eats of this bread he will live forever. The bread that I will give for the life of the world is My flesh.* (John 6:44-51)

Notice how He said that they ate and they died, but if you take Christ, you never die!

> *At that, the Jews argued among themselves, "How can this man give us His flesh to eat?"*

So Jesus said to them, "I assure you: Unless you eat the flesh of the Son of Man and drink His blood, you do not have life in yourselves. Anyone who eats My flesh and drinks My blood has eternal life, and I will raise him up on the last day, because My flesh is real food and My blood is real drink. The one who eats My flesh and drinks My blood lives in Me, and I in him. Just as the living Father sent Me and I live because of the Father, so the one who feeds on Me will live because of Me. This is the bread that came down from heaven; it is not like the manna your fathers ate—and they died. The one who eats this bread will live forever." (John 6:52-58)

Obviously, Jesus was not speaking about literally eating Him. He was speaking about believing in Him (notice the repetition of "believe"). Believe in Him and find satisfaction for your soul, and live forever. The religious leaders were looking for a list of things to do to have this bread. They had their pad and paper. Jesus said you simply need to believe.

Christ Is the Rock that Was Struck for Our Salvation (1 Cor 10:1-5)

In 1 Corinthians 10 Paul said that the rock was Christ. I take this to mean that the rock was a type or foreshadowing of Christ. Moses struck the rock instead of the striking the people, and water flowed to save people. Jesus, the rock, was struck for our salvation. Instead of striking us, God struck the Son.

Moses is told *not to strike the rock again*. The second time he is told to *speak to the rock*. Like this rock, Jesus was struck only one time! After that, He is to be spoken to. Like the rock, when He was struck water flowed from His side (John 19:34). He died the death we deserved to die. Now, by believing in Jesus, we drink from the water of life for eternal life (John 7:37-38). So Jesus gave us the water we desperately needed, and that water could only come through striking. One time. You do not strike the rock after that.

Think back to what Isaiah said:

Yet He Himself bore our sicknesses,
and He carried our pains;
but we in turn regarded Him stricken,
struck down by God, and afflicted.
But He was pierced because of our transgressions,
crushed because of our iniquities;
punishment for our peace was on Him,

and we are healed by His wounds.
We all went astray like sheep;
we all have turned to our own way;
and the Lord has punished Him
for the iniquity of us all. (Isa 53:4-6)

He was wounded, struck, pierced, crushed for our iniquity. He refrained from opening His mouth, like a lamb led to the slaughter. He submitted to God's will. He did not grumble. He took our judgment that we may know God's salvation. Praise the Rock!

Two Responses to the Wilderness Story

How should we respond to the wilderness story? First, *trust in God's providence for your daily needs.* Israel's wilderness experience shows us that God is with His people and God provides for His people. Will you trust Him, or grumble and worry? Second, *trust in God's Son for your deepest needs.* Trust in the One who lived the life you could not live. He passed the test we could not pass. Trust in the One who is the bread you cannot live without. Receive Him and live. Trust in the One who was struck for your salvation. Drink and live.

Reflect and Discuss

1. Where have you learned your most valuable information: in school, or in real-life experiences?
2. Have you ever been on a trip that was jeopardized or ruined because the food or drink was bad? Why can food and drink cause such strong reactions?
3. In what way are grumbling and anxiety symptoms of ingratitude and weak faith? How did God respond to the grumbling and anxiety of Israel?
4. Why do you think God provided manna to the children of Israel in the wilderness? How would you respond to someone who proposed a natural explanation for the manna and quail?
5. How did the provision of manna teach Israel faith and trust? How did it teach the Sabbath principle? What can we learn from their experience?
6. Can you think of a time in your life when God was faithful to you even though you questioned Him and grumbled against Him?

7. Why did we need Jesus to pass the test in the wilderness?
8. Why did the Jews grumble when Jesus said that He was the bread from heaven that gives life to the world? Why do people today resist this truth?
9. In what way was manna an undeserved blessing for Israel? How is Jesus as the bread of life even better than manna?
10. Why is it important that the Rock is only struck once? In what ways was the rock a "type" of Christ?

Essentials for a Healthy Community of Faith

EXODUS 17:8–18:27

Main Idea: A healthy community of faith relies on God's power, tells others about God, and shares the work of ministry.

I. **Essential 1: God's Power (17:8-16)**
   A. Who were they? (17:8)
   B. Why were they fighting?
   C. How did they engage the enemy? (17:9-13)
   D. What happened after the victory? (17:14-16)
   E. How should we apply this?
II. **Essential 2: Gospel Witness (18:1-12)**
   A. A family reunion (18:1-6)
   B. Displaying love and respect (18:5-7)
   C. Testifying to the good news (18:8-9)
   D. Believing in the real Savior (18:10-12)
III. **Essential 3: Shared Ministry (18:13-26)**

In this section of Exodus, we see God using the wilderness experience to form His people. He shaped them to display His glory among the nations. Previously, we began exploring the challenges that Israel faced in the wilderness, which included a lack of food and water. God was humbling His people and teaching them to trust Him and His word. Later He would give them His law and teach them how to live, and then He had them construct the tabernacle for worship.

We can learn several lessons from this portion of Exodus related to the idea of a healthy community of faith. I would like to point out three essentials for believers.

Essential 1: God's Power
EXODUS 17:8-16

A healthy community of faith relies on God's power. Here we see Israel's first outside enemy after the exodus. They represent the seed of the serpent rising up against the seed of Eve. As we examine this, let us consider five questions.

Who Were They? (17:8)

The Amalekites traced their lineage back to Esau. Amalek was the grandson of Esau (Gen 36:12). They inhabited the northern Sinai Peninsula (Gen 14:7; Num 13:29). Stuart says,

> [The Amalekites] organized themselves into a very early national nomadic group ("first among the nations," in the words of Balaam, Num 24:20) that lived partly by attacking other population groups and plundering their wealth (cf. Judg 3:13). The Amalekites had domesticated the camel and used its swiftness effectively in surprise attacks. Not only did the Amalekites attack Israel at Rephidim, but a year later they attacked them again at Hormah, when the Israelites had been driven out of southern Canaan and were on the run after their foolish attempt to enter the promised land in spite of God's command through Moses that they could not (Num 14:43-45). (*Exodus*, 393)

The struggles with the Amalekites continued after Israel crossed the Jordan (Num 14:43; 1 Sam 15; 30).

Israel's first enemy came from within. The difficulties at Marah, the Desert of Sin, and Massah and Meribah were caused by their own disbelief and discontentment. It led to grumbling against their leaders and against God. As a result, they were divided and discouraged. Here in Exodus 17:8-13, they have an outside enemy.

Healthy communities of faith must be aware of both threats. In the book of Acts, the people encountered opposition from the outside, like threats and persecution (Acts 4:29; 11:19). They also had problems on the inside, as in the case of Ananias and Sapphira (Acts 5:1-11).

Why Were They Fighting?

We cannot be sure why they were fighting. They might have felt threatened by Israel's sudden arrival, or they might have been trying to protect their resources. They could have just seen Israel as vulnerable and attacked them. When Moses looked back on the battle in Deuteronomy 25:17-18, he said they had attacked Israel when they were weary. They attacked men, women, and children, even from behind. They had no fear of God. Clearly the Amalekites were not in God's army, so they were taking orders from the enemy.

How Did They Engage the Enemy? (17:9-13)

Moses told Joshua, "Select some men for us and go fight against Amalek. Tomorrow I will stand on the hilltop with God's staff in my hand" (v. 9). I am not sure if Joshua thought, "Yeah, right. I will fight while you hold up a stick!" However, we know that he obeyed, and we actually see a powerful picture here.

Israel used physical weapons led by Joshua (17:9-10,13). Joshua was a warrior who would eventually become a dominant figure in Israel. Here he was introduced. He would be among the few who were faithful in the wilderness (see Num 14:6-9,30) and would succeed Moses, leading Israel into Canaan (Deut 34:9; Josh 1:1-9). Later, Joshua would be known for his courage and bravery.

Throughout Exodus God was showing little flashes of things to come. There would be a prophet, like Moses, and a warrior who will fight for you, like Joshua, all together in one person: Jesus Christ.

Moses told Joshua to choose some men and go fight. So Joshua selected his team and went. Moses used spiritual weapons. He went to the hillside and raised his shepherd's staff, a symbol of God's presence, His promises, and His power (vv. 9-12). Moses' actions demonstrated that he was dependent on God for victory. The battle was the Lord's.

Notice that it was not by physical force alone that the battle was won or lost. Though some might argue that this was not really "prayer" (the text never says Moses was praying), there are two reasons we can indeed call this "intercession."

Moses lifted up his hand(s), appealing to God to show His power. When Moses lowered his hands, they began to lose the battle (v. 11). Aaron and Hur helped Moses by giving him a seat and holding up his hands (v. 12). The result was that they overwhelmed the enemy (v. 13). This action reminds me of a roller coaster ride. Why do people raise their hands? (Well, some of them. Others of us close our eyes and hold our breath!) They are saying in a sense, "It is out of my control, and I'm OK with that."

Raising one's arms is a sign of dependent prayer elsewhere in the Bible. Remember Pharaoh asking Moses to pray for him?

Pharaoh sent for Moses and Aaron. "I have sinned this time," he said to them. "Yahweh is the Righteous One, and I and my people are the guilty ones. Make an appeal to Yahweh. There has been enough of

God's thunder and hail. I will let you go; you don't need to stay any longer."

Moses said to him, "When I have left the city, I will extend my hands to Yahweh. *The thunder will cease, and there will be no more hail, so that you may know the earth belongs to Yahweh.* (Exod 9:27-29; emphasis added)

Likewise, the psalmist spoke of uplifted hands, seeking God:

My lips will glorify You
because Your faithful love is better than life.
So I will praise You as long as I live;
at Your name, I will lift up my hands. (Ps 63:3-4; emphasis added)

May my prayer be set before You as incense,
the raising of my hands *as the evening offering.* (Ps 141:2; emphasis added)

In the New Testament, Paul commanded,

Therefore, I want the men in every place to pray, lifting up holy hands *without anger or argument.* (1 Tim 2:8; emphasis added)

The text might not say "prayer," but Moses was clearly depending on God for victory. We may fight like Joshua, but we must also cry out to God in prayer like Moses.

The idea of prayer seems to be confirmed by the last verse: "Indeed, my hand is lifted up toward the LORD's throne" (Exod 17:16). This phrase is hard to translate, but I like the ESV's translation: "A hand upon the throne of the LORD!" Elsewhere, the Bible describes prayer as coming to the throne. We can come to the throne because of Jesus' work, and we are now invited to the "throne of grace with boldness, so that we may receive mercy and find grace to help us at the proper time" (Heb 4:16).

In our battles we must fight like Joshua, but we also must hold up our hands to God's throne and say, "It is out of my control." We must go to the throne of grace and say, "Help me!" We need courageous, Joshua-like warriors who will take the gospel to hard places, fight injustice, and serve the needy—but all of it must be done in a spirit of dependent prayer.

What Happened After the Victory? (17:14-16)

The Lord said to Moses, "Write this down on a scroll as a reminder and recite it to Joshua" (v. 14). Here we see that Joshua was to be the successor. Notice also that God said, "Write this down." Why write it down? If anyone would remember this event, it would have been Joshua, right? We have all known those guys who used to play high school basketball who can recount specific games and how well they played back in the glory days! Why write it down? They needed to write it down because God knew that the people were going to be dealing with the Amalekites again, as well as other enemies of God. So God made them write it down so everyone might know that God fights for His people.

This is the first time we have this idea of "write this down." God has given us the Scriptures, showing us who He is, what He has done, and who we are. The Bible is a memorial of what God has done for us. He defeated the Amalekites for us, and conquered all the other enemies, bringing forth the Messiah. The New Testament authors wrote down for us the words and deeds of Jesus, and the good news has been passed down for generations to us. The Bible is the grand story of redemptive history.

God then predicted, "I will completely blot out the memory of Amalek under heaven" (v. 14). This would happen later.

Moses went on to build an altar (vv. 15-16). He did this in order to praise God and remind His people of His power. Altars were built to express gratitude. The patriarchs sometimes named altars, as Jacob did (Gen 33:20; 35:7). Moses does the same here, calling it "The Lord is My Banner" (Yahweh-nissi). This word was used "in military contexts, where the *nēs* is a signal pole around which an army or army unit can rally, regroup, or return for instructions" (Stuart, *Exodus*, 400). The Lord is where we regroup, rally, and get instructions.

How Should We Apply This?

Consider your need for God's power. There is a battle between the children of light and the powers of darkness. The church's spiritual warfare with the powers of darkness is noted in the New Testament in several places (e.g., Eph 5:8-14; 6:12). Jesus conquered our greatest enemies, but because a "mop up operation" still exists, we need God's power.

From reading Ephesians 6:10-12 we know that our enemy is deceptive. He uses all kinds of tactics. He is aggressive. Do not be naïve. Do not forget that you are in a battle. Israel's story is our story. They had been redeemed and were on their way to the promised land (like us), but on the way they faced enemies (so will we). Moses discovered that prayer is more powerful than the problem (cf. Eph 3:20-21; 6:18-20).

Also, consider how they got the power: a mediator. Moses interceded for them. On one hand, we can learn about seeking God from Moses, and on another, Moses points us to the ultimate intercessor, Jesus Christ. We have a greater mediator interceding for us. Many great intercessors stand out in the Old Testament—David, Solomon, Nehemiah—but none are like Jesus. How is Jesus a greater intercessor? Jesus is fully God and Man! He is the ultimate mediator. Jesus is the greater warrior than Joshua, defeating our ultimate enemies and making it possible for us to know God and commune with Him; and He is the greater Moses, praying for His people. But Jesus does not have to have His arms raised by anyone. He does not get tired of interceding! "Moses' hands grew heavy" (Exod 17:12), but Jesus "always lives to intercede for [us]" (Heb 7:25). Jesus does exactly what Moses did. While we fight the good fight, He intercedes for us. Oh, the wonder of the interceding Son of God (Rom 8:34)!

The Lord is our banner also, but in a way even Moses could hardly have imagined. Consider Isaiah 11:10:

> On that day the root of Jesse will stand as a banner for the peoples. The nations will seek Him, and His resting place will be glorious.

Jesus Christ is the banner for God's people, who rally to Him from every nation! Around His cross we are unified, encouraged, and instructed. It is through Jesus that we experience spiritual victories. Apart from His work and His intercession, we have no hope.

Essential 2: Gospel Witness
EXODUS 18:1-12

This section highlights Jethro's relationship with Moses (vv. 1-6) and new faith in the God of Israel. The Amalekites and Midianites were closely related. Jethro was a Midianite priest who came to rejoice in Yahweh's salvation.

A Family Reunion (18:1-6)

The news about Israel spread through the lands (v. 1). You could imagine Jethro and Zipporah asking travelers about the state of the Israelites. Stuart says,

> Moses may have prearranged for Jethro upon leaving Midian (4:18) to take Zipporah and their two sons into his home for safety after they had gone part of the way to Egypt with Moses (4:20-26) while he went about the dangerous business of confronting Pharaoh in Egypt, with the understanding that once the Israelites had left Egypt according to God's promise, they would reunite at Mount Sinai (3:12). If so, Jethro and Zipporah probably had been following Israelite progress and calculating when they should plan to leave for the prearranged rendezvous at the mountain of God. (*Exodus*, 404)

In verses 2-5 the two sons are with them and their names are mentioned: Gershom ("foreigner") and Eliezer ("God is my help"). Their names summarize Moses, the Israelites, and us!

Displaying Love and Respect (18:5-7)

Notice the love and respect in these verses. Moses went out to Jethro, bowed down, and kissed him. Except for the genealogies, there are no other mentions of Moses' wife and kids. The focus of the story is more on the conversion of his father-in-law, this Midianite priest. It is understandable that Moses' wife and kids would become believers, but it is an amazing thing to consider the faith of Jethro. Perhaps the story focuses on his confession because he was a public figure and a religious leader of another faith. His conversion would have been big news! Today this story should encourage believers. Keep spreading the good news to everyone, including your family members! Not only did Jethro receive the good news, but later in the passage, he also gave wonderfully helpful advice to Moses (and us).

Testifying to the Good News (18:8-9)

Was Moses trying to convert his father-in-law? Yes! Some want to argue that you cannot really call this a conversion here. Okay. Maybe it is a stretch to say that in verse 11 his conversion took place, but at some point Jethro got converted. That seems clear to me. And what also is clear is that Moses was telling him the good news. He wanted to see his father-in-law converted.

Notice the summary of the good news (v. 8). Before, there was hardship; after, there was deliverance. Moses probably spent several hours recounting this whole story. God has brought us from death to life, and we should testify to this good news as well.

Jethro rejoiced in all that God had done (v. 9). It seems that Jethro had been skeptical of Moses' initial call and had questions, but now his questions were answered by the facts of what had happened.

Believing in the Real Savior (18:10-12)

In verse 10 Jethro said, "Praise the LORD . . . who rescued you." What moved Jethro was this personal knowledge of Moses' story. He knew Moses before the exodus and now after the exodus. He repeated the phrase "from the power of the Egyptians" because this is what amazed him! The defeat of Pharaoh and this superpower nation by Moses and the Israelites could only be explained by the miraculous salvation of Yahweh. So he said, "Praise be to Yahweh." Based on this truth, Jethro made this awesome confession in verse 11:

> *Now I know that Yahweh is greater than all gods, because He did wonders when the Egyptians acted arrogantly against Israel.*

That is another way of saying a New Testament phrase "I know the One I have believed in" (2 Tim 1:12) or "I was blind, and now I can see!" (John 9:25). Jethro said, "Now I know who the real God is." Jesus said, "This is eternal life: that they may know You, the only true God, and the One You have sent—Jesus Christ" (John 17:3).

Jethro demonstrated that he had converted to faith in Yahweh (v. 12): he worshiped Yahweh according to the Israelite custom. He offered a "burnt offering," which was understood to atone for past sins and to appeal for forgiveness and acceptance before God. He also offered "sacrifices to God" to be sure to cover for any inadequacies in approaching Yahweh. All of this was to ensure that he was accepted in genuine fellowship with God. He ate a covenant meal with other worshipers of Yahweh in the presence of Yahweh. This signified Jethro's formal admission into Israel. Notice that the leaders had a meal with him "in God's presence."

Let us spread the gospel! How? *Be ready* to testify of God's grace in salvation as Moses was here (cf. Acts 20:24). Let us also spread the gospel *lovingly*. Look at the respect and warmth Moses had (cf. 1 Pet 3:15). And let us spread the gospel *to the nations*. God's plan for the nations was displayed in Jethro's conversion. He was outside the people of Israel, yet he was converted. God promised to bless all the nations through Israel. Israel was to be a "light to the nations." This story shows how their witness began reaching surrounding nations. This is consistent with Exodus 9:16. We all, from every tribe and tongue, are able to sit down with the bread and wine together and celebrate the grace of our Lord Jesus who has delivered us from sin and death.

Essential 3: Shared Ministry
EXODUS 18:13-26

As the story continues, Jethro gave some counsel to Moses telling him that he was trying to do too much. Moses had been attempting to settle multiple disputes. He was like the police, the law, the counselor, the department of motor vehicles, the judge, the theologian, and the pastor all in one. This task was too heavy. Get this picture:

The people stand around all day waiting for an appointment (v. 13). Jethro says, "What are you doing?" (v. 14). Moses basically says, "They need me. I have to tell them what to do" (vv. 15-16). I love Jethro's response: "What you're doing is not good" (v. 17). Why? Jethro tells him: "You will certainly wear out both yourself and these people who are with you, because the task is too heavy for you" (v. 18).

In regard to the church, our situation is not exactly the same, but part of what Moses was trying to do is shepherd the people. He was trying to take care of them and instruct them in the ways that please God. Shepherding is hard work. One person cannot do it all. This is similar to Acts 6. There were not enough apostles to take care of the widows, so the church appointed some qualified men to do that, and the apostles would focus on prayer and the ministry of the word.

As a pastor, I can sympathize with Moses. Sometimes people ask, "A 'Pastor'—is that a full-time job?" I almost laugh when I hear that! It is sort of like the question, "Does your wife work?" I actually tried to think about what I do. Here are a few things:

Sermons to prepare, worship services to prepare, vision to cast, mission to execute, meetings with elders to attend, people to counsel (some outside our church), bills to pay, phone calls to make, books to write, websites to monitor, funds to raise, outside speaking engagements to prepare for, groups to meet, classes to prepare for and teach, conflicts to resolve, reference letters to write, blogs to write, questions to answer, leaders to disciple, ministries to oversee, a building to work on, missionaries to send and support, people to pray for, visits to make, fellowships with other pastors to attend, social events to attend, weddings to officiate, funerals to lead—and more!

Before you are tempted to feel sorry for me, remember that my flock is nowhere near as large as Moses'! Imagine, six hundred thousand men, plus women and children! So, what solution gets put forward? The solution for Moses is the same solution for us: share the ministry.

Notice how Jethro counsels Moses. Jethro told Moses to fulfill his ministry (vv. 19-20). Moses was a mediator. He was taking the people to God in prayer and God to people in teaching. Jethro *did not* tell him to stop doing these tasks. He simply told him that he should develop some organizational structure and get some help.

Jethro told Moses to find capable leaders to help care for the people (vv. 21-23). He was to find "able men," from among the people, who would be capable of serving in this capacity. They were to be "God-fearing" men. God-fearing men realize that serving God is serious business, regardless of how big or small the job is. They were also to be "trustworthy" men. These are men you can count on. You do not have to question the motives of trustworthy men. They were to "hate bribes." They would be impartial, honest, and not in it for money. So these were leaders who would be capable and full of integrity. They were going to do the work with Moses.

Moses became the court of last resort or "supreme court" of Israel (v. 22). He remained as judge but delegated most situations to the other men. They "will bear [the burden] with you" Jethro said (v. 22). Notice the result: (1) God will direct you; (2) you will be able to endure; and (3) the people will go in peace (v. 23). In other words, this is best for everyone.

How do we apply this? What can we learn about shared ministry? As mentioned, our situation is different, but there is still the general connection to shared ministry and pastoral care. Let me point out two principles. The New Testament shows us how we should understand shared ministry. A healthy community practices shared ministry by having a plurality of qualified elders who care for the flock (Acts 20:17; 1 Tim 3:1-7; Titus 1:5-9; 1 Pet 5:1-4). But the elders do not do everything. They oversee the ministry of the church. They equip God's people to do the work of the ministry (Eph 4:11-16). Every member is to serve. Of course, Jesus Christ is the head, the chief Shepherd, and everyone must submit to Him. Under Him, He has appointed elders/pastors as undershepherds to equip God's people to do ministry together.

Therefore, healthy communities of faith practice shared ministry by having an "every-member ministry." While some are appointed to leadership, every Christian has a part to play in the body of Christ. Every Christian is a "priest" (Exod 19:6; 1 Pet 2:5-10). You can pray for people. You can care for people. You can teach others. Every Christian has spiritual gifts to use for the good of the body (1 Pet 4:10). Healthy communities of faith have active members serving, loving, and praying. Generally, those who serve best do not care about being known or having a title. We should do this in the spirit of "[carrying] one another's burdens; in this way you will fulfill the law of Christ" (Gal 6:2).

In verses 24-26 we see that Moses listens. He demonstrates humility. He receives counsel—even from his father-in-law! Will you follow his example and follow the counsel of the wise?

As a community of faith, we need power; we need to speak the good news; and we need a shared ministry. As a community of faith, we—like Jethro and Moses and the elders—gather around one table. We also rally around the cross, our banner, and we enjoy fellowship with one another because of the work of our great mediator, Jesus Christ.

Reflect and Discuss

1. Which enemies are more dangerous, those from inside or from outside? Why? What effects can an outside enemy have on a group? Can there be a benefit?

2. When Moses raised his hands and held up his staff, was he practicing magic? What is the difference between magic and intercessory prayer? Where does the power and control lie in each case?

3. When praying, what is the significance of kneeling, folding hands, and bowing, or standing, raising hands, and looking toward heaven? When would each be appropriate?

4. Compare Moses interceding for Israel, a Christian interceding for a friend, and Christ interceding for a Christian. What is the definition of intercession, and what is the ideal procedure and outcome?

5. How does Christ serve as a military banner? How can He help us avoid political infighting and succeed in spiritual warfare?

6. Why do you think Moses named his children "Foreigner" and "God Is My Help"? What were the reasons for the names of people in your family?

7. Moses told Jethro what God had done for him and his people. Is evangelism this simple, or is more involved?

8. When Jethro joined Israel, he praised God, acknowledged God's superiority, brought valid offerings, and had fellowship with Israelites. What evidence would you expect to see when someone becomes a Christian?

9. Jethro said overwork would wear out Moses and the people. In what ways does a leader's workload affect the followers?

10. Why do some leaders resist delegating? How do the qualities of "able," "God-fearing," "trustworthy," and "hating bribes" still apply to good managers today?

The Ten Words

EXODUS 19:1–20:21

Main Idea: Studying the Ten Commandments helps us to understand God's righteous character.

I. **Consider the Holy God Who Spoke Them (19:1–20:1).**
   A. The calling (19:1-6)
   B. The holiness of God (19:7-25)
II. **Consider the Gospel Pattern in Them (20:2).**
III. **Consider the Arrangement of Them (20:3-17).**
IV. **Consider the Attributes of God Displayed in Each of Them (20:3-17).**
   A. The first commandment (20:3)
   B. The second commandment (20:4-6)
   C. The third commandment (20:7)
   D. The fourth commandment (20:8-11)
   E. The fifth commandment (20:12)
   F. The sixth commandment (20:13)
   G. The seventh commandment (20:14)
   H. The eighth commandment (20:15)
   I. The ninth commandment (20:16)
   J. The tenth commandment (20:17)
V. **Consider How the New Testament Writers Emphasize Them.**
VI. **See How Jesus Fulfills Them.**

A few years ago, Stephen Colbert, American political satirist, comedian, and television host, interviewed a congressman about various issues. This particular Congressman cosponsored a bill to place the Ten Commandments in the House of Representatives and the Senate. He also sponsored a bill to place the Ten Commandments in courthouses in a historical setting. Colbert, in his witty way, went along with the discussion, and then he asked, "What are the commandments?"

The Congressman said, "What are all of them? You want me to name them all?"

"Yes," said Colbert.

The Congressman said, "Don't murder. Don't lie. Don't steal . . . [Colbert counts with his fingers]. I can't name them all." Colbert ended the exchange with some humorous facial expressions, and a parting shot about keeping the Sabbath day holy.

Can you name the commandments? I do not share this story to mock the Congressman. After all, he is not alone. Several reports have shown that Americans do not know the Ten Commandments. Many Christians cannot name them either.

Martin Luther, the great reformer, understood the value of teaching the Ten Commandments. He said, "I haven't progressed beyond the instruction of children in the Ten Commandments, the [Apostles'] Creed, and the Lord's Prayer. I still learn and pray these every day with my Hans and my little Lana" (Nichols, *Martin Luther*, 149).

Of course, we need to know more than what they actually are. Memorizing them is a good start, but we need to see some truths related to them. I would like to point out six concepts related to the Ten Commandments, or the "Ten Words" (Exod 34:28; Deut 4:13; 10:4).

Consider the Holy God Who Spoke Them
EXODUS 19:1–20:1

In Exodus 20:1 we read, "God spoke all these words." This fact is wonderful. God spoke the Ten Words directly to Israel rather than through the mediator, Moses. The people were so awestruck by this experience that when God finished, they asked for Moses to speak instead of Yahweh (20:19). Stuart says,

> [T]he people heard the voice of God for themselves and thus could not doubt his presence among them, a presence more directly manifest at Sinai than in any other mode previously since they had first learned of his interest in them (2:25; 4:31). All the people were hearing the voice of God just as Adam, Eve, Noah, Abraham, and the patriarchs had heard it and as Moses had heard it earlier at Mount Sinai when God first called him. And this time the voice of God was accompanied by such audio and visual displays (19:16-19; 20:18-21) as to leave no doubt in their minds as to both his presence and his uniqueness (*Exodus*, 445–46).

Isaiah says of these audio and visual displays, "The LORD was pleased, because of His righteousness, to magnify His instruction and make it glorious" (Isa 42:21).

Exodus 19 sets the stage for the Ten Words. Chapters 19 and 24 serve as the bookends of the "covenant scroll" (24:7), which included the Ten Words (20:2-17) and the "ordinances" in chapters 21–23 (Gentry and Wellum, *Kingdom*, 307). Gentry and Wellum say, "Central to the book of Exodus—and indeed the entire Pentateuch—is the covenant made between Yahweh and Israel at Sinai, comprised in Exodus 19–24" (ibid., 301).

Chapter 19 focuses on Yahweh setting the terms of the relationship between Israel and Himself. He has delivered the people but the terms of the relationship have not been set (Hamilton, *God's Glory*, 98). So they know Yahweh, but not like they are about to know Yahweh. Chapter 19 shows us how Yahweh stuns the Israelites with His blazing holiness and overwhelming glory. This is the God who calls them and makes His covenant with them. He is both gracious and holy. Many people want to isolate the commandments from this context; however, it is essential to know the God who gave them.

The Calling (19:1-6)

As the people continued through the wilderness, a time period of three new moons had gone by—about seven weeks after the exodus. Being at Sinai would have reminded Moses of his first encounter with God at the burning bush (3:1,12). God promised to bring Moses to this mountain, and He did. The text says "the mountain" and later identifies it as Mt. Sinai (19:20). As the people camped, "Moses went up the mountain to God" (v. 3). There he would receive this amazing covenant. God said, "This is what you must say to the house of Jacob, and explain to the Israelites: 'You have seen what I did to the Egyptians and how I carried you on eagles' wings and brought you to Me'" (vv. 3-4). What a beautiful picture of God's grace! God has brought them out, lifted them up, and drawn them close. An eagle is a good picture because it is a bird of prey and is also portrayed as a bird of rescue. Egypt would be prey, while Israel would be rescued.

God began by reminding them of what He had accomplished for them. God was their healer and redeemer who delivered them from the mighty Pharaoh. In light of this, God said, "Now if you will listen to Me and carefully keep My covenant, you will be My own possession out of all the peoples, although all the earth is Mine, and you will be My kingdom of priests and My holy nation" (vv. 5-6). God set the terms for the relationship.

God called them (and us) to Himself for faith and obedience. First He rescues us like an eagle, then He gives us His Word and expects us to live for His glory. Those who believe and obey the Word of the Lord will be considered God's "own possession." What a title! Out of all creation, the Creator selected this seemingly insignificant nation. So to enjoy the benefits of the covenant, Israel was to follow God's demands. We too are saved through Christ then called to live for Christ.

God also said, "all the earth is Mine" (v. 5). This phrase stands as one of the earliest direct statements of monotheism. There is one God in all the earth.

Next, just as Adam was a priest, worshiping in the garden sanctuary, so Israel would be a "kingdom of priests," devoted to worship and ministry (v. 6). They would make the ways of God's kingdom known to the nations (See Gentry and Wellum, *Kingdom,* 301–56). Through this people, this "holy nation," God would bless the nations and bring forth the Messiah.

Christians, likewise, are priests today, who worship and serve the living God, and who can call out to God in prayer (1 Pet 2:4-6,9; Rev 1:5-6; 20:6). Perhaps you have never been told this. You ask, "Who, me? A priest?" Yes, you! As a believer, you can take people to God in prayer and God to people in witness. Many people minimize the importance of prayer, but it is fundamental to who we are as Christians and to our mission (2 Cor 1:11).

The Holiness of God (19:7-25)

As we read on to the end of the chapter, we see the awe-inspiring holiness of God. In telling Moses these things, God directed him to tell the people what He had said (v. 6). As a result, Moses went before the elders and the people and told them the word from God (v. 7). Again, he was functioning like a prophet, saying, "Thus says the Lord." Then, it says, "all the people" agreed together and said they would do what God had commanded them (v. 8). (Soon we learn that they did not keep this promise.) God then announced that He would come in a thick cloud, that the people might hear Him speak and believe what Moses says (v. 9).

In the New Testament, Moses appeared again on a mountain, with Peter, James, and John. And there was a cloud, and it was majestic. And he was there with Jesus when the Father announced, "This is My beloved

Son; listen to Him!" (Mark 9:2-8). The three disciples saw glory and were told to listen to Christ. We too must "listen to Him."

God told the people to "consecrate" themselves for their meeting with Him, which would take place on the "third day" (Exod 19:10-15). This consecration consisted of several things such as washing their garments and abstaining from sex. On the third day, Yahweh descended on Mount Sinai. Look at this: heaven thunders, the lightning flashes, the earth quakes, and the *shofar* blasts! And the people? They tremble (v. 16). Moses told them to go to the foot of the mountain—which they must not touch or they would die (vv. 12-13)—that they might meet God. Then we are told that the mountain was wrapped in smoke because Yahweh descended on it in fire (v. 18).

The Lord called Moses to the top of the mountain (v. 20). God told Moses to tell the people not to gawk at Him, or they would die, and for the priests to consecrate themselves, or He would "break out in anger against them" (vv. 21-22). Then he is told to go down and get Aaron (v. 24). God was preparing Aaron for ministry as high priest. With Moses present, he was permitted to go up the holy mountain and meet with God. The top of the mountain was like a "sanctuary." Later, he would do the same thing in the tabernacle—he would go into the most holy place while the people kept their distance.

Now, to lead us to the most holy place, we have a high priest whom God has chosen: Jesus. And we too should stand in awe of God's holiness. Further, the New Testament teaches that actually we have more to stand in awe of, as new covenant believers, since we come into the presence of God through Jesus. In Hebrews 12:18-24 the author spoke of a new heavenly Zion/Jerusalem. He said that Christians have access in the invisible, spiritual realm into the heavenly Jerusalem, and we participate in worship with innumerable angels (cf. Heb 1:7; Deut 33:2; Dan 7:10) and the great assembly of the faithful dead who are already in God's presence (Heb 12:1). How do we come here? Our mediator, Jesus, stands as the mediator of the new covenant. His blood makes us able to worship. His blood speaks a better word than the blood of Abel (Heb 10:24). Abel was murdered. His blood cries out for vengeance; Jesus' blood cries out with forgiveness and pardon. We who have received an unshakable kingdom must "serve God acceptably, with reverence and awe, for our God is a consuming fire" (Heb 12:28-29).

A lot of people think the Old Testament was when God was to be feared, but now we can "skip into God's presence." This text says you have more reason to stand in awe. You are not standing back away from the mountain; you are in it through Christ!

As the story continues, God said, "Go down" (Exod 19:24). God's intention was for Moses to hear the Ten Words with the people. They would be audible to everyone. When God said, "come back with Aaron" (v. 24), it represented part of the plan to eventually bring Aaron. It was a call for Aaron to ascend the mountain with Moses the next time Moses went back up (Stuart, *Exodus*, 433). The last verse, "So Moses went down to the people and told them" (v. 25), shows us the awesomeness of God and the readiness of Moses and the people together at the bottom of Mount Sinai to hear the Ten Words thundered at them from the top of the mountain.

As you consider the Ten Words, consider the Holy God who spoke them. God is awesome in holiness yet amazing in His mercy. The God who was ablaze on Sinai is also the God who has rescued us like an eagle. He is to be loved and feared. His commandments are a divine gift from a gracious God who saves and divine truth from an awesome God who calls us to holiness. Hamilton says, "Yahweh is the most significant thing about the Ten Commandments" (Hamilton, *God's Glory*, 99). Do not miss the God who gave them.

Gentry and Wellum also point out that a connection is being made between the covenant at Sinai and the creation. They write,

> In the creation narrative, God creates the universe simply by speaking, i.e., by his word. . . . In a very real way, the entire creation depends or hangs upon the word of God. Here, the Book of the Covenant is what forges Israel into a nation. It is her national constitution, so to speak. And it is also Ten Words that brings about the birth of the nation. Like creation, Israel as a nation hangs upon the Ten Words for her very being. (*Kingdom*, 328)

Our God speaks. Do you see your need for Him and His word? Consider the holy God who gave these words.

Consider the Gospel Pattern in Them
EXODUS 20:2

Many people leap past verse 2 when reading the Ten Words, and they miss the important ordering here. Before the Ten Words, a statement about God's salvation is made: "I am the LORD your God, who brought you out of the land of Egypt, out of the place of slavery."

This is the gospel. We touched on it in chapter 19 and earlier in our study as well. God frees us by His grace, giving us new life, and then calls us to obedience to His words. Because Yahweh is Israel's God, who has brought them out of Egypt, they are to live for His glory by following His commands. In our teaching of the Ten Words, we should include verses 1-2! This highlights a very important gospel pattern. God's people desire to do God's will because they have already been saved, not to earn salvation.

Consider the Arrangement of Them
EXODUS 20:3-17

At a comprehensive level, the Ten Words may be divided into two parts: love God, and love people. One way you could summarize them, then, is by arranging them in a four-and-six pattern. The first four hang on the command to love God, since they describe ways to show covenantal loyalty directly to Him. The last six hang on the command to love neighbor as self. The first four are "vertical" commandments, and the last six are "horizontal" commandments. In this way, they express how we fulfill the "Greatest Commands" in Matthew 22:37-40.

To love God any way you please is illustrated by the words of Anthony Burgess in 1646—"like having the sun follow the clock" or "the tail wagging the dog" (Begg, *Pathway*, 41). In these commandments, God tells us how to love Him appropriately. Jesus said, "If you love Me, you will keep My commands" (John 14:15). My love for God is reflected by my obedience to His words.

The last six involve treating others properly. Gentry and Wellum say, "These entail basic and inalienable rights of every human and have been recognized by the customs and laws of every society. . . . No society can endure that does not respect the basic inalienable rights of every human person" (*Kingdom*, 328–29). While the last six are comparable to some other law codes in the ancient Near East, the first four are "unparalleled in the ancient Near East" (ibid., 329). Israel's exclusive devotion to Yahweh set them apart.

Our exclusive worship of God continues to mark Christians. In addition, our devotion to God will keep us from breaking the last six commandments. Since underneath every sin is idolatry, our obedience to the "vertical" commands inevitably affects our obedience to the last six. We will not scorn parents, murder, commit adultery, steal, bear false witness, or covet if God is our ultimate treasure, whom we honor with our lives and lips.

Consider the Attributes of God Displayed in Each of Them
EXODUS 20:3-17

The Ten Words display the character of God. God poured Himself into His law. Each of the Ten Words expresses particular attributes of God, who is the lawgiver.

Let us consider two questions for each commandment. First, "What does the command mean?" To help answer this first question, we can draw on other texts to understand various issues related to them. Some propose that Deuteronomy chapters 6–25 exposits the Ten Words. Second, "What does this command teach us about God?" Notice again verse 2—the character of God undergirds everything. God tells them to do something because of who He is.

The First Commandment (20:3)

The first commandment does away with atheism on one hand and pantheism or polytheism on the other. It assumes that there is one true God and no other. It also addresses the deep problem of the human heart: idolatry.

Everyone is a worshiper of someone or something. Idolatry is putting someone or something else in the place of God. Idolatry is exchanging the glory of the Creator for the creation, leading to a life of ignorance and moral corruption (Rom 1:18-25). Idols are not just on pagan altars but in the hearts of people (Ezek 14; Gal 5:19-20).

We must see our idols for what they are: they are stupid! After seeing this, we must crush them in repentance and turn to the living God instead. Idols will not satisfy. Only God will satisfy the human heart. We need to properly assess created things. Enjoy creation, steward creation, but worship the Creator!

What attribute of God comes to mind in the first command? Consider the command stated positively: "I shall be your only God." What does this teach? It teaches that our God is a *jealous* God. He will not share His glory with another.

The Second Commandment (20:4-6)

This commandment warns us against having the wrong object of worship and against worshiping the wrong way. Carved images were manmade objects for worship. These idols have no comparison to the true God. They are impersonal and powerless—deaf, dumb, and dead.

Sadly, Israel would fail in this commandment really soon. Think of what the psalmist said: "At Horeb they made a calf and worshiped the cast metal image. They exchanged their glory for the image of a grasseating ox. They forgot God their Savior" (Ps 106:19-21).

Once again, in this second command, God's jealousy and supremacy is highlighted (Exod 20:5). Later God said, "You are never to bow down to another god because Yahweh, *being jealous by nature*, is a jealous God" (34:14; emphasis added).

God promised to show "faithful love to a thousand generations of those who love Me and keep My commands" (v. 6; cf. 34:6-7). This is the first mention of loving God. It had been implied already in the exodus story, but it is explicit here. Loving God is foundational for everything else. Everything is a spillover of the heart.

The Third Commandment (20:7)

To understand this commandment, it helps to see it in its parts. First, the focus is on "the name of the LORD your God" (v. 7). This does not simply mean the name, "LORD" or "Yahweh." Rather, it has to do with all that is connected to that name. The focus is on God's essence. God is to be highly valued. He is worthy of the highest honor. This is understood in the fact that God names Himself. We all were given names, whether we like them or not. Only God names Himself, revealing His supreme authority, dominion, and power.

Understand what it means to "take" His name in vain. It does not mean to simply speak God's name; it means to carry or bear God's name. People who have publicly declared themselves to be followers of God are to exalt God's reputation by living in a way that honors Him.

This command also has the idea of not taking God's name falsely or using it meaninglessly. This might happen in corporate worship, as people mouth songs without actually thinking about God. As Christians, we bear His name (Acts 4:12; Rom 10:13; 1 John 5:13). In this way, His reputation is attached to us; as a result, we ought to live for Him and His glory.

The Fourth Commandment (20:8-11)

Notice that this commandment is based out of creation (v. 11). It describes how God made the heavens and the earth and then rested on the seventh day. This Sabbath commandment is found in Deuteronomy 5:12-15 as well. In Deuteronomy the commandment is modeled after God's provision in bringing the Israelites out of Egypt. So in Exodus it is related to God's model of rest in creation, and in Deuteronomy it is related to redemption. God's people are therefore called to remember God, the Creator and Redeemer, on the Sabbath.

While there are a number of views on what it means to keep the Sabbath today, it seems that the focus is on rest, remembering, and worship. God said, "Remember the Sabbath day." This calls us to think back to creation, as pointed out in verse 11, and to remember redemption, as pointed out in Deuteronomy 5. God's people are to remember God's creating and redeeming work and God's rest. Further, the Sabbath ultimately points us to a final resting day, which is affirmed in the New Testament (Heb 4:9-10).

Some are very strict in insisting that this happen on the seventh day of the week. However, I do not think the moral demand is on the seventh day of the week. I think the responsibility that is laid on us is to follow the biblical pattern of working six days and resting and worshiping one day.

When Paul wrote to the Colossians he said, "Therefore, don't let anyone judge you in regard to food and drink or in the matter of a festival or a new moon or a Sabbath day. These are a shadow of what was to come; the substance is the Messiah" (Col 2:16-17). These verses, along with Romans 14:5-6 and Galatians 4:10-11, also demonstrate that Paul seemed to lay aside the seventh-day Sabbath with all the Jewish ceremonies as shadows. But I do not think Paul intended to abandon the principle of the Sabbath. What seems to have happened is that the early church chose the first day of the week as their day for rest and worship. After the resurrection, the Jewish Sabbath almost disappeared; the seventh-day Sabbath is never mentioned except as to be tolerated by Jewish Christians (Rom 14:5).

We worship on the Lord's Day (first day of the week), following the early church (Acts 20:7; 1 Cor 16:2). In so doing, we recognize the resurrection. Already by the first century, Ignatius wrote that Christians "no longer observe the Sabbath, but direct their lives toward the Lord's Day in which our lives are refreshed by him and his death" (Ryken,

Exodus, 597). Begg says, "Just as the deliverance from Egypt was at the heart of the Mosaic Sabbath, so the redemption accomplished through Jesus Christ is remembered on the Lord's Day" (Begg, *Pathway*, 106). He adds,

> The change not only bore witness to the resurrection, but it emphasized the difference between the Christian Sunday and the Jewish Sabbath. The Jewish Sabbath came at the end of six days and spoke of a rest to come; the Christian Sunday comes at the beginning of the week symbolizing the "rest" that Jesus Christ has won for those who trust in him. (ibid.)

You need a Sabbath. It is rooted in creation and redemption. Some may argue over the day, but no one should argue over the principle. The Sabbath is God's gift to us. It benefits us to keep it, and it helps us anticipate the final rest to come.

Next notice that verse 9 says, "You are to labor six days and do all your work." Remember also that God created us to work! If you work hard during the week, you should be able to take a Sabbath. Your body and heart and mind will need it as well. Work hard to the glory of God, and enjoy the worship on the Lord's Day.

What do we learn about God here? He is a working and resting God. He is creator God. He is sovereign God. He is eternal God. He is the redeeming God.

The Fifth Commandment (20:12)

God commands each person to honor his or her father and mother. The word for "honor" implies acknowledging the "weight" of something. In this context, it implies that people give the proper "weight" or "respect" to their parents' position. The opposite of this would be to despise or scorn one's parents. One who did this was in danger of being put to death (Lev 20:9), in some cases by stoning (Deut 21:18-21). Thus, respect for parents, and for authority figures in general, should be taken seriously.

What do we learn about God here? We learn of His authority. We also learn about His provision. The clause on the end of the commandment provides a motivation for keeping the commandment—to live long in the land given by God. This reveals the generosity of God. As fathers, we should also seek to imitate our God, who is the perfect Father.

The Sixth Commandment (20:13)

This commandment is expressed with one of eight words in Hebrew for killing someone or something. It includes intentional, premeditated killing as well as accidental killing. This word for "murder" in Hebrew is specific to "putting to death improperly, for selfish reasons rather than with authorization" (Stuart, *Exodus*, 462). With this in mind, one is not to kill unlawfully. Stuart says, "No Israelite acting on his own could decide that he had the right to end someone's life" (ibid.). God is showing us that life is sacred!

What do we learn about God? We should not murder because God alone gives life (Deut 32:39) and people are made in His image. Jesus deepened it by saying that anger was like murder (Matt 5:22). James also said we should not curse people because people are made in God's image (Jas 3:9).

The Seventh Commandment (20:14)

This commandment addresses sexual purity. The purpose of the commandment is to promote, positively, the purity of the heart, especially in regard to the marriage relationship. The commandment specifically addresses adultery, or marital infidelity. As Jesus told us, everyone who looks at a woman with lustful intent has already committed adultery with her in his heart (Matt 5:27-28). Again, the underlying principle is a pure heart.

What does this command teach us about God? It reminds us of God's faithfulness and holiness. God is holy and He commands His people to be holy (1 Pet 1:15-16). God expects His people to faithfully follow His word in regard to relationships. Another note: God is not trying to spoil your fun. *Inside* the covenant of marriage there is great enjoyment and intimacy in a one-flesh union. God's commandments are for your good as well as the good of others.

The Eighth Commandment (20:15)

This commandment deals with taking that which does not belong to you. This can manifest itself in a number of ways. This even goes back to the beginning when man sought to take what did not belong to him— the fruit from the tree in the garden of Eden. The opposite of this is to remember what God has graciously given us. Rather than stealing, we should have thankful hearts that rejoice in what God has provided for us. We should be good stewards with what God has given us. Otherwise, we may be more tempted to steal and commit sin against our Lord. We must remember that what we have is not our own, but it is the Lord's; as He has given freely, so we too should give freely.

God is our provider. Because God gives His people everything they need, we do not steal. Paul tells Timothy that the rich must not "set their hope on the uncertainty of wealth, but on God, who richly provides us with all things to enjoy" (1 Tim 6:17).

The Ninth Commandment (20:16)

Traditionally, a lot of people summarize this command by saying, "You shall not lie." While this does provide a good summary, the language used here points to some other important aspects of this commandment. It is directly connected to the idea of legal testimony and the witness. Rather than providing false testimony, the individual should give truthful and honest testimony. This idea, however, is not limited to the courtroom, for nothing extends outside "the courtroom of God." All will be held accountable for their words.

From this command we recognize God's attribute of truthfulness. It is impossible for God to lie (Titus 1:2).

The Tenth Commandment (20:17)

This commandment highlights the twisted desires of mankind and the sin of discontentment. Instead of having a thankful heart, the coveter desires what others have. Notice also that this commandment is about the inward nature of the law. Covetousness is about the heart. It is about desire. It may or may not lead to an act, but even if there is no act, it is still wrong because our desire should be on the God who made us and redeemed us. Covetousness, then, involves breaking the first commandment.

Jesus said, "Watch out and be on guard against all greed because one's life is not in the abundance of his possessions" (Luke 12:15). In Hebrews 13:5 we read about the need to live free from the love of money. Do not trust in your wealth. Do not have excessive anxiety about wealth. Do not be devoted to wealth.

This command teaches us about God's faithfulness, goodness, and provision. We need not worry about provisions or desire other people's stuff, for our Father knows our needs (Matt 6:25-34) and satisfies our deepest longings.

Therefore, understand the commands and see how God has poured Himself into them. They reflect His holy character. The commandments are not just a list of rules; they are a reflection of God. How awesome it is that we have a God who has given us His Word! The psalmist reflects on God's law saying, "How I love Your instruction! It is my meditation all day long" (Ps 119:97).

Consider How the New Testament Writers Emphasize Them

Some argue that the Ten Words speak of the "moral law," not the "civil law" or "ceremonial law." Some contend that the civil laws are useful, and both the ceremonial and the civil law contain some of God's moral law, but what is reconfirmed in the New Testament is God's moral law. The moral law is still binding on us, they say. While I understand this argument and affirm some clear discontinuity between these laws and the new covenant, I think one should be careful in pressing this three-part categorization too much. We should remember that these laws are mixed together "not only in the Judgments or ordinances [Exod 21–23] but in the Ten Words as well (the Sabbath may be properly classified as ceremonial)" (Gentry and Wellum, *Kingdom*, 355). Gentry and Wellum seem to point us in a good direction when they say, "What we can say to represent the teaching of Scripture is that the righteousness of God codified, enshrined, and encapsulated in the old covenant has not changed, and that this same righteousness is now codified and enshrined in the new" (ibid.).

Indeed, the righteous character of God continued to receive emphasis in the New Testament as the writers spoke of the nature of God and as they touched on the Ten Words. Authors often named the Ten Words in outline form (see Matt 15:19-20; Luke 18:20; Rom 13:8-10) and also separately (see John 14:6; 5:23; 1 John 5:21; Col 3:23; Matt 12:8; Heb 4:9; Eph 6:1-2; Matt 5:21-22,27-30; Eph 4:28; Col 3:9; Luke 12:15), reconfirming the same righteousness put forward in Exodus. All of these commands show us how to live righteously, but we realize that we have failed miserably; thankfully, the Righteous One lived them out perfectly for us and then died in our place. This good news leads us to the final concept.

See How Jesus Fulfills Them

At the end of the giving of the Ten Words, the people stood in fear and trembling (vv. 18-21). They had a sense of awe toward God. We know that they also failed repeatedly. Even their mediator, Moses, would fail. However, there is a greater mediator who did not fail—the Lord Jesus Christ.

The Ten Words point us to the Savior. Christ was "born under the law, to redeem those under the law" (Gal 4:4-5). He fulfilled the law in every respect (Matt 5:17-18). He paid the penalty of the law and bore the curse of the law on the cross (Gal 3:10-14; Col 2:13-14). We cannot keep God's law perfectly. We need another to do this for us. The law drives us to Jesus for forgiveness and a new heart, and the Spirit then empowers for obedience. While in this life we cannot keep the law perfectly and are always in need of grace, we are never crushed by the law because there is no condemnation for those in Christ Jesus (Rom 8:1). Because the weight has been lifted, we are able to delight in God's law. We do not see His commandments as burdensome (1 John 5:3).

Therefore, our hope and power does not come from *our* law keeping but from *His* law keeping. He lived the life we could not live (keeping the law) then died the death we should have died (for our law breaking). That is why we love Jesus.

> Not the labors of my hands
> Can fulfill Thy law's demands;
> Could my zeal no respite know,
> Could my tears forever flow,
> All for sin could not atone;
> Thou must save, and Thou alone. (Augustus Toplady,
>   "Rock of Ages")

Praise Jesus Christ, the One who saves those who cannot keep God's holy law.

My non-Christian friend, did you read the Ten Words and ask, "How can I be saved when I cannot keep God's law?" There is only one way: Jesus. Look to Him and believe. Receive His perfect righteousness by faith alone. He is your hope. Look to the One who kept these commands perfectly and then died for those who broke them. Christian friend, rejoice that you have a Savior who lived for you and died for you. And by the power of the Spirit, as a new creation, live out these commands to the glory of our great and awesome God.

Reflect and Discuss

1. How many of the Ten Commandments do you know? Beyond memorizing them, how else can they be made profitable?

2. How are God's holiness and grace demonstrated in His giving Israel the Ten Words? Why is it important to remember that God delivered Israel from slavery first, then gave the Ten Words?

3. What is the connection between God saying, "All the earth is Mine," and our status as a "kingdom of priests"? What is our mandate?

4. How does obedience to the four "vertical" commands cause a person to obey the six "horizontal" commands? That is, how does the first "greatest command" give rise to the second?

5. How does the first command address atheism, agnosticism, and idolatry? What do people in your culture tend to worship, and how do they express that worship?

6. How is jealousy a virtue in God but generally a vice in humans? Why is it good for God to demand His own worship and defend His own glory?

7. How does human pride subvert each of the commands? How are coveting and stealing related to the first command?

8. How do you observe your Sabbath? Which receives more time and emphasis: rest or worship?

9. Why is it not always helpful to distinguish moral law, civil law, and ceremonial law? Which category does each of the Ten Words fall in?

10. Why does the perfect righteousness incorporated in the Ten Words cause people to lose hope? What restores that hope?

Loving God and Neighbor

EXODUS 20:22–23:19

Main Idea: Studying these ordinances helps us glorify God in our everyday lives by the way we honor Him and treat each other.

I. **Concerning Worship (20:22-26)**
   A. Principle of simplicity (20:24a, 25b)
   B. Principle of purity (20:26)
   C. Principle of locality (20:24)
   D. Principle of sacrifice (20:24)

II. **Concerning Slaves (21:1-11)**
   A. Laws on slaves (21:1-6)
   B. Female slaves (21:7-11)

III. **Concerning Behavior (21:12–32)**
   A. Intentional and unintentional homicide laws (21:12-14)
   B. The sanctity of life and the image of God (21:12-17)
   C. Assault on parents, kidnapping, and cursing parents (21:15-17)
   D. Life-threatening injuries (21:18-21)
   E. Permanent injuries (21:22-27)
   F. Injuries associated with animals (21:28-32)

IV. **Concerning Restitution (21:33–22:15)**

V. **Concerning Holiness (22:16-20)**

VI. **Concerning Social Justice (22:21–23:9)**
   A. Compassion to the foreigner, widow, and fatherless (22:21-24; 23:9)
   B. Compassion for the poor (22:25-27)
   C. Respect for God and leaders (22:28)
   D. Giving offerings (22:29-30)
   E. Consecration (22:31)
   F. Do not pervert justice (23:1-3,6-8)
   G. Loving enemies (23:4-5)

VII. **Concerning Sabbath and Festivals (23:10-19)**

VIII. **We Need a Savior!**

In our slow jog through these chapters, we run into some intriguing passages (e.g., "You must not boil a young goat in its mother's milk," 23:19) as well as some contemporary hot topics such as the death penalty, slavery, premarital sex, orphan care, lawsuits, fistfights, property, the poor, loving our enemies, and more.

In Exodus, God formed a people to display His glory. He taught them how to live in community with one another. Before we pass this section off as irrelevant, think about how important this section was for Israel. They needed some guidelines for living.

We can understand this need. Have you ever had a roommate? If so, then you know proximity brings drama, even if you have wonderful roommates. I have had a number of difficult roommates, and with each problem, I insisted on some guidelines. For my snoring friend, Philip, I made him go to sleep after I went to sleep! For my friend Calvin, I asked him not to play rap music at 2:00 a.m.! For Jamie, I demanded that he stop locking me out of the room! With this in mind, you can imagine six hundred thousand men, plus women and children, living together in a desert! They needed some guidelines. They needed instruction to help them not only to get along with each other, but also to learn how to glorify God in their daily lives.

The rules or "ordinances" we find here essentially *apply* the Ten Words to specific situations. Is there anything more relevant than glorifying God by loving Him and our neighbor? Since all true Christians long to obey the Greatest Command, they should consider these chapters carefully. This section shows us that God is concerned with how we relate to one another in day-to-day life. God calls us to holiness, integrity, mercy, justice, and fairness *in the ordinariness of life*. We spend most of our days in the ordinary: going to work, seeing neighbors, raising kids, and other seemingly routine affairs. Occasionally, the Christian may attend conferences, go on a vacation, or head out on a mission trip, but these events are the exceptional times of life. How can we glorify God in the ebb and flow of our day-to-day dealings?

"Loving our neighbor" may sound like an abstract idea, but here we see some real-life examples and principles. We will seek to draw out the principles and view them in light of the New Testament's teaching, just as we did with the Ten Words. Just like the nation of Israel, who sought to apply the Ten Words, we too must learn to apply God's Word to our situation today.

This section of Scripture also reveals the character of God to us. One of the most important things we ask when we read the Bible is, What does this text teach me about God? Here we see a just and compassionate God who expects His people to live before Him in humility and with justice and mercy toward others. Perhaps we could hang this verse over this section of Exodus:

> *Mankind, He has told you what is good*
> *and what it is the LORD requires of you:*
> *to act justly,*
> *to love faithfulness,*
> *and to walk humbly with your God.* (Mic 6:8)

We should be careful to avoid two mistakes with this section: (1) throwing these laws out completely, thinking they have nothing to teach us or (2) urging our city to adopt them as they are. We should see both continuity and discontinuity here. We are not a theocracy, so we need to be careful not to make a one-to-one correlation. At the same time, God's character is revealed in His law, and this makes these laws relevant. We should seek to learn what these laws mean, then make responsible, Christ-centered, new covenant application.

These case laws were written to deal with specific situations. However, even in their specificity, they were never intended to address every possible situation. They were guidelines. Judges would take these case laws and apply them with care. The selected laws were probably stated because of how they related to Israel's prior situation in Egypt. Israel was exploited in various ways in Egypt, and God did not free them to abuse others, either on a major life/death scale or in ordinary day-to-day matters.

Let us now look at how God expected His people to love Him and their neighbors. To help us jog through the material, I have grouped them in seven parts.

Concerning Worship
EXODUS 20:22-26

God's instructions about building idols (vv. 22-23) reflect the first four of the Ten Commandments. God's people must worship God alone. Israel failed to obey this word in chapter 32 when they bowed down to a golden calf.

God then told them how to worship (vv. 24-26). The reference to altars and sacrifices reminds us of the patriarchs who built altars, and points us forward to further instruction to come. God not only wanted Israel to avoid worshiping pagan gods, He also wanted them to avoid worshiping like the pagans. God told them about four particular differences in their worship, all of which apply to us today.

Principle of Simplicity (20:24a,25b)

God told them to make their altar out of the earth and stone that He created. The Canaanites worshiped idols, and they did so on altars of finished stone. John Mackay says, "An altar made from such costly and aesthetically pleasing stone would be a tribute to human craftsmanship, but it would be defiled from the Lord's point of view because it distracted attention from him and his goodness" (Ryken, *Exodus*, 692). Pagan altars were built with costly items and built high to show off. But God told Israel to build it out of earth. He did not want them to be distracted from the heart of worship. If an ornate, costly altar was built, one might be tempted to worship it! The altar was simple—just stones fitted together into a waist high rectangle upon which wood would be laid for cooking meat for the sacrifice.

Nothing in corporate worship services today should be done for show. At the church where I serve as a pastor, we intentionally avoid being gimmicky or ornate. God should be the focus of worship, not a building or even a leader. God delights in the praise of His people, as they gather in simple, modest buildings or as they exalt Him in a mud hut in a third world country. Impressive structures should never capture our hearts and take us away from the object of worship: the triune God.

Principle of Purity (20:26)

Because Canaanite worship was often obscene, God provided instruction for purity. God told His people to avoid going up steps in order to preserve their modesty (men wore robes). Later, God made the priests wear linen undergarments to avoid being exposed. God still expects purity from His people, especially among leaders.

Principle of Locality (20:24)

These verses also teach something important about the location of worship. God said, "I will come to you and bless you in every place where I cause My name to be remembered" (v. 24). This meant that Israel did not have to go to Sinai to experience God's presence. There would be other places to meet God (later, in the tabernacle, then in the temple).

We now understand that through the Holy Spirit, God can be worshiped all over the world. Jesus told the woman at the well that worship was not about a location but about worshiping the living God in spirit and truth (John 4:24). We do not have to make a pilgrimage to a certain place to experience God's power in worship. We come through Christ (our new temple) by the Spirit to meet with God. Whether we are offering corporate worship or dealing with a case of discipline, God is with us.

Principle of Sacrifice (20:24)

The most important thing about the altar was what happened *on* the altar. The altar was the place for making sacrifice for sin. The burnt offering was an offering of atonement for sin (Lev 1). A perfect animal was placed on an altar, and it was consumed with fire, with the smoke rising to heaven.

The second type of offering was a fellowship or peace offering (Lev 3). It also dealt with sin but had a different emphasis. These offerings were given on special occasions to give thanks to God, and they symbolized the fellowship one had with God. In recognition of God's reconciliation with people, the offering was not consumed with fire. So they ate the animal in the presence of God. (By contrast, the burnt offering was burnt to ashes.)

Even after the giving of the law, God knew that His people would need forgiveness. Of course, these sacrifices pointed to the once-and-for-all sacrifice of Jesus, who paid the penalty for our sin by being slaughtered. His sacrifice pleased God, and now we can be reconciled to God (Rom 3:25). In fact, the author of Hebrews referred to Jesus as our "altar" (Heb 13:10). He was the burnt offering that made sacrifice for our sin and the fellowship offering that reconciles us to God.

Therefore, when it comes to worship, the most important thing we do is remember Jesus. Apart from Him, we cannot worship and know God. The only sacrifice that now remains is the sacrifice of our very lives (Rom 12:1-2; Heb 13:15-16).

Concerning Slaves
EXODUS 21:1-11

Laws on Slaves (21:1-6)

We should note first that this is not "slavery" like we think about in American history. Most people ran small family businesses, and their "slaves" were more like simple workers or employees in the business who lived at the master's place. They were basically "contract workers."

Further, other variables made this situation different from American slavery. During the time of Moses, it was *voluntary* (people hired themselves into service of others, often because of debt). They worked hard in exchange for room, board, and an honest wage. Involuntary slavery was forbidden in this very section of Scripture (see 21:16). This type of service was also *temporary*. The slave worked for six years and then went free. Hebrew slaves were given a Sabbatical. Further, they did not leave empty-handed (see Deut 15:12-15). This form of service was also *civil*. The master could not abuse the slave (see Exod 21:26-27). Receiving slaves could even be seen as benevolent if the master intentionally sought to get the slave out of debt. It also was neither *oppressive* nor *racially based*. Israel just came out of slavery and God did not free them in order for them to oppress others.

A final difference of this form of service is that it preserved *the sanctity of the family*. American slavery often separated families, but not this system. We read, "If he arrives alone, he is to leave alone; if he arrives with a wife, his wife is to leave with him" (Exod 21:3). But if the master gave a slave a wife, in an arranged marriage situation, then the husband might have to "leave alone" (21:4). This seems unfair at first glance. But remember a few things. The female slave committed to a contract for six years of labor. She could not just up and leave if she got married before her term expired. The husband could do one of the three things: (1) wait; (2) get a good job and purchase the freedom of his wife and kids; or (3) commit himself to work permanently for the master (vv. 5-6). In the last case, the husband-slave was brought before God and a sharp object went through his ear at the doorpost (symbolizing covenant and the permanent commitment).

This piercing of the ear at the doorpost illustrates a beautiful picture of service. David might have had this in mind in Psalm 40:6 when he said, "In sacrifice and offering you have not delighted, but you have given me an open ear" (ESV). Worship without a lifelong commitment to obedience is no worship at all. David said that God desires lifelong, loving obedience to Him. We too have bound ourselves to Christ, our Master—a kind, generous, sacrificial Master—who actually became a slave Himself (Phil 2:5-11); to Him we should gladly say, "Because I adore You, I am Yours forever."

Female Slaves (21:7-11)

After first glance, this sounds harsh. Why did God allow men to sell their daughters to service of another? We do not know all the details here, but it seems that the father was not trying to get rid of her but trying to improve her prospects for marriage (arranged marriages were common). A poor man could send his daughter to a rich home in hopes that she would be part of that family. She could also be designated for the master's son (v. 9).

The lady received protection in three ways: (1) If it did not work out, the family could ransom her. She could not be sold to foreigners. (2) If she became engaged to one of the sons, she was treated as a daughter. She would have full rights as a free citizen. (3) If the engagement ended, the man had the duty of providing food, clothing, and marital rights. God loves His daughters and wanted them treated lovingly and fairly. God still cares for ladies physically and emotionally and expects men to defend them and treat them lovingly and justly!

Concerning Behavior
EXODUS 21:12-32

As we move through this section, we see laws on injuries to people and animals. The underlying principle is that the punishment should fit the crime.

Intentional and Unintentional Homicide Laws (21:12-14)

The first and third scenario (vv. 12,14) deal with murder and the consequence: capital punishment; the middle one (v. 13) addresses an accidental homicide and the response to it: protection of the guilty in a city of refuge. The middle scenario could be a case in which you accidently ran over someone with a wagon, hit someone with a tool, or killed an ally in battle. This distinction made Israel different from other cultures of the day, which did not consider *intent*. The covenant law anticipated the cities of refuge that would be spread throughout Israel to protect the offender from an avenger (Num 35:9-15). No such refuge existed for those who planned to murder ("willfully"). They could not run to the altar, as in some societies, for protection. There was no place one could run to escape from the consequence of such sin.

The Sanctity of Life and the Image of God (21:12-17)

Many modern readers of the biblical laws have a hard time with capital punishment mentioned here in these chapters. The specific crimes calling for it include murder, kidnapping, physical or verbal assaults on one's parents, sorcery, bestiality, and idolatry (21:12-17; 22:18-20). It appears extremely harsh to some. But we must not forget what belief this action was based on: the value of human life, the honor of family, and the purity of worship. Concerning the value of human life, Alexander says,

> The death penalty was invoked, not out of indifference
> for human life, but rather because each human life is of
> tremendous value (cf. Gen 9:6). A life for life does not express
> vengefulness, but rather the idea that the only payment that
> can be made for taking human life is a human life itself.
> (*Paradise,* 216)

God established this principle before these laws in Exodus: "Whoever sheds man's blood, his blood will be shed by man, for God made man in His image" (Gen 9:6). Whatever you believe about the death penalty, at least grab this principle: people matter to God. They bear His image.

This law was distinctive to Israel because of this principle. In some cultures, breaking and entering, stealing, or looting at a fire brought the death penalty! Some considered a crime related to possessions as more serious than a crime against a human being. In the Code of Hammurabi, if one committed murder he could pay it back with money alone (Alexander, *Paradise,* 184). God, however, placed a distinction here on the various objects of creation. Nothing is more valuable than human life. Further, God's law gave safeguards to protect the innocent (cf. 23:7). In Deuteronomy 17:6-7 we read where one could not be executed on the basis of a single witness. To carry out this serious penalty it had to be administered justly.

A perfectly just process in a fallen world will never exist; therefore, there will be times to oppose the death penalty, even if you agree with the principle of it. What we should not oppose is a severe punishment for those who do not honor the image of God.

Assault on Parents, Kidnapping, and Cursing Parents (21:15-17)

Notice the gravity of honoring one's parents. The verses describe ways of "attacking" one's parents. They help to explain the meaning of "honor your father and mother." The assault envisioned in verse 15 does not have a minor slap in view, but a serious attack—with the intent to kill, perhaps. It is a "beat down" (Stuart, *Exodus,* 487).

Probably what is envisioned in verse 17 is not a one-time fit of rage that leads a child to disrespect their parents, but a total repudiation of their authority and failure to care for them. Jesus understood this law and challenged the Pharisees, who were trying to sidestep caring for their parents by hiding behind religious tradition (Matt 15:3-6). The bottom line is, if you speak against your parents—or worse, strike them—you are guilty of a great sin against God. Honor them and care for them, even if the situation is not ideal.

In verse 16 the verb "kidnaps" is the same as "steal" in the eighth commandment. If a person stole another person and sold him, or if a person was in possession of a stolen person, then the death penalty was required (1 Tim 1:10). Kidnappers were to be put to death immediately. Again, in the Code of Hammurabi (around 1772 BC), the prohibition against kidnapping applied only to the upper class. Common people could be kidnapped without it being viewed as a crime (Ryken, *Exodus,* 712). But Israel was different. Because people are made in the image of God, they could not be treated in such a way.

Is this a problem today? Yes! Kidnapping people and trafficking them as slaves is the second largest, fastest growing international crime today. Some estimate that we have about 27 million slaves in the world today. "Nearly 2 million children are exploited in commercial sex industry" (www.ijm.org). We need people to rise up to defend the enslaved and defenseless. Recently, a team from our church spent an entire day praying for justice at the International Justice Mission Global Prayer Gathering. We went to rooms that represented particular injustices in places like Uganda, Cambodia, Thailand, and the Philippines. After hearing from field officers about the abuse of widows, land grabbing, corrupt police, the cries of orphans, taking of bribes, girls sold in brothels, and more heart-breaking cases, we prayed and learned what the church might do to respond to these awful situations. Let us seek justice for those in need, as Isaiah said: "Learn to do what is good. Seek justice. Correct the oppressor. Defend the rights of the fatherless. Plead the widow's cause" (Isa 1:17).

Life-Threatening Injuries (21:18-21)

In verses 18-19 we see an example of a situation in which the judges would make their decisions regarding a fight. If a man got in a brawl with another man but the loser did not die, then the winner of the fight had to pay for the loss of time and see that the loser was healed. Again, we see the punishment fitting the crime. God did not say, "Put the man to death."

In verses 20-21 we see that the master did have the right to physically punish his slave, but he was not permitted to seriously injure or kill the slave. If he did, he could be tried as a murderer.

Permanent Injuries (21:22-27)

In regard to verse 22, Stuart says, "This verse contains some wording that is without parallel elsewhere in the Old Testament and thus challenging to translate" (*Exodus*, 491). Assuming the HCSB or ESV translation is correct, this verse implies that there was a penalty for hitting a pregnant woman, even if she was not injured. The situation seems to be a case in which the lady was an innocent bystander of a fight and got struck in the process. The law considered both the mother and the child. Notice that the fetus was treated *as a person* ("life for life").

Verses 23-25 show that if someone was severely injured or killed, the punishment should fit the crime. Here we are introduced to the Bible's *lex talionis*, the laws of retaliation: "life for life, eye for eye, tooth for tooth," etc. At first this sounds barbaric, but it was actually an advance in justice compared to other Near Eastern codes. Alexander writes,

> In the earliest known collection of laws, monetary fines were imposed in cases of assault and bodily injury. The weakness of such fines was that they failed to take into account an individual's ability to pay. (For an unemployed laborer, a fine of a thousand pounds imposes great hardship; to a millionaire

it is a mere trifle.) The law of talion removes all such discrepancies by ensuring that the punishment should be no less, or no more, than the crime demands. (*Paradise*, 215–16)

These laws did not allow the rich to buy their way out of criminal penalties, which continues to be a problem around the world. The powerful have often been able to buy escape from justice.

We should also keep in mind that, other than the case of the death penalty, the *lex talionis* was not necessarily applied literally. In verses 18-19 a wounded person received the cost of medical expenses and lost wages instead of wounding the guilty person in return.

In the next scenario (vv. 26-27), a slave who lost his eye was to be released. Nothing is said of the master losing his eye! Stuart says,

Instead, expressions like "eye for eye" were understood idiomatically to mean "a penalty that hurts the person who ruined someone else's eye as much as he would be hurt if his own eye were actually ruined also." The precise penalty was left up to the judges by talion law; it might involve anything from banishment to loss of property (and/or property rights) to punitive confinement to special financial penalties to corporal punishment to public humiliation, or to any combination of these. (*Exodus*, 493–94)

In other words, the goal was for justice to be served. Favoritism was unacceptable.

Jesus referred to the *lex talionis* in Matthew 5:38-42, in which He said to "turn the other cheek." But Jesus' point was different. These laws in Exodus provided guidelines for *judges* in assessing damages. Jesus' teaching was more about guidelines for *ordinary relationships.* Christians should seek to imitate God's own generosity and mercy in personal relationships, as Jesus described in the Sermon on the Mount.

At the cross, Jesus cried out, "Father, forgive them," as they crucified Him. Peter said, "[W]hen He was reviled, He did not revile in return; when He was suffering, He did not threaten but entrusted Himself to the One who judges justly" (1 Pet 2:23). The heart of the Christian must be a heart of mercy, not retaliation. Paul said, "And be kind and compassionate to one another, forgiving one another, just as God also forgave you in Christ" (Eph 4:32).

Yes, there are times for appealing to the authorities for just consequences, and we need the civil authorities to carry out justice, but we who have experienced mercy through the cross should be willing to suffer in order to show mercy in our relationships.

Finally, verses 26-27 do not allow a master to abuse a slave. If he did, he lost his ownership immediately. Once again Moses underlined the principle of mercy and fairness.

Injuries Associated with Animals (21:28-32)

Because virtually everyone farmed in the ancient world, laws had to be put in place regarding animals. If it was written in our day, it might include laws related to automobiles. If an ox killed a man, the ox was to be killed. Once again we see the value of human life. Moses explained that if the animal had a history of violence and the owner did not properly monitor it, and if the animal killed a person, then the owner was guilty of negligent homicide. If called for, a ransom could be paid. The same applied if the victim was a child.

If the victim was a slave, it was different because of the social structure (v. 32). Perhaps the slave was working closer to the animal by command of the master. If he was struck, the owner was to pay the master thirty shekels.

Concerning Restitution
EXODUS 21:33–22:15

Now we move to the loss of animals and property. These ordinances show us what would happen if someone "got ripped off"—basic property laws. The offender was to make restitution. The required amount was related to the nature of the crime. The amount was normally multiples of the value of the loss.

Notice a "jail sentence" is never mentioned. Offenders had to deal face to face with the offended; they had to generously compensate the victim.

Irresponsible action, like not covering a pit or not controlling one's wild ox, is dealt with in 21:33-36. Theft was addressed in the first four verses of chapter 22. Notice, like modern laws, there was a distinction in breaking and entering at nighttime versus the daytime. Verses 5-6 involve cases of negligence that led to the loss of someone's property. Verses 7-13 deal with giving someone property for safekeeping, but having that trust breached (there were no banks in those days). Verses 14-15 deal with borrowed property.

In each of these cases, the laws appear sensible. You had to respect one another's property. Again, these laws were wonderful gifts because they showed people how to live in community, loving their neighbors as themselves. The laws also helped to solve disputes. Further, by demanding more than the value of the item, it deterred possible criminals. It also protected life—the life of the thief. As mentioned, in other cultures the authorities killed thieves. But God's law placed primacy on life, not possessions. And the punishment fit the crime. If the thief could not pay off his debt, he was forced to work it off until the victim got what he deserved.

How do these property laws relate to us? Let me ask you, can you think of a biblical character that went from a thief to a generous slave after experiencing salvation in Christ—who went to make things right with others? A wee little man comes to my mind: Zacchaeus. After encountering Christ, he said, "'Look, I'll give half of my possessions to the poor, Lord! And if I have extorted anything from anyone, I'll pay back four times as much!'" (Luke 19:8). He wanted to give to those in need and return four-fold what he owed others. Why? Because the gospel changes us—it creates in us a new heart of love for God and neighbor. The gospel creates not just a heart to make things right with others that we have offended, but to go beyond—to lovingly serve and to generously give.

Concerning Holiness
EXODUS 22:16-20

Verses 16-17 relate to premarital sex and to the seventh commandment. The details seem to focus on mutual consent, not rape. If it had been rape, the penalty would have been death (Deut 22:25-27). The man here "seduces" the lady to have sex. The text shows us that anyone who committed this sin violated the purity of ladies, showing blatant disregard for their worth.

Here the man had the responsibility to provide for the lady, both through marrying the woman (unless the father utterly refused) and by paying her father (Deut 22:28-29). So the consequence of premarital sex was huge! These verses show us two important concepts: (1) the value of the lady (you could not run around and have sex with anyone without facing consequences) and (2) the family's involvement in marriage.

Do you see how much God values purity? Today we live in a sex-saturated culture. Reportedly, more money is spent on pornography than on pro baseball, football, and basketball. More are exposed to pornography than ever before. Premarital sex and cohabitation are commonplace. People think little about modesty.

God still calls His people to a life of holiness and purity. Now we have great power with the Holy Spirit to live out this calling (see 1 Cor 6:18-20; 1 Thess 4:3-5).

In verses 18-20 Moses broadly surveyed capital crimes. God called Israel to be holy and worship Him alone; therefore, these rules carried the ultimate consequence. Each of the three cases mentioned made Israel unclean. Further, they involved the reasons God was about to judge the nations in Canaan (Lev 20:22-26). This seems too severe, but in one sense it was gracious. Anyone engaged in these activities was turning from the real God, hence God graciously warned them; and anyone engaged in them was also leading others astray.

Concerning Social Justice
EXODUS 22:21–23:9

As most commentators suggest (e.g., Alexander, *Paradise*, 184), there are three reasons these verses form a new section with a different emphasis: (1) The section is framed by verses related to the treatment of foreigners (22:21; 3:9). Alexander also notes that the material is presented in a form more like the Ten Commandments than those in the previous section. (2) There are no penalties enforced from a human court (the only statement of a penalty is from God who says He will "kill you with the sword" [v. 24], which may refer to Israel's enemies being used as means of judgment). (3) The subject matter differs. It encourages a caring attitude toward the vulnerable and disadvantaged. God's people are called not just to obey the laws, but to care for those in need.

Compassion to the Foreigner, Widow, and Fatherless (22:21-24; 23:9)

The call to care for foreigners was rooted in this idea: "you were foreigners in the land of Egypt" (22:21; 23:9). God called Israel to show the same type of care they received from Him.

This principle of caring for strangers also applies to internationals that flood our city, either for school, for work, or as refugees. Let us be quick to welcome them, as Christ has welcomed us.

We also read, "You must not mistreat any widow or fatherless child" (22:22). Taking advantage of the weak continues to be a huge problem today. The text adds that if anyone mistreats the widow and fatherless, God will "kill [them] with the sword" and make their wives "widows" and children "fatherless" (v. 24). God expected His people to care for those in need. Widows and orphans were in great need in that society. They were alone and had a hard time surviving.

God expects us to care for those in need because He cared for us when we were in desperate need. When you were fatherless, He adopted you; when you were a widow, He became your groom; when you were a stranger to His grace, He welcomed you. Those who know such love should be the very ones showing it to this broken world. Notice also that it said God would "hear their cry" (v. 23). God hears the cry of the desperate.

I have written on this subject elsewhere (see *Orphanology* in "Works Cited"), and I do not have time or space to say everything that could be said here. The Old Testament and New Testament consistently give attention to these weaker groups (Exod 22:21-22; Deut 10:18; 14:28-29; 24:17-22; 27:19; Pss 10:14,16-18; 68:5-6; 82:3-4; 146:9; Isa 1:17-18; Zech 7:10; 1 Tim 5:3-16; Jas 1:27). Tim Keller points out this biblical emphasis:

> When people ask me, "How do you want to be introduced?"
> I usually propose they say, "This is Tim Keller, minister of the
> Redeemer Presbyterian Church in New York City." Of course,
> I am many other things, but that is the main thing I spend
> my time doing in public life. Realize, then, how significant it
> is that the Biblical writers introduce God as a "father to the
> fatherless, a defender of widows" (Psalm 68:4-5). This is one
> of the main things he does in the world. He identifies with the
> powerless, he takes up their cause. (*Generous Justice*, 6)

Remember that God calls us to imitate Him (Eph 5:1). One important way we can do this is by caring for the vulnerable.

Compassion for the Poor (22:25-27)

Borrowing and lending are not forbidden in verse 25. God simply forbids exploiting the poor with exorbitant interest. Other verses in the

Pentateuch show that God told His people not to charge excessive interest to any other Israelite, not just the poor (Deut 23:19-20). Once again, this was a command to show mercy and compassion.

The law addressed the properties people might put up for collateral for loans (vv. 26-27). God made a distinction between a poor person and the non-poor. Some of the poor might have to give "the shirt off their back." If they had to pledge an item essential for survival to obtain a loan, then they were to be exempt from the requirement of putting up a surety, or were at least permitted to have it returned to them at night.

God provided amazing detail here, especially for the sake of the poor. Why did He do this? We read, "And if he cries out to Me, I will listen because I am compassionate" (v. 27). Again, we are to imitate God by showing compassion to the poor. Jesus referred to this and other ideas found in these case laws in Luke 6:27-36. He said that even those who do not know God love those who love them; so be different! Love your enemies. Give without expecting a return. Granted, there may be times that it is more merciful not to give to someone in need if you are supporting a lifestyle that is not pleasing to God; but there are times simply to give a gift. In short, "Be merciful, just as your Father also is merciful" (Luke 6:36).

Respect for God and Leaders (22:28)

Ancient people understood the power of the tongue, perhaps more than those who live in a country with "free speech." They took the Proverb seriously, "Life and death are in the power of the tongue" (18:21). One daily way that you live out a just life, with compassion and integrity, is by watching what you say about God and others, especially leaders. In the New Testament, Paul and Peter both echoed the call to respect those in leadership (Acts 23:5; Rom 13:1-7; 1 Tim 2:1-2; 1 Pet 3:13-17). Paul also spoke of the calling of Christians to respect those in leadership in the church as well (1 Thess 5:12-13).

Giving Offerings (22:29-30)

A love for God means that we give Him those things that belong to Him, including our gifts and offerings. Israelites may have been tempted to withhold these things, like people today, but such an act would not please God. "God loves a cheerful giver" (2 Cor 9:7). We also find another reference here to the consecration of the firstborn son, as explained in Exodus 13.

Consecration (22:31)

This prohibition from eating flesh that was torn by beasts in the field probably was due to it being considered ritually unclean as well as it being unhealthy. God still wants pervasive holiness from His people (Mark 7:20-23).

Do Not Pervert Justice (23:1-3,6-8)

These laws expanded on the ninth commandment. They spoke against "following the crowd" if that meant you had to pervert justice. Notice how verses 3 and 6 cover both temptations: to side with the rich or to side with the poor. Verse 3 says not to be partial to the poor in a lawsuit, and verse 6 says not to pervert justice against the poor in a lawsuit. Verses 7-8 tell us that God expected justice, not partiality, and forbade taking bribes (which are a worldwide problem today).

Loving Enemies (23:4-5)

These verses show us that loving our neighbor includes our enemies. Instructions are given here for helping your neighbor, not just being civil. This makes us think of Jesus' instruction to love those who hate you (Luke 6).

Concerning Sabbath and Festivals
EXODUS 23:10-19

As the "covenant scroll" continues, we come to laws regarding the Sabbath and three specific festivals. Concerning the Sabbath, the law said it should be a day in which all rest—including the animals, the slaves, and the foreigners (v. 12). Not only this, on the seventh year the people were also to rest from sowing and gathering so that the poor might benefit from the land (vv. 10-11). God then reminded the people to "Pay strict attention to everything I have said to you. You must not invoke the names of other gods; they must not be heard on your lips" (v. 13). God is not interested in partial or half-hearted obedience.

To commemorate what God had done, He established three feasts. First, the Festival of Unleavened Bread was established to celebrate Israel's liberation (vv. 14-17). Second, the Festival of Harvest would celebrate God's provision for His people. Third, the Festival of Ingathering, which is also the Festival of Booths or the Festival of Tabernacles, would celebrate God's salvation.

The blood of the sacrifices was not to be offered with leaven, which represented sin (v. 18). Thus, getting rid of the leaven represented getting rid of sin. Also, the firstfruits were to be used during the feasts (v. 19). The first and best of one's harvest was given to God. God still deserves our best, not our leftovers. These feasts point us to God's salvation. They ultimately point us to Christ. Ryken says,

> The three major Old Testament feasts were rich in their teaching about salvation. Jesus Christ is the Savior God always planned to send; so already in the Old Testament he gave his people experiences that would help them (and us) understand the meaning of their salvation. Jesus is the source of our sanctification, the firstfruits of our resurrection, the Lord of the harvest, the water of life, and the sacrifice for our sin. This is the gospel according to Moses, as recorded in Exodus 23. (*Exodus,* 761)

The end of verse 19 is odd (cf. 34:26; Deut 14:21). It may be a word against the creative order: do not take that which is source of life and use it as a source of death. But I think it probably forbids this act because such a practice occurred in magical arts and fertility religions. God's people were to trust their Creator and Redeemer to make a flock strong. Even though surrounding countries practiced pagan rituals, Israel had to abstain. They were to glorify God alone for the giving of life and strength and health.

We Need a Savior!

In the exposition on the Ten Words, we noted that the law drives us to Jesus, and Jesus empowers us for obedience. If these laws demonstrate ways in which Israel was to live out the Decalogue, then we can make the same application again. We cannot keep God's law. But there is One who lived the life we could not live and died the death we should have died. Jesus obeyed for us and died in place of lawbreakers.

Because Jesus saves sinners and gives us His Spirit, we can now glorify Him in our ordinary, daily lives in each of these seven ways (in a new covenant sense). Concerning worship, because of Jesus, we can now worship Him in spirit and truth anywhere around the world (John 4:24).

Concerning the workplace, all of our work is to be done as an act of worship to the Lord (Col 3:22-25). Concerning behavior, God's people should demonstrate an ethic that is characterized by integrity and sacrificial love (Rom 12:9-21). Concerning restitution, we should seek to make all things right and be generous since Jesus has changed our selfish hearts. Concerning holiness, because God has given us His Spirit, let us bear the fruit of the Spirit and not gratify the desires of the flesh (Gal 5:16-26). Concerning social justice, we should desire to care for those who are weak and vulnerable because God cared for us when we were the orphan, the widow, the foreigner, and the poor. Concerning Sabbath and Festivals, we should remember God's grace by worshiping Him, obeying His Word, resting in His promises, and enjoying the Lord's Supper. This supper points us back to the Passover, to our Lord's death, and then forward to the new kingdom to come. There, in that kingdom, we will finally know what it is to live in a perfectly loving and just society. There, the lion will lie down with the lamb. There, peace and righteousness will dwell (2 Pet 3:13).

May God grant His fresh strength through the Spirit to love Him more passionately and love neighbor justly and compassionately.

Reflect and Discuss

1. What are some bad experiences you have had with roommates? What rules, if enacted and obeyed, might have prevented those problems?

2. Why should we not expect to enact all of these biblical ordinances in the country where we live? What value do the ordinances have with regard to civil laws?

3. How do we balance the principle of simplicity with the idea of giving our best to God? Compare honoring God by building a simple chapel or a magnificent cathedral.

4. How was Israelite servitude different from slavery, especially Western racial slavery? What aspects of these ordinances demonstrated grace and benevolence? How is the gospel even more gracious?

5. How should the fact that humans are created in the image of God influence civil legislation?

6. How would you respond to someone who said that Israel's laws and ordinances were based on earlier Near Eastern law codes? How were Israel's laws better than the others?

7. What would be a strictly literal enforcement of the *lex talionis*, the law of retaliation? Why would such an interpretation be impractical, unfair, and unenforceable? When is mercy appropriate?

8. Was the call to holiness specific to Israel, or does it have application to church bylaws and civil ordinances?

9. Who are the weak, disadvantaged, powerless, and vulnerable people today? How can we help them?

10. How are the three Festivals—Unleavened Bread, Harvest, and Booths—fulfilled in the work of Christ? How do all these laws point out our need for a Savior?

Conquest and Covenant

EXODUS 23:20–24:18

Main Idea: God rescues and redeems us, and we should follow and worship, trust and obey Him.

I. **The Conquest Promised (23:20-33)**
  A. Trust in God's victory (23:20,22b-23,27-31).
  B. Obey God's commands (23:21-22a,24-25a,31b,32-33).
  C. Receive God's blessing (23:25b-26,29-30).

II. **The Covenant Confirmed (24:1-8)**

III. **The Glory of God Beheld (24:9-18)**

If you are at all familiar with the military, you know that rankings exist. From privates to the commander in chief, some have leadership and authority over others. Privates follow sergeants who follow lieutenants who follow captains who follow majors who follow colonels who follow generals. Moreover, when a superior is highly respected because of his character and leadership, those under him actually delight in obeying the superior. A student of mine once told me about his grandfather who served in World War II. His grandfather was in a foxhole seeking shelter when all of a sudden General Patton jumped in! They exchanged words, and they continued to fight. This soldier gladly obeyed Patton because of his respect for him.

Soldiers know the voice of their leader. We likewise must pay attention to God's voice, the ultimate Commander in Chief! Be careful to listen to His voice and follow His instruction. Jesus said that His sheep know His voice and follow Him, but His sheep do not follow the voice of a stranger (John 10:4-5). Christ has led with holy character and unparalleled sacrifice, and we who follow Him should delight in His word.

In this passage, we see a number of important expressions related to the idea of obeying God's word (see 23:21-22; 24:3,7). We also find important truths related to trusting in God, following Him, receiving His blessing, the covenant, and living for God's glory. If you briefly scan this passage, you can see that God is the main character of the story. God gave the victory. God's voice was to be obeyed. God provided the blessing. God made and sealed the covenant. God was to be worshiped forever.

God rescues and redeems us, and we should follow and worship, trust and obey Him. With this in mind, let us see why and how we should do this. I will divide the passage into three main parts: (1) the conquest promised, (2) the covenant confirmed, and (3) the glory of God beheld.

The Conquest Promised
EXODUS 23:20-33

God began by explaining that He would send an angel. People today are fascinated with angels (and demons). We see them in books, TV shows, and movies, yet people have great misconceptions and misunderstandings about angels. We should be careful not to get our understanding of angels from our culture. We need to understand the role and character of angels from God's perspective through Scripture.

The angel in Exodus 23 was a warrior angel. Do not imagine a plump, cherubic angel with pretty wings and a harp, lounging on a cloud. This angel was quite different from that cartoonish picture. Think of the angel in Psalm 91:11: "[God] will give His angels orders concerning you, to protect you in all your ways." Instead of picturing a delicate, baby-like angel, imagine a majestic warrior angel (see also Josh 5:13-15, "the commander of the LORD's army").

Theologians provide at least five possible identities of this angel. (1) The angel could be *the glory cloud* that led the Israelites day and night. However, a cloud is an inanimate object, whereas the angel described here is a living, moving, and speaking being. (2) The angel could be *a metaphor* for the guidance and help of the Lord Himself. Yet the text clearly says God would send the angel who would do certain things. This does not seem like a metaphor. (3) The angel could be *a human being*, or *a messenger*. While some speculate this messenger was Moses, we know that he did not enter the promised land, making this option unlikely. Or, the messenger could have been Joshua. The text says God's name was "in him" (v. 21). This is possible since Joshua is the Hebrew name of Jesus. Yet the text also implies the angel has the authority to forgive sin, which is problematic if it refers to Joshua. (4) The angel could be *an actual angel*, perhaps Michael the archangel. We see him at work battling the Devil in Jude 9 and Revelation 12:7. While this is plausible, it is still problematic because the angel is able to forgive sin. (5) The angel could be *the pre-incarnate Christ*. The description that God's "name is in him" fits well here, along with his having the authority to forgive sins. However, why would God refer to him as an angel? Despite not having clarity of the angel's identity, we certainly think of Christ. Like the angel, Christ is our guardian and guide (Matt 8:20; John 14:6); like the angel, Jesus speaks to us with the authority and message of God (Luke 9:35); like the angel, Jesus bears the name of God, for He is the image of the invisible God (Heb 1:3).

Consider three applications from this text: trust in God's victory, obey God's commands, and receive God's blessing.

Trust in God's Victory (23:20,22b-23,27-31)

Notice first how often God is spoken of in these verses. See the first person singular pronoun, "I." God was going to win the victory. God would work on behalf of His people to bring about His purposes for their lives. God even sent hornets to protect His people (v. 28)! While this could be figurative, imagine thousands of hornets going after the Canaanites. It would be chaos! Think in your own life. Do you panic when there is a bee around you? I understand if you are allergic to them, but even if you are not, no one wants to be stung by a bee. In fact, I bet some of you go downright crazy. You get scared, panic, and run for cover. If so, that gives you a good idea of what was going to happen in Canaan.

For the Israelites, God was their holy bouncer, if you will. He went before them, and through His agents and power He would strike fear into their enemies. God, the all-powerful Creator and Sustainer, goes before you in the battle. How can you be concerned about losing? Why would you not trust Him and have faith in the victory? We see this later when Moses sent in the 12 spies, including Caleb and Joshua. While ten did not have faith that they could conquer the land, the other two had no doubts.

Now for us, we likewise must trust God to win the victory. As far as our eternal salvation, the victory is already won. Therefore, since God has won the ultimate battle, we can rest assured that He will be with us in our smaller battles. This does not allow us to be passive observers; it simply means that we do not fight alone. We should be on watch; and pray, study, and apply God's Word; and "be strengthened by the Lord and by His vast strength" (Eph 6:10).

Obey God's Commands (23:21-22a,24-25a,31b,32-33)

God also promised to provide the victory. And what were the Israelites to do? Sit back and watch? Be spectators and enjoy the blessing? What did God expect of His people? Obedience! But how? What were they to do and not do? Notice the instructions in 21-22a, 24-25a, 31b, and 32-33:

> *Be attentive to him and listen to his voice. Do not defy him, because he will not forgive your acts of rebellion, for My name is in him. But if you will carefully obey him and do everything I say, then I will be an enemy to your enemies and a foe to your foes. . . . You must not bow down to their gods or worship them. Do not imitate their practices. Instead, demolish them and smash their sacred pillars to pieces. Worship the Lord your God. . . . I will place the inhabitants of the land under your control, and you will drive them out ahead of you. You must not make a covenant with them or their gods. They must not remain in your land, or else they will make you sin against Me. If you worship their gods, it will be a snare for you.*

God made two essential demands on the Israelites. First, they were forbidden to worship the gods of the Canaanites (v. 24a). Second, God told them to destroy the idols and sacred stones of the Canaanites (v. 24b).

For us, we should never compromise in giving God all our worship. We too should do everything we can to distance ourselves from sin, destroying the idols of our hearts. The Lord demands and deserves our exclusive allegiance.

How are you doing at detecting and destroying idols in your life? What are the idols in your heart that compete with the Holy One for your affections, your heart, your time, your resources, your attention, your love? We must remember that idols are not always innately bad things. When we make good things a "god thing," then they must be destroyed. We often times deny recognizing idols in our own lives. However, you can know it is an idol *when you sin to get it or sin when it is taken away.* When those good desires become idols, we are worshiping and loving something more than God. God warns the Israelites and us against this. These things will trap us and draw us away from God. And God doesn't simply say to avoid those idols. He says destroy them! Will you obediently destroy your idols?

Receive God's Blessing (23:25b-26,29-30)

Next God promised to bless His people as His people served Him. How was the Lord going to do that for Israel? In 25b-26 and 29-30, He promised to provide plenty of food and water, good health, large families, long life, and most of all the promised land, the inheritance He had prepared for them.

Understand this word of caution: God gave these promises for a specific people at a specific time for a specific purpose. God promised to protect and provide for His chosen people from which the Messiah would come. This does not mean that if you obey the Ten Commandments and the rest of the law you will never get sick, never starve, have lots of children, and live a long life. It also does not mean that when Christians suffer it is necessarily due to their disobedience. We do know that Jesus suffered. He promised His followers they would not only suffer but they would even be hated (John 15:18-20). Suffering will not end until we get to Heaven. And when we do, we will no longer hunger, or suffer, or mourn. John said, "He will wipe away every tear from their eyes. Death will no longer exist; grief, crying, and pain will exist no longer, because the previous things have passed away" (Rev 21:4).

God gave the people of Israel a specific promise, at a specific time, for a specific purpose—and it was a good promise. But with the new covenant, for those who have faith in Christ Jesus, we have a better promise and we will receive a better promised land. Are you ready for that? Do you long for that? Do you savor the certainty that God keeps His promises and will lead you into His eternal promised land? I hope you do!

The Covenant Confirmed
EXODUS 24:1-8

When talking about covenants, remember that for any covenant to be established it has to be confirmed by both parties. This happens in chapter 24. Chapters 20–23 lay out the terms of the covenant, and chapter 24 tells us how it was confirmed. Exodus 24 is also the story of a worship service, the first of its kind. In this one chapter, we have the following:

- a call to worship,
- the reading of God's Word,
- a confession of faith and commitment to obedience,
- and the sharing of a holy meal.

All of this is under the oversight of an appointed servant of God and the elders, and in the presence of a holy and glorious God.

Nadab and Abihu were present (v. 1). They were Aaron's two eldest sons who would have been the next high priests in the line. However, they died later under God's judgment because of their unauthorized sacrifice (Lev 10:1-2; Num 3:4). In verse 2 Moses was alone. He was the chosen mediator between God and the Israelites. He represented the people before God. He went between a holy God and a sinful people. He was the only one permitted to draw near. In this, God taught His people to honor and respect His holiness.

We can only draw close to God and be in His presence if we come on His terms, in the way He has appointed—through an appointed mediator. Back then it was through Moses and the priests. Now it is only through Jesus Christ, the "one mediator between God and humanity" (1 Tim 2:5).

After God had set the terms for the covenant, the people affirmed the covenant (vv. 3,7). They promised to do all the words He had said. Moses told all the people the "commands" and the "ordinances" that God had given. The "commands" likely refer to the Ten Commandments themselves (20:2-17). The "ordinances" were the laws that provided specific instruction, which followed the commandments (chs. 21–23). This, then, is the "covenant scroll" (24:7). After hearing the "commands" and "ordinances," the people unanimously agreed to keep them—to be obedient. They even did this a second time, after Moses had written them down (v. 4) and read them aloud (v. 7). Thus they doubly confirmed the covenant with their current verbal promise in addition to the promise they had made in 19:8.

Why did he read it twice, and why did they promise to obey twice? The first time was so they could understand and accept it. They declared their intent. The second time was so they could promise to obey and confirm it. They took their vows. This is not foreign to us. We do the same thing in our wedding ceremonies. First, you declare your intent ("I will" or "I do"); second, you say your vows. In the case of the Israelites, their obedience did not last long. Moses stepped away for a few days and they immediately disobeyed.

Notice some other important components to this covenant process. Moses wrote down all the words of the Lord. In ancient times, covenants were always written down. Unless they were written, they were not finalized. As we saw in our introduction to the book, this verse also confirms

Mosaic authorship of the Pentateuch. Another component was the building of an altar. After writing down the words, Moses came to build an altar, for the covenant was to be sealed with blood. The altar was used for burnt offerings and sacrificial peace offerings. With a burnt offering, the whole animal was consumed by fire. With a peace offering, the animal was not consumed by fire. Instead, meat was grilled and eaten after the blood had been drained. This is where the blood comes from in verses 6 and 8. The blood sprinkled on the altar was God's blood, signifying that He was one party to the covenant. The portion of blood that Moses put in bowls was for sprinkling on the people, as a sign that they were recipients of the benefit the shed blood provided.

We are told in Hebrews, "without the shedding of blood there is no forgiveness" (Heb 9:22). Since the fall, blood has been the basis of man's relationship with God—in terms of sin and forgiveness. Without the blood, there can be no access to God because there is no forgiveness of sin (cf. Eph 1:7; Rev 1:5).

This idea of "the blood of the covenant" is expanded in the New Testament. Hebrews 9 provides a glorious description of this idea. We see confirmation that Jesus ushered in a new covenant through the shedding of His blood. This new covenant is also seen specifically in regard to the Lord's Supper (Matt 26:28; Mark 14:24; Luke 22:20; 1 Cor 11:25; Heb 9:20; 10:29; 12:24; 13:20).

When you consider the confirmation of God's covenant, are you determined to obey the word of God? When Moses told the people the words and laws of the Lord, they responded twice in unity, "We will do and obey everything that the LORD has commanded." Are you resolved to obey God no matter the circumstances, by His grace, for His glory?

The truth is we all, like Israel, fail to obey. But when this happens, we must look to the One who did obey perfectly, the One who provides us with His righteousness. Jesus Christ—the radiance of God's glory, Who holds the universe by His power—shed His own blood for you.

Perhaps you have heard the phrase in corporate worship, "The blood of Christ, shed for you." What a powerful statement and reminder of the work of the Lord Jesus. Do you dwell on this truth? Do you cherish the fact that Christ poured out His blood for you? He ushered in a new covenant, sealed with His own blood. This gives us reason to celebrate with joy inexpressible, for our King has paid our ransom. This moves us to humble obedience for the glory of our Lord and Savior Jesus Christ. Some of you reading this undoubtedly do not know this

Jesus and His provision of grace. How I pray that you will rest in the work of Jesus today!

The Glory of God Beheld
EXODUS 24:9-18

Seventy-four people ascended Mount Sinai to represent all Israel in the covenant meal. Can you imagine this scene? Do you get nervous when you eat a meal with someone important? Imagine dining with God on His mountain! Verses 10-11 tell us that they saw God. What does this mean? What did they actually see? They probably saw some sort of general shape that He allowed them to see vaguely. Ezekiel and Amos had similar visions (Ezek 1:26-28; Amos 7:7). Quite possibly they saw God from below since the description we have is of His feet and the pavement. It is also possible this was a vision of the pre-incarnate Christ. No matter what conclusion you arrive at, we know that "no one can see [God] and live" (Exod 33:20).

God did not raise His hand against these leaders; they did not die after seeing Him (v. 11). There are two likely reasons. First, they did not see God fully, but only a vague or partial vision of Him. Second, God deliberately chose not to "send His hand" (divine judgment through a display of supernatural power) against them. It was not God's intention to punish them. This meeting and meal was part of His plan. They had an invitation! But why did God show Himself, albeit only vaguely and partially? It was so that Israel would understand He was a willing party to the covenant. They would remember that they agreed to the keep His covenant in His actual, unmistakable presence.

God gave them a glimpse of His majesty. They ate and drank in His presence. It just keeps getting better! If getting a glimpse of God was not enough, they were given a further privilege—to share a meal with Him. Sharing a meal was a symbolic act of friendship. It showed that they had fellowship (communion) with God.

We should remember the importance of sharing a meal. Whether it is with your small group, your church, a few friends, your family, your neighbors, or your coworkers, the table is a big deal. You do the work of and follow the example of God. Later, Jesus earned the reputation of being a "glutton and a drunkard" (Luke 7:34; cf. 14:12-14; 15:1-2) because of His pattern of using the table as a place to express fellowship with others and to live out the mission of reaching sinners. Use your meals for the good of others and the glory of God! And remember, there is another meal coming. Look forward to the "marriage feast of the Lamb" (Rev 19:9). Believers will dine with the risen Jesus.

In the meantime, God has given us a special meal to remind us we belong to Him by covenant. Some call this meal the Lord's Supper. At the congregation where I serve as a pastor, we enjoy it every week. Every week we remember the sacrifice of Jesus and we look forward to the wedding supper of the Lamb.

In verse 12 God spoke to Moses individually: "The LORD said to Moses, 'Come up to Me on the mountain and stay there so that I may give you the stone tablets with the law and commandments I have written for their instruction.'" Moses received these tablets in writing, a sign of an authenticated covenant.

Verses 15-18 tell us more of Moses' experience with God in His glory cloud. The cloud reminds us of chapters 13–14. There we read of the pillar of cloud that appeared during the day and the pillar of fire that appeared at night to guide the Israelites. The cloud had already served as a protection and guide for the Israelites in their flight from the Egyptians. This current manifestation only confirmed that the cloud represented God's glorious presence: awesome, multifaceted, partly mysterious, but also protective and encompassing.

Now we must ask, "What about us?" Remember, this was a big worship service, and like Moses and the Israelites, we are invited to participate. This is the story of their salvation and in a sense ours, too. Like the Israelites, God calls us to worship Him and speaks to us by His Word. Like the Israelites, we are separated from God because of our sin and therefore have to keep our distance. But then God, in His grace, provided a sacrifice of atonement through the blood of His covenant. For the Israelites it was the blood of an animal; for us it is the blood of Jesus. Once our sins have been forgiven, we can enjoy fellowship with God. We can sit down and enjoy His banquet. Now we do it through the Lord's Supper; later in Heaven we will enjoy the meal at His table.

Reflect and Discuss

1. What qualities in a military officer cause people to consider insubordination? What qualities cause unswerving obedience and devotion? Which of these qualities can be seen in God?

2. What are the popular ways of picturing angels in current culture? What do biblical angels do? What do their activities imply about their appearance? How are they described?

3. God promised to bring victory in Israel's battles. What specific battles in your life are certain to be won because God fights for you?

4. What happens to an army when the soldiers refuse to obey the commands they are given? What happens when some soldiers take orders from the enemy? How does this apply to the church?

5. God promised the children of Israel health, prosperity, and the promised land. What does that mean for Christians? How would you respond to someone who teaches otherwise?

6. God could have demanded obedience unilaterally, but He initiated a covenant between Himself and His people. How is this an indication of grace? How do fear and gratitude play parts in our obedience to God in the new covenant?

7. How would you respond to a non-Christian who said, "If God showed up right now, I'd give Him a piece of my mind! I'd get in His face and tell Him what for!" What should be our attitude in worship and prayer?

8. Have you ever had the privilege of sharing a meal with an important or famous person? How does that compare with God's invitation to have a close relationship with Him through Christ? How can we learn to appreciate the grace and mercy and privilege that is ours?

9. How can meals and other forms of hospitality be used as an opportunity to invite others to know Christ?

10. How does the Lord's Supper compare with this covenant confirmation feast? Does celebrating the Lord's Supper imply that we promise to affirm and obey our covenant with God through Christ?

He Tabernacled Among Us

EXODUS 25–27 & 35–40

Main Idea: God dwelt with the people of Israel by way of the tabernacle and its furniture, foreshadowing the presence of God in Christ with His church.

I. **Contributions for the Sanctuary (25:1-9)**
II. **The Tabernacle (25:10–27:21)**
    A. The ark of the covenant: God's presence is majestic and merciful (25:10-22).
    B. The table for the bread: God's presence through provision (25:23-30)
    C. The golden lamp stand: God's presence through light (25:31-40)
    D. The tabernacle structure: God's presence among His people (26:1-37)
    E. The bronze altar: entrance into God's presence through a sacrifice (27:1-8)
    F. The court of the tabernacle: God's presence guarded (27:9-19)
    G. The oil for the lamp: God's presence with us (27:20-21)
III. **He Dwelt Among Us.**

Whenever I go out of town, my kids are downhearted. They like having me present with them. Whenever I tell them that I have to go out of town, their reaction is not positive. I felt the same way when I was a child. I loved the presence of my father. My dad's presence was calming, but his presence also brought a sense of fear.

As God begins to introduce the instructions for the tabernacle, we observe the awesome presence of God described. God graciously chose to dwell with His people. He was not an absent father. He was deeply involved and invested in the lives of His people. His presence brought both reassurance and holy fear. His presence set apart Israel from all other nations. The almighty God dwelt among them.

In chapters 25–31 God provided the *instructions* for building the tabernacle. In chapters 35–40 we see the *execution* of the project. One could read these two sections alongside of each other since so much overlap exists. Later I will simply touch on the execution of the tabernacle construction because we will highlight the details in this exposition (25–27) and the next (28–31).

To see the comparison between chapters 25–31 and 35–40 (with a few references to Leviticus and Deuteronomy), consider Stuart's helpful chart:

Verse(s)	Command	Fulfillment
25:1-7	call for offerings of various materials	35:4-9; 35:21-29
25:10-22	the ark	37:1-9
25:23-30	the table	37:10-16
25:31-39	the lamp stand	37:17-24
26:1-37	the tabernacle proper	36:8-38
27:1-8	bronze altar for burnt offerings	38:1-7
27:20-21	oil for the lamp stand	command renewed in Lev 24:1-3
28:1-5	priests' dress summary	command renewed in 35:19; fulfilled in 39:1,41; cf. 40:13-14; Lev 8:7-8
28:6-14	ephod	39:2-7
28:15-30	breastpiece	39:8-21; Lev 8:8
28:31-43	remaining priests' garments	39:22-31
29:1-37	consecrating priests	Lev 8:1-36
29:38-43	daily offerings	command renewed in Num 28:1-8
29:44	consecration of tabernacle and altar	command renewed in 40:9 command renewed in 40:10; fulfilled in Lev 8:11
29:44	consecration of priests	command renewed in 40:13
30:1-5	incense altar	37:25-28

30:6	incense altar placement	command renewed in 40:6; fulfilled in 40:26
30:7-9	rules for incense burning	40:27
30:10	atonement for incense altar	command renewed in Lev 4:7
30:17-21	bronze washing basin	38:8; 40:30
30:22-33	anointing oil for objects and priests	35:28; 37:29; 40:9; Lev 8:10-12,30
30:34-38	incense	35:28; 37:29; 39:38; 40:27
31:1-11	Bezalel and Oholiab: work overview	35:30-35; 36:1-7
31:12-17	Sabbath	command renewed in 35:1-3; Lev 23:3; cf. Num 15:32-36; Deut 5:12-15

One can see the large amount of repetition (or complement) in these chapters. Though arranged in a different order, and sometimes stated more concisely in one place or the other, the same basic material gets covered. The reason for the different order seems to be based on the fact that chapters 35–40 explain the order in which the tabernacle was constructed. The order was dictated by "common sense and necessity" (Stuart, *Exodus,* 745). In chapters 25–31, the objects seem to be arranged by order of importance and holiness, moving from the most sacred (the ark) to the least sacred (the courtyard perimeter; ibid.).

Let us take a look at the tabernacle and consider the awesome presence of God. Then let us mediate on how the tabernacle points us to Jesus.

Contributions for the Sanctuary
EXODUS 25:1-9

The instructions for the tabernacle began with a heart-check. God is first and foremost concerned with the heart. He began by requesting a contribution from the people. He asked the people to contribute their resources to make what would be His dwelling place among them. He did not demand compulsory giving. He wanted those who were "willing to give" to contribute (v. 2). God does not force your worship and giving, but He does call for it. Such an offering called for sacrifice. The people denied themselves and followed the path God set for them.

God requested specific contributions. The materials for the tabernacle were unique and valuable. They included gold, silver, bronze, colored yarn, and more. God told them exactly what to collect. They knew what was expected and required. The level of detail demonstrates that God is not approached spontaneously or casually. He is holy. He is not your "homeboy," "the big man upstairs," or a "genie" that you approach on your own terms to get wishes. He is the Almighty, the Creator and Redeemer.

The resources given to make the tabernacle were not their own resources. They were formerly the Egyptians' materials. Remember, before the Israelites left Egypt, God promised they would not leave empty-handed (3:21-22). God kept His promise and sent the Israelites out of Egypt with great wealth (12:36). God provided these goods. Now the people were to return to Him a portion of what had been given to them.

The same holds true of us today. We give of our resources, but they are resources that God has entrusted to us. Sometimes our stinginess with our money, time, and talent demonstrates that we do not believe this. We should see ourselves as entrusted with blessings from our great God. Then we would freely give as joyful worshipers of our Redeemer.

In verses 8-9 we find the purpose of the tabernacle. This would be a sanctuary, meaning "holy place," for God to dwell in their midst. Here is the purpose of this structure: that God would dwell among them. What made the place holy? Was it how it was made? No. The place became holy once God's presence engulfed it. God made the place holy, not men. And once He made it holy, it was only to be used as God intended for it to be used.

Young children love games. They especially love to make rules for their own games. If you want to play their game, you must keep their rules (even if they change them in the middle of the game!). God made His standards and expectations clear. They do not change. The making of this tent had to be specific. It was going to house the King of glory. Therefore, it had to be built on His terms, not the people's terms. This was vital because it would show their obedience to their king. It would also help them understand how a holy God might dwell in midst of a sinful people. In this passage, we observe the main point of the exodus being strengthened: Yahweh was showing that He is the Lord and that He would be their God.

A clear application emerges for us. We can approach God because He has initiated a relationship with us by His grace. We come because He is merciful. We are only able to approach Him by grace through faith in Christ by the power of the Holy Spirit. He has also revealed Himself to us in the Scriptures. We do not worship the god of our imagination but the God of biblical revelation. We must see Him for who He is in the Word and pattern our personal worship of Him, as well as our corporate worship of Him, based on Scripture. Biblical worship done in spirit and truth will have a sense of gravity (because God is holy) as well as a sense of gladness (because God welcomes us through Christ).

The Tabernacle
EXODUS 25:10–27:21

God was dwelling in the midst of His people in vivid, powerful ways. While the tabernacle was not as large or grand as some of the other nations' buildings and landmarks, God designed the tabernacle perfectly. It was flawless (Ryken, *Exodus,* 813–14). In it, God manifested His presence, and this was seen in the ark of the covenant, the table for the bread of the Presence, the golden lamp stand, the structure of the tabernacle, the bronze altar, the court of the tabernacle, and the oil for the lamp. Let us consider God's presence in the tabernacle.

The Ark of the Covenant: God's Presence Is Majestic and Merciful (25:10-22)

The first item mentioned is the most important: the ark of the covenant or testimony. Here God would meet with and speak to Moses. It was the only furniture in the most holy place, which was the innermost part of the tabernacle. The presence of God would dwell particularly powerfully in this one spot when God descended. This majestic holiness required two transport poles, to prevent any man from directly touching the ark, for if they were to touch it, they would die (Num 4:15; 2 Sam 6:6-7).

The mercy seat or atonement cover served as a lid on the ark. Here the Lord met with His people. Ultimately, His mercy would be revealed here on the Day of Atonement when the high priest made reparation for the people by sprinkling blood on the mercy seat. There was a way for God to be specifically present with His people, even to commune with them like He did in the garden. This could only take place now one day a year, and through blood. Through the atonement cover, God revealed that sinners cannot come to God without a mediator. At the mercy seat, God and sinners met. Scripture later revealed that Christ's work and provision of salvation was described like what happened at the mercy seat (Ryken, *Exodus*, 821; see Heb 2:17; Rom 3:25; 1 John 4:10).

On top of the mercy seat, cherubim of gold faced each other with their faces bowed toward it. These tremendous angels bowing down remind us of the great reverence we must have for our majestic God. Do not have a misconception about angels. They are the warriors who are mentioned in Genesis 3 to protect Eden with flaming swords. They are mighty, but in God's presence they must bow. Angels also serve as a sign of the presence and work of God. If they are near, God is working.

There were also a few items that would be placed inside the ark. The author of Hebrews tells us that it contained the Ten Commandments, a pot with manna, and Aaron's rod that budded (Heb 9:4). These served as reminders of where the Lord had brought them. He was faithful and worthy of worship.

One can read an amazing story of the ark in 1 Samuel 4–7. The Israelites went to war with the Philistines, but because of their idolatry, they were defeated. The loss was symbolic of the curse for covenant disobedience. The Israelites proposed to use the ark as a magic trick, taking it to the front lines to win, but instead it fell into the hands of the Philistines. When the high priest heard of this he fell over dead. The Philistines then placed the ark in the temple of Dagon, as if Yahweh were bowing before the Philistine god. The next day, as the people of Ashdod entered, they found that Dagon had fallen over as if to bow before Yahweh. They stood him up, but when they entered the temple the following morning, Dagon had fallen again, and his head and hands were crushed as well.

Israel deserved the punishment for their disobedience. They deserved exile among the enemies, and instead the ark took the punishment. We will see later the very presence of God taking on the punishment for the people and gaining victory by substituting Himself for the people and bearing their curse.

The Table for the Bread: God's Presence through Provision (25:23-30)

God began to describe what would be placed outside the most holy place. A table was to be made of acacia wood, covered in gold like the ark. This table was set up in the holy place. The table, however, was not the most important; what the table held was much more significant. It was to hold 12 loaves of bread, symbolizing God's people Israel. There was one loaf for each of the 12 tribes. The bread served as a reminder that every tribe played a role in God's family. Each tribe had a seat at the table (Ryken, *Exodus*, 831).

The table also reminded them of God's provision. This was the Lord's table and His bread. He provided it for them. The priests were later told to eat it, reminding them that God provided their daily bread. God was their sustainer. God's fellowship was displayed through provision.

It is by God's grace that we too are fed. He sustains us. In John 6, Jesus told us that God is the One who gives bread from heaven, and the true bread is Himself. Jesus is the bread of life. Those who come to Him will never hunger or thirst again. Do you recognize that today? Will you eat of this bread and drink of this cup? God has provided for all of our daily needs and has provided us ultimately with the bread of life, Jesus Christ.

The Golden Lamp Stand: God's Presence through Light (25:31-40)

The golden lamp stand was positioned in the holy place directly across from the table. It was handcrafted and made from around 75 pounds—one talent—of pure gold (v. 39). This was no lamp from your local department store! This was an incredibly valuable lamb. From the base of the lamp came many branches with the design of almond blossoms at the top. Today, this would be most similar to a menorah. God also instructed Moses to make certain instruments that were used to care for the lamps, like snuffers and firepans (v. 38).

The lamp was to shine on what was in front of it (v. 37). Lamps were often placed on a stand to provide more light in the darkness. This was later seen in Numbers 8:1-4: Aaron was to set up the lamps to provide light to what was before them.

Was there something symbolic about this? Yes! As we see throughout Scripture, God is light. His light symbolizes His presence and His holiness. We see in Revelation that the removal of a lamp stand means God's presence has departed (Rev 2:5). In addition to the sacrifices, God's people were also to bring olive oil for the lamp in the tabernacle (see 27:20-21). The priests were to keep this lamp burning continually, signifying the continual presence of God. God is, always has been, and forever will be the light of the world.

This light later came to live among us as the light of men in Jesus (John 1:4). But we also know that the light of men was also life. Light is often related to life. David tells us in Psalm 36:9, "For with You is life's fountain. In Your light we will see light." God is both light and life. He created life and light, He sustains life and light, and He offers hope of life and light in Him.

Israel was called to reflect His light to the nations. We likewise are to show the glory of God in word and deed. We must fight to keep the light shining brightly. God has blessed us in allowing us to reflect the light of His glory. Jesus tells us,

> *You are the light of the world. A city situated on a hill cannot be hidden. No one lights a lamp and puts it under a basket, but rather on a lampstand, and it gives light for all who are in the house. In the same way, let your light shine before men, so that they may see your good works and give glory to your Father in heaven.* (Matt 5:14-16)

God's light is intended to shine through us. When we allow it, people will give glory to God. The light from the lamp stand was to point us to God's glory; now the light of His people should point others to God's glory.

The Tabernacle Structure: God's Presence among His People (26:1-37)

In this section, God described how to build the curtains for the tabernacle. Cherubim were woven into the curtain to protect the entrance to God's presence, just like Eden. This reminds us of paradise lost. Though God would dwell among them, access to Him was limited. God's presence was guarded.

The curtains were constructed, not to keep people out of the presence of God, but to protect the people from God's presence. There were three divisions: the courtyard, the holy place, and the most holy place. The final separation was a veil into the most holy place where God would meet with them once a year. He was teaching the people that forever they can only approach Him through blood sacrifice at that for now His holiness must be veiled.

Here we must see the parallel between the tabernacle and Eden. The whole point of God dwelling with them was the idea that they could return to Eden where they could commune with God as it was intended in the beginning. We may note six parallels between Eden and the tabernacle (see Hamilton, *God's Indwelling Presence*). The tabernacle creation parallels God's creation where God would commune and fellowship with mankind.

First, there were seven speaking acts of creation in both. In the creating acts of the tabernacle, they were signaled with the phrase, "The LORD spoke/said to Moses," which parallels the seven speaking acts in Genesis, "Then God said . . ."

Second, both were the place where God would dwell in the midst of His people and Moses. God is present everywhere but chooses to manifest His presence strongly in certain places. Some even draw a parallel of the dark, cool room of the high priest with the garden account of meeting with God in the cool of the day.

Third, both indicated the quality of the creation after a time of observing what was made. Moses would say the tabernacle was a blessed place, and God said of creation it was "very good." This is another reason the tabernacle had to have such specific commands on how to create it.

Fourth, both narratives end with a focus on the Sabbath. On the seventh day, God instituted the Sabbath. At the end of this narrative in chapter 31, God once again drew Moses' attention to the Sabbath rest.

Fifth, a "fall" follows both narratives, where people try to substitute creation for God. Man, with his idolatrous heart, is prone to substitute something or someone else for God.

Sixth, both narratives have cherubim guarding the presence to God at the east entrance. But now in Exodus, the cherubim are welcoming people back into Eden through blood at the atonement seat. Some even suggest that the lamp stand was a type of tree of life.

These parallels show that the tabernacle was a step toward paradise regained. The breach that had caused separation was being overturned slowly. This was a step toward realizing the final dwelling place of God and man. Hebrews sees the tabernacle as not only looking forward but also as looking up. It was a copy of the throne room of God. We are now seeing how God will make a way for us into that throne room.

All of this is showing us the gospel. God wants a relationship with His people, but we are all sinners. None of us can come into the presence of God on our own. We cannot make it back to Eden on our own. But God provided a way to have access back to Him by blood, through a sacrifice offered by a high priest.

The Bronze Altar: Entrance into God's Presence through a Sacrifice (27:1-8)

The next instructions include the bronze altar construction. It stood in the outer courtyard so that people approached it as soon as they entered. It stood 7 ½ feet long, 7 ½ feet wide, and 4 ½ feet high. Clearly, this was a very large altar. God told His people to make it out of acacia wood and to cover it with bronze. God also said to make the utensils of bronze. Only gold was used *inside* the tabernacle.

However, the altar was not permanently fixed, for it had poles like the ark and the table so that it could be moved. God had promised to live among His people. When they traveled, God went with them. God's people were desperate for His presence to go with them (33:14-15). God traveling with His people—what a blessing! Even greater is this truth today in the New Covenant: "I will never leave you or forsake you" (Heb 13:5)!

God's people constructed the altar to make sacrifices. Again, people come before God and His presence only by way of sacrifice. Communion with God requires sacrifice. The altar was the first thing a worshiper would see when entering. The massive size of the altar confronted them with the massive gap between them and God. There had to be a sacrifice. Remember: without the shedding of blood, there is no forgiveness of sins (Heb 9:22). The people were reminded of that as they entered the courtyard. And we know that Christ is the ultimate sacrifice. He is the only One to bridge the gap between man and God. The gospel reminds us of these truths, and the Lord's Supper gives us a holy ordinance to remember them. We approach God only because of blood. Christ's blood is that of the new covenant. His body was torn for us; His blood was poured out for us. It is only through Him that we have access to God.

The Court of the Tabernacle: God's Presence Guarded (27:9-19)

Though God would dwell in the middle of the Israelite encampment, it was clear that He was still separate from them. Walls and curtains would guard and separate His presence from them. He is holy, but He is also merciful and gracious in making a way back to Him.

Around this tent was a fence. Inside the fence was the bronze altar. The fence guarded about ten thousand square feet (Ryken, *Exodus*, 858). There was one entrance into this courtyard. People entered only from the east, as in the garden of Eden (Gen 3:24).

The materials for the court were like those used on the tent. For the person entering the courtyard this served as a reminder of what was before them. It prepared them for the glory ahead.

Ryken notes that the setup is similar to the Israelites' situation at the mountain. On the mountain, Moses went up and experienced God's presence; at the tabernacle, only the high priest might enter the most holy place. On the mountain, the elders were able to come up half way; at the tabernacle, the priests were able to go into the holy place. On the mountain, the people waited at the bottom of the mountain; at the tabernacle, the people were only able to enter as far as the courtyard. Inside the tent, Israel was separated from the world (Ryken, *Exodus,* 860).

From all this, we see that there are limitations on interacting with God. For the people, they needed the high priest. For us, we have the great high priest who works on our behalf and enables us to approach the throne of grace with confidence (Heb 4:16).

The Oil for the Lamp: God's Presence with Us (27:20-21)

The priests were responsible for collecting oil from the people for the lamps. There was a high standard for the oil. It was to be "pure oil from crushed olives." The oil was for the lamp stand, which provided light in the holy place of the tabernacle. It continuously burned. Even in the night, the light reminded the people that God's presence was among them. Even when darkness covered the land, God's light still shone brightly. The priests tended to the lamps in shifts to ensure God's light continued to burn. This light also reminded people to worship day or night (cf. Ps 134:1-2). God's light was shining on them. They were His people. His presence was with them. This reminds us of the Holy Spirit, who is God's light in us. What joy to know that God's presence lives in us as believers always! May His light shine from us!

He Dwelt Among Us

Ultimately, the tabernacle points us to someone, to the true presence of God dwelling with us: Christ. How can a holy God dwell among sinful people? How can sinful man enter the holy place? The tabernacle has shown us the furniture and the process for bringing sinners and the Holy One together. All of this points us to *Christ,* the greater and truer tabernacle. John said that Jesus "took up residence" or "tabernacled" among us (John 1:14).

Regarding the better tabernacle, John Owen said, "Everything Moses did in erecting the tabernacle and instituting all its services was intended to testify to the person and glory of Christ which would later be revealed (Heb 3:5)" (*Glory*, 69). Indeed, the tabernacle provides an amazing representation of Jesus Christ that we need to behold. We could spend days meditating on the connections. I will simply mention a few of them and close with some more application.

Jesus is "the true light" (John 1:9) and the true lamp stand—"the light of the world" (John 8:12). We "were once darkness, but now [we] are light in the Lord," therefore, through Christ, we must "walk as children of light" (Eph 5:8).

God's presence is also portable in the new covenant. God's Spirit comes and lives within His people (Rom 8:9).

Christ is the mediator who shed His own blood to redeem sinful man (Eph 2:13). While He was forsaken, we, by grace through faith, can enter God's presence.

Jesus was the better ark of God. He, like the ark in the story in 1 Samuel 4–7, was taken captive by a foreign army and took the punishment the people deserved. Then what seemed like defeat ended with His triumphant victory, as He crushed the serpent's head by the third day.

Jesus also represents the ultimate provision of God. He called Himself the "bread of life," and whoever comes to Him will never perish (John 6:35,51,58). He is the bread we desperately need.

Jesus is the better altar (Heb 13:10). His ultimate sacrifice is the source of our salvation and the source of grace by which our hearts are strengthened (cf. Heb 13:9).

We now enter through the torn veil. The torn body of our Christ provides direct access to God (Eph 2:13-17). He can provide access past the cherubim. Instead of defending against access, they are now welcoming back in because blood has been applied.

Jesus is bringing us back to Eden as the high priest who enters the holy place for us and tears the veil for our entrance. And what amazing grace that we can now come boldly (Heb 4:14-16)! The Israelites came trembling. Yet in John 20:17 we read these amazing words: "To My Father and your Father!" He is our Father!

For us, God is building a new dwelling place. God's Spirit dwells in us individually as believers and corporately as the church, a building made of living stones where Christ is the cornerstone (Eph 2:19-22; 1 Pet 2:4-8).

May the glory of Christ represented in the tabernacle lead you to worship. As you behold Christ's glory, you will find your greatest joy and will overflow with praise. John Owen said,

> By beholding the glory of Christ we shall experience what it means to be everlastingly blessed. "We shall always be with the Lord" (1 Thess 4:17). We shall "be with Christ," which is best of all (Phil 1:23). For there we shall "behold his glory" (John 17:24). And by seeing him as he is, "we shall be made like him" (1 John 3:2). This is our everlasting blessedness. (*Glory*, 9)

Everlasting blessedness is found in Christ.

What is more, as you behold His glory, God, by the Spirit, transforms us into Christ's image (2 Cor 3:18). This is a fundamental principle for Christian growth. As you behold Christ, you become like Christ. Therefore, gaze on His glory by faith.

In addition, let the glory of Christ represented in the tabernacle drive you into unhurried and unhindered communion with the Father. What an amazing privilege to know that God welcomes us into His presence because of the priestly work of Christ. The author of Hebrews exhorted his hearers,

> *Therefore, brothers, since we have boldness to enter the sanctuary through the blood of Jesus, by a new and living way He has opened for us through the curtain (that is, His flesh), and since we have a great high priest over the house of God, let us draw near with a true heart in full assurance of faith, our hearts sprinkled clean from an evil conscience and our bodies washed in pure water.* (Heb 10:19-22)

What a privilege we have as believers! How can other things fill our days and capture our attention when this privilege is ours? Let us draw near to God and pour out our hearts to Him in worship and supplication.

Finally, let the glory of Christ represented in the tabernacle fix your eyes on the glorious future hope that is ours as believers. Revelation 21 points forward to a glorious day, when the dwelling place of God is with man. In this place, God's dwelling place will not just be overlaid with gold but will be made of pure solid gold. We will not need a lamp stand or the sun, for God will be the city's light.

Do you want to be a part of His people? Do you want to dwell in God's presence? Do you want to return to Eden? There is one way: Christ! We approach God only on His terms, and His terms are: "Christ."

For the rest of our eternal lives, we can and will only enter into His presence through blood—blood poured out by the Savior. Just as the tabernacle was a dwelling place where God abides, Jesus told us that to be in the presence of God we must abide in Him (John 15:1-11).

Reflect and Discuss

1. What aspects of love should be present in the ideal relationship of a child with his or her father? What kind of fear or respect? How do the love and fear of human child-parent relationships compare with that of human-God relationships?
2. How is knowing what to give (head doctrine) different from willingness to give (heart commitment)? In what way does a person's willingness to give reflect a genuine relationship with God?
3. How have some people tried to change the rules concerning how God is to be worshiped? What unbiblical rules have some people added?
4. How have angels been portrayed in art and popular culture? How does that compare with the biblical description of angels and their duties?
5. How does the ark represent God's glory? How does it represent His mercy?
6. How does the presence of God in His tabernacle imply His mercy? How does this translate to the church?
7. In what way is a Christian like a lamp that produces light? In what way do Christians merely reflect God's light?
8. What are some of the ways the tabernacle and its various furnishings were fulfilled in Christ and His church? How might the consciousness of this fulfillment enhance your worship experience?
9. What is the significance of the curtains separating the courtyard from the holy place and most holy place? What did it mean when the curtain was torn in two (Matt 27:51)?
10. How would you explain the broad theme of Eden, the tabernacle, Christ, and paradise to an adult Sunday School class?

Holy Work and Holy Rest

EXODUS 28–31 & 39

Main Idea: Tabernacle construction foreshadowed the Holy Spirit, who works in us, as well as the Sabbath rest, and tabernacle worship foreshadowed Christ, our great high priest.

I. **We Have a High Priest Who Worked and Works on Behalf of Us (28–29).**
    A. The clothes for the priests (28:1-43)
    B. The consecration of the priests (29:1-46)
    C. Our great high priest
II. **We Have the Spirit of God Working through Us (31:1-11).**
III. **We Have a Sabbath Rest Provided for Us (31:12-17).**

Previously, we examined the instructions for building the tabernacle. As we continue our study of the tabernacle, we are introduced to those who worked *in* the tabernacle: *the priests*; and those who worked *on* the tabernacle and on the priests' garments: *the craftsmen*. As this section on the tabernacle closes, the Sabbath gets emphasized again. As a reminder, one should also consider chapters 35–40 for additional information about the tabernacle and the priesthood.

The themes of *work* and *rest* teach us about the gospel. Here we learn about our great high priest *who works on our behalf*, the Holy Spirit *who works in us* to do God's work, and a *holy rest* that we need. Here we find "gospel gold" in what is probably an unfamiliar part of the Bible for many Christians.

For those of you who may not believe this gospel or are not familiar with the Bible, please know that the Old Testament is the backstory of the New Testament. You might compare it to the first act of a drama. We need to know this portion of the Bible because the New Testament extends the drama. If you do not understand some of the backstory, you will be like the person who arrives late to the movie and keeps asking everyone, "Who is this guy? What does that mean? Where did that come from?" Many important parts of the faith begin here in the Old Testament and introduce categories that get filled up later with more meaning in the New Testament. In this section, these categories involve *the priesthood, the Spirit,* and *the Sabbath.*

We Have a High Priest Who Worked and Works on Behalf of Us

EXODUS 28–29

Chapter 28 focuses on the priests who serve in the tabernacle. We see how Aaron and his sons would serve as priests and how God told them to make the priestly garments. In chapter 29 we observe the consecration of Aaron and his sons—like an ordination—and how they were to make daily offerings. God called Aaron to this office. Aaron did not "run for office" or appoint himself (cf. 1 Sam 2:28; 1 Kgs 13:33).

You can see a few obvious lessons in these chapters. First, *worship is important!* A major theme in Exodus 25–40 is worship. The focus is on the tabernacle. Here we learn about true worship versus unacceptable worship. The tabernacle was also a portable sanctuary. God went with His people. Chapters 28–29 reinforce this principle of worship. The people could only worship God on His terms. Aaron and his sons were to follow God's directions exactly in their priestly service (the mention of Nadab and Abihu in v. 1 is important, since they failed to do this later).

A second observation is that these *priests must be set apart for service.* The priests were unique. They worshiped God "in the splendor of His holiness." In 28:2-4 we see the purpose of the priestly garments: "make holy garments . . . for glory and beauty . . . for consecrating him . . . so that they may serve Me as priests." In addition, the color and material of the priest's clothing corresponded to the color and material of the tabernacle. You could say the priest embodied the tabernacle. His clothing would have been absolutely stunning. Like the tabernacle, the priest points us to God, who is beautiful (Pss 27:4; 29:2). Like the priests, we, as the priesthood of believers, are to be set apart to walk in the beauty of holiness before God—not with clothing, but in the beauty of a life devoted to God.

The Clothes for the Priests (28:1-43)

Notice the outline provided for this clothing and the description of it. In verse 4 God provided the names of six of the eight priestly items: (1) a breastpiece, (2) an ephod, (3) a robe, (4) a specially woven tunic, (5) a turban, and (6) a sash. Verse 5 gives an outline of the material needed to make the items. Later, God explained these garments and added to the list the linen undergarments (vv. 42-43) and the gold medallion on the front of the turban (vv. 36-38).

We read about the details of the clothing worn by Aaron and his sons in verses 6-43. In 39:1-31 we see that the worker fulfilled these instructions as the Lord commanded. The section breaks down as follows: the *ephod* (vv. 6-14; fulfilled in 39:2-7); the *breastpiece* (vv. 15-30; fulfilled in 39:8-21); the *robe* (vv. 31-35; fulfilled in 39:22-26); the *turban, tunic,* and *sash* (vv. 36-41 [with differences between the high priest and the regular priests/sons of Aaron in v. 40]; fulfilled in 39:27-31); and the *linen undergarments* for purity (vv. 42-43; fulfilled in 39:28).

No footwear gets mentioned. In Moses' encounter with God at the burning bush, God told him to remove his shoes because the ground was "holy." Likewise, we understand that the ground of the tabernacle was holy; thus, no shoes were to be worn.

Figure 1 (from the *HCSB Study Bible*) gives us an idea of what the clothing looked like. What a detailed garment!

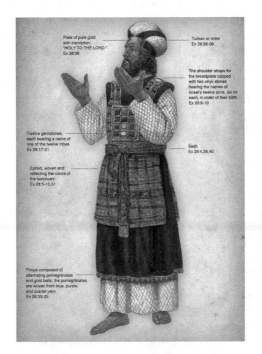

In verses 6-14 we learn that the ephod was like an apron—a long, sleeveless vest. It had two shoulder straps, each holding an onyx stone. The names of the 12 sons of Israel were engraved on these stones. The purpose of the engraving was to show the role of the high priest. He bore their names as a memorial before the Lord.

In verses 15-30 God described a "breastpiece for making decisions." It consisted of a small pouch worn on the breast. It was adorned with gemstones. It had four rows of three stones. Each stone had the name of one of the 12 tribes of Israel engraved on it. Like the ephod, the act of representation gets noted again.

Strikingly, the stones mentioned in verses 17-19 appeared in the garden of Eden (Ezek 28:13) and in Revelation (Rev 21:19-20). This should not surprise us given what we have learned about the tabernacle. It pointed backward and forward. From glory to glory, we see the story of God dwelling with His people. The language used through this section reminds us of the garden where Adam the priest worshiped God, working in Eden, the garden sanctuary.

We also find that it contained the Urim and Thummim, perhaps meaning "lights" and "darks" (Stuart, *Exodus,* 613), which were items used for discerning the will of God (v. 30). The people knew that God controlled "chance" (Prov 16:33). We do not know exactly what these items were or how they were used. They might have been thrown like dice. Or, after asking God a question, the priest may have pulled one out of his pocket to see the answer. We do not know (see Num 27:21; 1 Sam 14:41-42; 23:9-12; 28:6; 30:7-8; Ezra 2:63). It seems that they were only used for decisions related to the whole nation and that they could only answer a yes or no question. They could not ask, "Whom should I marry?" or "Where should I eat?" So the high priest was an intercessor, taking the concerns of the people to God. What is clear is that the people knew what these items were. It is probably a good thing that we do not know what they are! Otherwise, we would have people offering them to you on an 800 number or having tables set up in the cities along with fortune-tellers!

Even with the allowance of the practice, we should note that this method was not the first resort. God's people were to obey the written covenant and listen to the prophets. Today we have something better then these mysterious stones: the Spirit and the Word. Plus, we have a great high priest who hears our concerns and takes them before the Father. As a practical note, it is good to get counsel from people on major decisions in your life, especially your leaders who are performing the duties of prayer and ministry of the Word.

In verses 31-43 we find a number of items. The blue robe was worn under the ephod. On the hem of the robe were imitation pomegranates alternating with golden bells. These bells jingled when he was in the holy place so that he might not die (v. 35). It may have been a reminder for the priest to make sure the garments were being worn appropriately, as a "greeting" to God, or as a reminder to the people that he was in the holy place. We are unsure about this, as well.

The turban was made of fine linen. It had a golden plate with "Holy to the LORD" engraved on it (v. 36). The tunic was the basic garment for the priest (v. 39a). The embroidered sash probably secured the tunic (v. 39b).

The undergarments were made of linen (vv. 42-43). They kept the priest from being exposed. This reminds us of the garden, in which garments had to be made to cover the shame and nakedness of Adam and Eve.

These garments pointed to the idea that the priest must be righteous. The psalmist wrote, "May Your priests be clothed with righteousness" (Ps 132:9). Ultimately, only one high priest would be "Holy to the LORD" and would be clothed with righteousness: Jesus. By faith in Him, we receive His righteousness (see 2 Cor 5:21). That is the only way we can stand before God.

The Consecration of the Priests (29:1-46)

As the priests prepared to be consecrated, they were first washed from head to toe, symbolizing spiritual cleansing (v. 4). Next they were clothed with the garments (vv. 5-6) mentioned in chapter 28. Then they were ready to be ordained. There was anointing oil to pour on their heads, showing that they were set apart for their ministry (v. 7).

God told Moses to use some special spices for this occasion (30:22-33). Everything was anointed, including the priests. You can imagine the change in smell from the wilderness, which was filled with animals, to this tabernacle! The oil ran down the head onto the garments of the priests, as Psalm 133:2 mentions. What did this picture? The oil was a picture of God pouring out His Spirit on the man. Like the elements in the tabernacle, the priest was also "set apart" and was to be used for special purposes.

The sacrifices in 29:10-28 for Aaron and the priests get mentioned next. A bull and two rams were required. They were slaughtered "before the LORD at the entrance to the tent of meeting" (v. 11). The bull was a "sin offering" (vv. 14,36; Lev 8:14). As for the rams, the first was a "burnt offering" (v. 18), and the second was an offering "for ordination" (v. 22). Notice the symbolism of transference in verses 10-14. They placed their hands on the head on the bull and then killed it, symbolizing that their sin was transferred to the bull; this applied to the rams as well. Concerning the bull, its flesh, skin, and dung were burned "outside the camp" (v. 14), an idea picked up in Hebrews about how Jesus was crucified outside the gate of Jerusalem "that He might sanctify the people by His own blood" (Heb 13:12).

After the bull was killed, the blood was applied on the altar and on the priests' right ears, right thumbs, and great toes of their right feet, representing the exposed parts of the priests. The "right" parts of the body probably signified honor, the way the "right hand" was considered a place of honor (Gen 48:17-19). Then the priests and their garments were sprinkled with blood. This reminds us, once again, that no one can enter God's presence apart from blood.

As they obeyed the Lord's instruction, the sacrifice produced a "pleasing aroma" (vv. 18,25). God was pleased with their sacrifice. Similarly, we read in Ephesians 5:1-2, "Therefore, be imitators of God, as dearly loved children. And walk in love, as the Messiah also loved us and gave Himself for us, a sacrificial and fragrant offering to God." Jesus' sacrifice was a fragrant offering; it filled heaven with holy perfume. God's people must imitate Him through the sacrifice of love to others.

The second ram was to be prepared as a sacred meal for Aaron and the priests (vv. 31-34). Remember how in chapter 24 Israel's elders ate a meal on the mountain in God's presence? Now we see that Israel's priests ate with God at the tabernacle during the seven days of their ordination. This meal displayed the fact that they were in a covenant relationship with God and that they enjoyed fellowship with Him.

The entire ceremony of offering the bull and the rams was repeated for seven days (vv. 35-37). Each day a fresh bull was sacrificed on the altar. This purified the altar. The altar was set apart; it was where God accepted sacrifices for people's sin. These sacrifices were also for the priests since they were sinners also.

Once ordained, the priests offered these sacrifices every day (vv. 38-42). Two lambs were offered, one in the morning and one at twilight. These daily sacrifices were combined with grain, oil, and wine and were a sign of devotion. They gave a pleasing aroma to God. Israel began and ended each day with God in devotion. We should consider this pattern for our lives, as well. Also, notice the "pleasing aroma" mentioned again. Every day, our lives are to be a worship offering (Rom 12:1-2; 2 Cor 2:14-15).

The big idea with the tabernacle and the whole process was about God dwelling with a sinful people. "And they will know that I am Yahweh their God, who brought them out of the land of Egypt, so that I might dwell among them" (v. 46). And so it is with us: God has brought us out of slavery to sin and we worship Him in the glory of His presence. In the new covenant, through the Spirit, He now dwells in us (Rom 8:9; 1 Cor 3:16; 6:19, John 14:17). In the book of Revelation, God promised to dwell with His people. In the same way, He dwells within us now and will dwell among us in the days to come.

Our Great High Priest

These two chapters call our attention to the very important person and work of the high priest. We understand Jesus as "prophet, priest, and king." We have already noted how He is a prophet better than Moses. Now we see He is a priest better than Aaron.

The book of Hebrews has so much to say about the superiority of Jesus' priesthood that I can only summarize a few points (see Heb 8:1-2). Hebrews calls Jesus

- "a merciful and faithful high priest in service to God" (2:17),
- "high priest of our confession" (3:1),
- "a great high priest" (4:14),
- "a high priest forever" (6:20),
- "high priest of the good things that have come" (9:11), and
- "a great high priest over the house of God" (10:21).

Jesus, as the great high priest, stands superior in numerous ways. First, *Jesus is superior in holiness.* The problem facing the priests in Exodus was that they were sinners. They had to make sacrifices and had to wear external garments, but that was not enough. Throughout the Old Testament, the priests were imperfect. Jesus, however, never failed. He was not clothed with beautiful garments but with perfect holiness. He was clothed with glory (Heb 1:3). He did not need to offer sacrifice for Himself. He was and is sinless (Heb 7:26-28).

Second, as our great high priest, Jesus had a *superior anointing.* He too was anointed for His priestly ministry. His baptism was part of this ordination. Instead of oil symbolizing the Spirit, the Spirit Himself descended on Jesus (Luke 3:21-22). Luke said, "God anointed Jesus of Nazareth with the Holy Spirit and with power" (Acts 10:38).

Third, as our great high priest, Jesus is *superior in representation*. The high priest *was* Israel federally. Every Israelite understood that he represented him or her. He carried their names with him. Yet we have a better representation! Jesus, the Son of God, represents us. Instead of stones on His shoulders, He carried a cross on His shoulders. He carried *us* on His shoulders—bearing our judgment in our place (2 Cor 5:21). Further, He carried our names not on a breastpiece, but in His heart—for we are in Christ. We died with Him; we were raised with Him. We are united with Christ. Isaiah said He engraved us on His hands (Isa 49:16)! Further, our representative provided a better sacrifice. He did not offer sacrifices of animals, but Himself (see Heb 9:11-14; 9:24-26). Here is the good news for believers: The Father now sees us through our representative. The Father accepted the great high priest's work, and if you are in Christ, you are accepted just as much as Christ is!

Fourth, as our great high priest, Jesus is *superior in intercession*. The breastpiece was a reminder that the priest interceded for the people. As he took the items for making decisions, it was a reminder of this act. He carried their concerns. In a greater way, Jesus continues to carry our concerns on His heart. One of the things He is doing now is praying to the Father on our behalf. In contrast to the former priesthood, Jesus' priesthood is permanent and there is no one else like Him.

> *Now many have become Levitical priests, since they are prevented by death from remaining in office. But because He remains forever, He holds His priesthood permanently. Therefore, He is always able to save those who come to God through Him, since He always lives to intercede for them.* (Heb 7:23-25)

We have an intercessor. When we get tempted to despair, we can say like Paul, "Who is the one who condemns? Christ Jesus is the One who died, but even more, has been raised; He also is at the right hand of God and intercedes for us" (Rom 8:34). He is forever pleading for us. On earth Jesus was an intercessor. Remember what He told Peter? "Simon, Simon, look out! Satan has asked to sift you like wheat. But I have prayed for you that your faith may not fail. And you, when you have turned back, strengthen your brothers" (Luke 22:31-32). Take courage in this truth! In John 17, we see a picture of His great intercessory work. Right now, because of Jesus, we may approach the throne of grace with boldness to find help in our time of need (Heb 4:14-16).

In light of Jesus' superior priestly work, Hebrews says we should draw near, hold fast to our confession, and find ways to encourage one another (Heb 10:19-25). We have a great high priest who worked on behalf of us and cried, "It is finished," and a great high priest who continues to work on behalf of us through His ongoing intercession.

> Before the throne of God above
> I have a strong and perfect plea:
> A great High Priest, whose name is Love,
> Who ever lives and pleads for me.
> My name is graven on His hands,
> My name is written on His heart;
> I know that while in heaven He stands
> No tongue can bid me thence depart
> No tongue can bid me thence depart.
>
> When Satan tempts me to despair,
> And tells me of the guilt within,
> Upward I look, and see Him there
> Who made an end to all my sin.
> Because the sinless Savior died,
> My sinful soul is counted free;
> For God the just is satisfied
> To look on Him and pardon me
> To look on Him and pardon me. (Charitie Lees Bancroft,
>   "The Advocate," 1863)

Before we move on to the second point, I want to summarize Exodus 30 because its contents have previously been covered. In 30:1-10 we see an altar of incense. This altar had raised corners or "horns" like the sacrificial altar and was overlaid with gold. It was put just in front of the most holy place. It continually burned incense before the presence of the Lord. The high priest lit it every morning and evening. In 30:11-16 we read about the atonement money. All the Israelites shared the expense of the tabernacle. In 30:17-21 the basin for washing is mentioned. A bronze basin was constructed for the priests. Before they worked at the altar they washed their hands and feet. In 30:22-33 we see the anointing oil. This was a special type of oil that was used for anointing the tabernacle and the priests. They could not use the oil for any other purpose.

Finally, in 30:34-38 we see the incense that, like the oil, was a special type that could not be used for any other purposes.

Once again we see the themes of being holy and devoting ourselves to the worship of God. What service to God are you performing? Are you using your talents and resources for the kingdom? Let your life be a daily offering of worship to God.

We Have the Spirit of God Working through Us
EXODUS 31:1-11

What we learn from the high priest is that we need someone to represent us and to work on behalf of us. What we learn from the craftsmen is that the Spirit of God enables us to serve God's people for God's glory. The work of God was accomplished by the Spirit of God.

Another parallel to the creation narrative exists here (Gen 1:2–2:3). Just as God did His work in creation by the Spirit, so He did His work in the tabernacle, this little Eden, by the Spirit. God chose Bezalel from Judah and Oholiab from Dan as His craftsmen. Their skill did not originate in themselves but from God.

Let us use our gifts for God's glory as well. In the next chapter, we will see how men used their gifts to make a golden calf for idol worship. Will you use your gifts for God's glory or for your own gratification?

Look at how the Spirit's work is described. Of Bezalel, it says, "I have filled him with God's Spirit" (v. 3), and later, "I have placed wisdom within every skilled craftsman in order to make all that I have commanded you" (v. 6). God enabled this man to build the tabernacle by His Spirit. When we read of "wisdom, understanding, and ability" (v. 3) these are not additional qualities that went along with the Spirit. Instead, God gave him one thing: the Spirit (Stuart, *Exodus*, 650). The Spirit sanctified his ability, intelligence, and knowledge. Sometimes God may do something supernatural and totally beyond a person's normal ability, but more often I think He perfects an existing God-given gift, as we see here.

Consider also that God empowered the craftsmen to perform tasks for the well-being of the people. Later, in 35:31, the work of the Spirit of God is mentioned again. The repetition reveals its importance. Then observe how Bezalel executed the plan with skill and precise obedience (e.g., 36:1; 37:1,10,17).

The Spirit enables obedience. Joseph and Joshua were two other key characters in the Pentateuch who were filled with the Spirit of God

(Gen 41:38; Deut 34:9). Like Bezalel and Oholiab, they were obedient to God as a result. Likewise, Micah was "filled with . . . the Spirit" (Mic 3:8) to declare God's word forcefully and effectively to the people. This section of Exodus may be the background for the phrase "filled with the Spirit" used later in the New Testament (Luke 1:15; Acts 13:9; Eph 5:18).

From the craftsmen we can learn at least two truths. First, we need the Spirit of God to accomplish the work of God. God gifted these men with the Spirit. We too need God's Spirit to carry out God's work.

When I was in Ukraine recently, I had an interesting discussion with a missionary friend about the Holy Spirit. Apparently, around 1960 the Pentecostal Church did not want to register with the government, so they merged with the Baptist Union. Then, to avoid controversy, an administrative policy was put in place. The policy stated that no one could teach, preach, or discuss the Holy Spirit. This lasted until about 1990 (though not every leader followed the policy!). My friend told me that this created sort of a deistic, rationalistic religion. People talked about God and His power in general, but few ever talked about the personal influence of the Holy Spirit or about gifts. They were attempting to "do church" apart from the Spirit!

Never stop thanking God for the Spirit's work. Never stop relying on the Spirit's work. Do not become a "mechanical Christian," that is, just going through the motions, serving in the energy of the flesh. We need the Spirit of God to do the work of God.

Second, we learn that the Spirit fills us to do tasks that are not always considered "sensational" in the eyes of others. I love how the text says that they were empowered to make stuff! I love it because people have the craziest ideas about the Spirit's work. Many are sensationalists. They have "the Incredible Hulk syndrome," thinking when the Spirit blesses you, you turn green and into a different creature. Yet in the text we find that God blessed them with intelligence and ability to construct things.

In regard to miracles and giftings, we can say a couple of things. Yes, the Spirit does miracles. But in the New Testament you see things that are not what people would call "spectacular." When the Spirit filled the early church, one of the things that they needed was to be able to "speak God's message with boldness" (Acts 4:31). They talked about Jesus a lot in the face of opposition. I like Peter's instruction. He simply said that some *serve* and some *speak*; both should use their gifts to serve one another for God's glory (1 Pet 4:10-11). As for the gifts in the New Testament that are listed, many of them are not glamorous. Paul mentioned gifts like service, teaching, giving, mercy (Rom 12:7-8), helping, and managing (1 Cor 12:28). Sure, others are listed like prophecy, tongues, and miracles, but let us remember that the greatest gift is love (1 Cor 13).

Think also about Acts 6. When the church grew, the needs increased. So they decided to appoint some men to meet the needs. What did they look for? They looked for men who were "full of the Spirit and wisdom . . . full of faith and the Holy Spirit" (6:3,5). That is awesome, right? Yes it is! But what were they going to do? Their job involved serving widows. Those who are filled with the Spirit, who are walking with Jesus, will gladly serve widows, visit the sick, care for orphans, make coffee on Sunday, care for children in the nursery, tutor a disadvantaged student, give generous offerings, and help those in need. Is that you? Do you think these things are beneath you? May God help us, in this age of celebrity Christianity, not to lose sight of this biblical vision of the Spirit's work. The Spirit of God enables us to do the work of God, and the Spirit's work through us may not be considered "sensational work," but it is "important work."

We Have a Sabbath Rest Provided for Us
EXODUS 31:12-17

The similarity between God's work of creation and Israel's construction of the tabernacle emerges here with the reference to the Sabbath. After six days of creation, God rested. Now Israel is to do the same. Further, the phrase "The LORD spoke/said" appears seven times in Exodus 25–31, echoing the creation account. The first six are related to creating, and the seventh, here, concerns rest.

God's creation rest occurred once; the weekly Sabbath is a reminder of that divine rest. There remains a permanent rest awaiting us (Heb 4:9). Without getting into details about what is permissible on the Sabbath (see comments on 20:8-11), consider this idea: there is a resting in Christ for God's people. We find our rest in Jesus, who has done the work for us. There is a resting that takes place now for Christians as well as a permanent ultimate Sabbath in the new creation. Many Christians avoid work on the Lord's Day but they still are not keeping the Sabbath because they worry themselves into knots over things. They are not trusting in Christ. Do you find yourself in the same situation? Rest in Christ!

God had been talking to Moses on the mountain (v. 18). When He finished, He gave Moses two tablets with the Ten Words written on them. In the next chapter, Moses would come down and see the opposite of true worship of this glorious God. We go from a return to Eden to a return to the fall.

How should we wrap this up? Let us recap these glorious, gospel truths:

- We have a great high priest who worked/works on behalf of us.
- We have the Spirit of God working through us.
- We have a Sabbath rest provided for us.

Worship the true and living God, who is worthy of our praise!

Reflect and Discuss

1. How has studying the Old Testament helped you to understand the New Testament?
2. Is worshiping God together with other Christians an obligation or a benefit? Explain.
3. In what way are Christian pastors set apart? What part does a pastor's clothing play in current culture? In what way are all Christians set apart like priests?
4. Rather than the Urim and Thummim or flipping a coin, how have you determined God's will and guidance in your life?
5. How is ordination accomplished in your church? How does the symbolism compare with what was done in Exodus 29?
6. Why was it important that Jesus surpass the priests in Exodus in holiness?
7. In what way is Jesus—as the ultimate, perfect high priest—the ideal intercessor and advocate who speaks on our behalf before the throne of God?
8. What are some of the most challenging tasks you have faced? How did God prepare you beforehand to accomplish those tasks? How did He empower you while you were working?
9. When you think of Spirit-empowered ministry, what do you think of? What is the value of recognizing that the unspectacular gifts also come from the Spirit?
10. Which is easier for you on your Sabbath, rest from working or rest from worrying? How do both indicate our faith in God?

Idol Factory

EXODUS 32

Main Idea: We must avoid the idols of our hearts: we must not put anything in the place of God.

I. **Be Careful Not to Fall (32:1-9).**
    A. We fall when we disobey the word of God (32:1a).
    B. We fall when we fail to trust the purposes of God (32:1b).
    C. We fall when we forget the grace of God (32:2).
    D. We fall when we fail to use our gifts to the glory of God (32:3-4).
    E. We fall when we distort the worship of God (32:5-6).
    F. We fall when we exchange the glory of God (32:8).
II. **See the Power of Intercession (32:10-14).**
    A. We should appeal to God's character and faithfulness in prayer.
    B. We must seek the will of God, not our own selfish desires in prayer.
    C. We must believe that God answers prayer!
III. **Repent of Sin; Do Not Shift Blame or Minimize Sin (32:15-29).**
    A. Confrontation (32:15-20)
    B. Shifting blame and minimizing sin (32:21-24)
    C. Who is on the Lord's side? (32:25-29)
IV. **See Our Need for a Substitute (32:30-35).**

A few of our pastors and interns took a trip to Boston recently to explore the idea of sending a church planting team to New England. The need for churches in the Northeast is great. One Christian leader there calls the area north of Boston "the desert." Some estimate that it is currently 1-percent evangelical at best.

As our friends described their culture to us, they pointed out that people actually worship in the Northeast. Some people worship the Red Sox. Others, in the world of academia and research, are slaves to ambition. In Salem, Massachusetts, they statistically have more witches than Christians. The Northeast is really no different from anywhere else in the world. Left to ourselves, we will worship something other than the living God. To paraphrase Calvin, "The human heart is an idol factory."

Because of this universal problem, we need to understand this subject. Os Guiness and John Seel comment on the how important this topic is: "Idolatry is the most discussed problem in the Bible. . . . There can be no believing communities without an unswerving eye to the detection and destruction of idols" (*No God but God*, 23).

What is idolatry? Idolatry is putting something or someone in the place of God. Idols are counterfeit gods. Anything you seek to give you what only Christ can give you (joy, security, peace, meaning, significance, identity, and salvation) becomes an idol. Many do not believe idolatry is a problem because they only associate idolatry with shrines, temples, and carved images. But heart idolatry exists everywhere. Common idols include money, sex, a romantic relationship, peer approval, competence and skill, secure and comfortable circumstances, beauty, brains, and success and ambition.

Israel's worship of the golden calf idol appears in this passage. Perhaps you think, "I do not struggle with worshiping a cow; I like to eat them too much, but I am not tempted to worship them." Maybe so, but remember that this story has everything to do with you because it is not ultimately about a calf. It centers on the human heart. The martyr Stephen proclaimed that God's people "in their *hearts* turned back to Egypt. They told Aaron: 'Make us gods who will go before us'" (Acts 7:39-40; emphasis added).

While Moses was on the mountain getting instructions for the tabernacle for the proper worship of the living God, the people were back at the camp making a calf for the worship of a false god. Even though the people had gotten out of Egypt, Egypt remained in the people. Moses was absent for about 40 days, and Aaron, his older brother, assumed leadership. The people told Aaron how they wanted to worship, and Aaron demonstrated what a leader without conviction looks like. He gave these sinful people exactly what they wanted.

This is a story of "another fall." We were in "Eden," receiving instructions about the tabernacle, but now we are looking at a huge plunge into sin. Remember what Paul said about this in 1 Corinthians 10:6-8 and 11-14:

> *Now these things became examples for us, so that we will not desire evil things as they did. Don't become idolaters as some of them were; as it is written, The people sat down to eat and drink, and got up to play.*

Let us not commit sexual immorality as some of them did, and in a single day 23,000 people fell dead. . . . Now these things happened to them as examples, and they were written as a warning to us, on whom the ends of the ages have come. So, whoever thinks he stands must be careful not to fall. No temptation has overtaken you except what is common to humanity. God is faithful, and He will not allow you to be tempted beyond what you are able, but with the temptation He will also provide a way of escape so that you are able to bear it. Therefore, my dear friends, flee from idolatry.

Paul said that we must not desire evil. We must not become idolaters. After mentioning other Old Testament examples, he said that one of the reasons we have this story is to learn from their example. It teaches us important truths. Paul said that we too must be careful not to fall. We will be tempted, but we must flee from idolatry. In Corinth, they were tempted with the local pagan gods, and in Exodus, the people were tempted with the local Egyptian gods. In each culture, the gods may look different but the principle is the same: we must avoid the idols of our hearts. Consider four challenges from chapter 32 regarding idolatry.

Be Careful Not to Fall
EXODUS 32:1-9

Why did Israel fall into idolatry? For the same reasons we fall.

We Fall When We Disobey the Word of God (32:1a)

The people called for Aaron to make them gods. The Israelites were supposed to know the Ten Commandments. They knew the first commandment, which said to have no other gods, and they knew the second, which was not to make any images. But they disobeyed God's clear commands. Israel previously said, "We will do everything that the Lord has commanded" (Exod 24:3). Yet we see them rejecting God's word.

Notice how sin works. We do not want to be told what to do. This is as old as the garden. We still battle with "garden thoughts," like "Did God really say?" (Gen 3:1), and "You will not die" (Gen 3:4). We do not want to be under authority.

They claimed to be worshiping "the Lord," and they proceeded to give offerings (Exod 32:5), yet they made an image to do so. While "Elohim" ("God" in v. 4) is plural, it can refer to "god" in the singular. Perhaps they thought they were worshiping the real God, but they were worshiping in a way that clearly violated what God had said. Their hearts craved Egypt, with its false but tangible gods, as evidenced by this godless practice.

This scene shows us the importance of knowing God for who He truly is, not how we imagine Him to be. Worship is built on a right perception of God revealed through Scripture. Tozer said, "The essence of idolatry is the entertainment of thoughts about God that are unworthy of Him" (*Knowledge*, 3).

We Fall When We Fail to Trust the Purposes of God (32:1b)

The people said they did not know what happened to Moses. But they knew where he was! They simply did not trust his involvement with God's purposes, which included His instruction and guidance in His timing. Notice the reason for their idol making. They grew frustrated with Moses' extended absence. Instead of trusting in God's purposes, they moved on. Failure to trust God is sin, and it leads to countless other sins. Israel wanted to get on with their journey. God, however, had not told them the itinerary; He only promised to go with them. But the impatient Israelites failed to trust God. Did they have any reason to doubt Him? Of course not—think of all the miracles and His provision up to this point!

The same is true for us. God has not given us a script. He says, "I will be with you. Trust me. Trust in my timing. My purposes are good and best." When you try to do things your way, in your time, you fall into sin. Perhaps you find yourself in a wilderness and you want out of it. If so, trust in God's goodness and wait for Him.

We Fall When We Forget the Grace of God (32:2)

The people were instructed to remove the rings that reminded them of God's grace. Notice how they got the gold to make the idol: it came from their plundering of Egypt. Why did they get it? God gave it to them (32:20-22). The gold came from God's victory. It pictured His grace and His faithfulness. Israel minimized His grace. What God gave to them, they gave to an idol, instead of using God's gifts for His glory. Read Psalm 106:19-21:

> At Horeb they made a calf and worshiped the cast metal image. They exchanged their glory for the image of a grass-eating ox. They forgot God their Savior, who did great things in Egypt.

We Fall When We Fail to Use Our Gifts to the Glory of God (32:3-4)

We should enjoy God's gifts, be thankful for His gifts, and use His gifts to build the kingdom, not for idolatrous devotion. Think about not just the gold but the skill and time it took to make this idol. Instead of using this skill, this time, and this gold to honor God, they used it for idolatry. It leads us to a question: Are you using God's gifts—your time, talent, and treasure—for His glory?

Many today want "salvation without dedication." God delivered Israel from Egypt, but now they fail to live for His glory. Many people want to be forgiven and go to heaven, but they want to hold on to the idols of the world. But God is not mocked.

In verse 4 they said to each other, "Israel, this is your God, who brought you up from the land of Egypt!" This is similar to the later worship of a golden cow instigated by Jeroboam I in 1 Kings 12:28. They forgot who saved them. We must be careful not to forget. Do not stop thanking God for His grace and living for His glory.

We Fall When We Distort the Worship of God (32:5-6)

This whole scene was a picture of distorted worship. They were doing everything their way instead of God's way. Consider how twisted their worship was from the way God prescribed it:

- They took the initiative, instead of God.
- Offerings were demanded not offered freely.
- They did not prepare themselves for worship.
- There was no guarding of the presence of God.
- The invisible God was exchanged for a visible image.
- The personal, living God was exchanged for a lifeless, dumb idol.

They did what was popular instead of doing what was right with regard to worship. And Aaron listened to them—perhaps out of fear (a real possibility) or a desire for acceptance. He displayed terrible spiritual leadership.

Today there is a whole church culture that reflects this story. We want to do away with what Scripture says about worship and do it our way. As a result, the attenders are mere consumers of worship, and they are led by Aaron-like individuals who pander to the people. By contrast, God's way of worship puts the gospel on display. God-centered, gospel-saturated worship shows sinners how they can be forgiven and worship the Holy One. That is what the tabernacle displayed—the gospel.

We must remember that worship is about glorifying God, not gratifying self. The golden calf is what people wanted. The calf could not talk. The calf was not feared. The calf could be manipulated for one's own desires. People do not want a holy God who speaks and confronts them. Be careful: you can do things "in the name" of the Lord but still not worship the Lord. Be careful: you can have some orthodox acts of worship (they had a feast and made offerings) but worship unacceptably.

We Fall When We Exchange the Glory of God (32:8)

The Lord said they chose to worship a created thing instead of worshiping Him, their Creator and Redeemer (v. 8; cf. Ps 106:19-20). Paul described this awful exchange:

> *Claiming to be wise, they became fools and exchanged the glory of the immortal God for images resembling mortal man, birds, four-footed animals, and reptiles. Therefore God delivered them over in the cravings of their hearts to sexual impurity, so that their bodies were degraded among themselves. They exchanged the truth of God for a lie, and worshiped and served something created instead of the Creator, who is praised forever. Amen.* (Rom 1:22-25)

Any created thing can be an object of idolatry. Usually, the better something is, the more likely people will idolize it. People live in bondage to sexual sin, in part, because the human body is an amazing creation. But people take a good thing, turn it into a god thing, and end up in a life of total bondage and corruption. You will worship something. Will it be creation or Creator?

Two results of idol worship stand out in this story. First, consider the *moral corruption* that resulted. Wrong worship leads to a corrupt life (vv. 6-7; cf. Rom 1:18-32). The word "corruptly" appears in verse 7. In verse 6 "the people sat down to eat and drink, then got up to play." Some point out that this description has sexual overtones. It should not surprise us. When you worship the wrong god, you are capable of all types of sin. Later, when Joshua heard loud sounds as they came off the mountain, he said, "There is a sound of war" (32:17), and Moses told him that he was mistaken. In verse 19 we read of "dancing." Dancing itself is not a sin, but the sounds and the dancing may indicate wild, dishonorable activity. In Romans 1 Paul said that God had given over those who worship creation instead of Creator to their "degrading passions" (v. 26).

Therefore, sin problems are worship problems. Your pornography addiction is a worship problem; your anger problem is a worship problem; your love of money is a worship problem. The idol of money ("the god of mammon") got exposed vividly with the recent collapse of the economy. "Some hung themselves, shot themselves behind the wheel of their expensive sport cars, slit their wrists, leapt from their office buildings" (Keller, *Counterfeit Gods*, ix-x). Why? Their god was taken from them. The psalmist wrote, "The sorrows of those who take another god for themselves will multiply" (16:4). Sorrows multiply when you chase other gods. This only leads to self-destruction. Love creation, use creation, steward creation, but worship the Creator, the triune God.

The second result of idolatry illustrated here is *imitation*. We become like what we worship (vv. 7-10). This point, illustrated in Exodus 32:7-10, was also made in Psalm 115:4-8:

> *Their idols are silver and gold,*
> *made by human hands.*
> *They have mouths but cannot speak,*
> *eyes, but cannot see.*
> *They have ears but cannot hear,*
> *noses, but cannot smell.*
> *They have hands but cannot feel,*
> *feet, but cannot walk.*
> *They cannot make a sound with their throats.*
> *Those who make them are just like them,*
> *as are all who trust in them.*

Israel illustrated this truth in a number of ways. They became spiritually lifeless like the idol. They became corrupt and nasty like cattle. Psalm 106 said they exchanged the glory of God for the image of an ox that eats grass (v. 20). The psalmist noted the disgusting digestive process of cattle. This may be why the story in Exodus included Moses grinding up the bull and serving it to them. He might have put it into the water supply so that it could get digested and become unusable filth.

Notice also that Israel became "stiff-necked" and stubborn like unruly cattle (Exod 32:9). They had gotten "out of control" like cattle (32:25). They had to be led like cattle (32:34). Hosea 4:16 said, "Israel is as obstinate as a stubborn cow."

Some propose that Satan actually entered the cow, and people were dancing as a result of their imitation of Satan, their cheerleader. In other words, Satan became the ultimate owner and builder of the calf (Beale, *Worship*, 152–53). I think Satan definitely got involved in this whole thing. Scripture refers to satanic influence in relation to idolatry in several passages. "They sacrificed to demons, not God, to gods they had not known, new gods that had just arrived, which your fathers did not fear" (Deut 32:17). Likewise, Paul said in 1 Corinthians 10:19-20, "What am I saying then? That food offered to idols is anything, or that an idol is anything? No, but I do say that what they sacrifice, they sacrifice to demons and not to God. I do not want you to participate with demons!"

What should we do to avoid falling? Worship God! As you behold the glory of God in the face of Christ, you become like Christ (2 Cor 3:18). This is how we are transformed. You resemble what you revere (Beale, *Worship*, 16).

See the Power of Intercession
EXODUS 32:10-14

The psalmist wrote in Psalm 106:23, "So He said He would have destroyed them—if Moses His chosen one had not stood before Him in the breach to turn His wrath away from destroying them." Here we learn about intercession, that is, praying for others. In Exodus 32:10 God said, "Now leave Me alone, so that My anger can burn against them and I can destroy them. Then I will make you into a great nation." God pushed Moses toward intercession. God could have destroyed the people in a second; instead He was making a "rhetorical demand." He challenged Moses to get involved, basically saying, "Here is what I will do unless you intervene" (Stuart, *Exodus,* 670). God declared His holy anger in other passages of Scripture as a way of inviting intervention (Gen 18:20-25; cf. Isa 59:15-16). In Amos 7:1-6, God showed Amos what He might do to Israel, but Amos interceded, and God relented.

The prophet Jonah announced God's threat to destroy Nineveh in "40 days," but Jonah knew this was actually an invitation for the Ninevites to repent. They did repent, and God did not destroy them. A similar thing happened here in Exodus. When verse 14 says, "the LORD relented," it does not mean God changed His mind. God was inviting Moses to pray, and Moses did, then God turned away His wrath. God was not changing His plans; Moses carried out God's plans. In the end, God did in fact send a plague, but it was less of a punishment compared to what was first mentioned (32:34-35).

What do we learn about prayer from this example? We learn that as sinners we need a mediator. We have the ultimate One in Jesus. He turned away the wrath of God from us through His intervention (John 3:16). But as followers of Jesus, we must also plead to God for others through Jesus, and to do so, I suggest that we learn three lessons from Moses.

We Should Appeal to God's Character and Faithfulness in Prayer

Notice how Moses appealed to the following:

- God's power—Why would You nullify Your power? (v. 11)
- God's past investment and public reputation—Why would You want the enemy to delight in seeing Your people crushed? (v. 12)
- God's covenant faithfulness—Why would You go back on Your promises? (v. 13)

Praying according to God's faithfulness is expressed again in Numbers 14:13-19. Let me encourage you to appeal to the character of God in prayer.

We Must Seek the Will of God, Not Our Own Selfish Desires in Prayer

Moses did not ask for personal glory here. God said that He would start all over with *Moses*: "I will make you into a great nation" (v. 10). This was flattering and tempting, but Moses cared more about the people who were in the process of fulfilling God's purposes of becoming a great nation. We too should pray in line with God's will; that is, making disciples of all nations, not desiring our own fame. This prayer points us to Jesus, who would be the ultimate offspring of this people. It is His glory that we should seek.

We Must Believe that God Answers Prayer!

This account in Exodus 32 is one of the best examples of how God responds to prayer. Those who have a high view of God's sovereignty often struggle with prayer. But remember, God is not a math equation.

He is not some abstraction. God is personal. He responds to prayer! I love what Spurgeon said:

> In God's Word we are over and over again commanded to pray. God's institutions are not folly. Can I believe that the infinitely wise God has ordained for me an exercise that is ineffective and is no more than child's play? Does He tell me to pray, and yet does prayer have no more of a result than if I whistled to the wind or sang to a grove of trees? If there is no answer to prayer, prayer is a monstrous absurdity, and God is the author of it, which is blasphemy. (*Power*, 9)

When you pray like Moses, you are not whistling to the wind. Believe that God hears the cries of His people. Is He pushing you to intervene through intercession? Draw near to God, through Jesus, and appeal to God, believing that He answers prayer.

Repent of Sin; Do Not Shift Blame or Minimize Sin
EXODUS 32:15-29

Notice the process here. First, Moses confronted the people. Second, Aaron shifted the blame and minimized sin, instead of repenting. Third, some joined Moses, turning from idolatry.

Confrontation (32:15-20)

Moses confronted them by doing two things: breaking the commandments and destroying their idol. Moses descended the mountain with the two tablets. They were inscribed on the front and back with the law of God. The text says God wrote it Himself. Here is a picture of the fact that the law came from God. It revealed His holy character.

Then Joshua joined him. He had gone halfway up the mountain and waited for Moses. He then commented on the sound, as mentioned earlier.

Next we see Moses' reaction. He had heard of what Israel was doing at the foot of the mountain, but now when he saw it, he was filled with anger. As a result, he threw the tablets down and broke them. Then he ground up the idol and made Israel drink it. I do not think Moses was acting sinfully here, since he was never rebuked for his anger (as he was later in Num 20:1-13). Instead, I think he illustrated the point that Israel broke God's law (cf. Zech 11:10).

Think about this: these tablets were the most valuable possession on earth! If a letter written by Abraham Lincoln can fetch $300,000, think what an inscription written by God is worth! When Moses broke the tablets, it symbolized the severity of sin. James said, "For whoever keeps the entire law, yet fails in one point, is guilty of breaking it all" (Jas 2:10). The Israelites had broken their covenant with God. That is serious. The Word confronts us.

Notice also that it was at the foot of the mountain (32:19). This was the official gathering place for worship, the place of meeting with God (19:12,17) as well as the location of the only proper worship altar (24:4). Moses confronted their sin publicly here, announcing the breach of the covenant in the place where the covenant should have been most honored.

Next Moses completely destroyed the calf (32:20). What a picture! Idols are not to be managed; they are to be destroyed. Moses probably put it in their water supply so they would drink it and digest it—passing it as waste, making it permanently ruined.

Shifting Blame and Minimizing Sin (32:21-24)

The next person Moses confronted was his big brother, Aaron, demanding, "What did these people do to you that you have led them into such a grave sin?" (v. 21). Moses correctly called this a "grave sin." Aaron, as the spiritual leader, rightly was singled out for allowing this to happen (see v. 35). But instead of repenting of sin, Aaron did what Adam (the first garden priest) did in the garden: he shifted blame. He put the blame on the people for their evil and tried to make it sound like Moses had the problem (v. 22; cf. 1 Sam 15:20-24). He essentially said, "Don't be so upset, little brother; you know how these people are. They are bent on evil." In other words, "Why are you getting so mad?"

We have seen our own versions of this approach. Instead of confessing sin, people prefer to make excuses for their sin. Sometimes there is truth to these excuses. In this case, Aaron was right: the people were evil. But that was not the issue. What they did was irrelevant in this discussion; Aaron chose to give into the temptation. You cannot control your situation and your circumstances all the time, but through Christ, you must not yield to temptation.

Aaron then said the people made him do it (v. 23). Once again, Aaron refused to admit his sin. He refused to acknowledge that he had yielded to temptation. He said, "They said to me . . ." as if he had no choice in the situation. The proper way to respond when confronted with sin is not by saying "Everyone was doing it!" or "She made me do it!" You may indeed be in a tempting situation, but you must respond appropriately, and when you sin, you need to repent.

His final excuse was the most pathetic. He blamed the fire (v. 24)! Aaron said that when they threw the gold in the fire, a calf came out! Aaron tried to cover up his sin with the spin game. He lied, made up things. Whether you admit your sin or not, you remain accountable for it. We need to own it and repent of it, like David, who said,

> Against You—You alone—I have sinned and done this evil in Your sight. . . . Purify me with hyssop, and I will be clean; wash me, and I will be whiter than snow. . . . God, create a clean heart for me and renew a steadfast spirit within me. (Ps 51:4,7,10)

We read in Proverbs, "The one who conceals his sins will not prosper, but whoever confesses and renounces them will find mercy" (28:13). The choice is yours: conceal or confess.

Who Is on the Lord's Side? (32:25-29)

In verses 25-29 God made it clear to Moses that those committed to idolatry must be cut off. As a result, 3,000 men fell.

I can imagine a modern person's reaction to this scene. They would struggle to justify this action. That is because you must understand the reason behind it, namely, leaving idolaters in the land would threaten the preservation of truth and the salvation of future generations. If idolatry continued to exist, many would never have the opportunity to obtain eternal life through Jesus. Jews and Gentiles would both be eternally affected by the continuation of Israel's idolatry. We must also point out that we must not imitate Moses' actions. In the new covenant, we are not given permission to kill as a means of preserving orthodoxy.

Additionally, there seems to be here an opportunity for repentance before the judgment is carried out. In verse 26 Moses said, "Whoever is for the LORD, come to me." Who chooses the Lord? The Levites do. Stuart said, "Since Aaron was a Levite and had led the move toward idolatry, it can hardly be doubted that other Levites had also succumbed to its attractions. But now, everyone was being given a chance to repent and re-establish loyalty to Yahweh's covenant" (*Exodus*, 681). This is how we are to respond when we are confronted with sin. The Levites turned from idolatry and chose the Lord.

In verses 27-29 we read of the Levites carrying out God's demand for judgment. They were told to show no partiality (v. 27). It appears that the Levites carefully and systematically saw who was returning to Yahweh. Those found in idolatry were put to death. Three thousand men died (about 0.05% of the male population, cf. 12:37).

Because the Levites had to "consider the cost" in carrying out this severe act (cf. Matt 10:37-38), they were told, "Today you have been dedicated to the LORD" (v. 29). God said He was setting them aside for special service and that they were recipients of His blessing. So here we see the severity of sin; the reality of judgment; and the need to repent of sin, not to shift blame or minimize sin.

See Our Need for a Substitute
EXODUS 32:30-35

Moses went back up Mount Sinai to intercede again for the people (vv. 30-31). He said, "perhaps I will be able to atone for your sin" (v. 30), which is "a concept that could also be translated literally as 'get your sins covered/forgiven'" (Stuart, *Exodus*, 684). The killing of the 3,000 was only the beginning of the process of restoring God's favor and blessing. The judgment of the 3,000 only corrected those who refused to return to God. It was a limited judgment. What about those still alive—those who had broken the covenant? Their hope was in the mediator who climbed the mountain to make atonement.

Moses appealed to God. He did not minimize their sin. He said it was a "grave sin" (v. 31). He sought forgiveness for their sin (v. 32a). Then he said something amazing: "But if not, please erase me from the book You have written" (v. 32b). Moses offered to lose his own life for the sake of Israel (cf. Rom 9:1-3). Moses understood the nature of salvation: when people sin, they need a substitute.

As mentioned with the priests, sin could be forgiven through a representative, with sacrifices. But here is a new approach! The representative offers Himself as the sacrifice! God responded with judgment and mercy. The judgment came with the immediate answer (v. 33); the mercy came when God agreed to continue with this stiff-necked people (v. 34; 33:1-17). God said, "I will erase whoever has sinned against Me from My book" (v. 33). This is a statement of God's practice of judgment.

Eternal life is not automatically granted to a person who tries to enter it without the forgiveness of sins. Stuart says, "Verse 33 is, then, one of the Bible's stronger statements about the absolute necessity for the forgiveness of sins, and therefore, for a savior. It can be regarded as messianic even if not overtly so" (*Exodus*, 685).

In verse 34 God told Moses to continue on the journey. Their idolatry did not result in total destruction. The punishment spoken of here might have referred to future punishment not the plague in the next verse (see Stuart, *Exodus*). The plague was a small-scale warning, a sample of God's wrath (v. 35). We are not told how many people died—even if any did. This plague might have only made them sick.

From this, it is clear that we need a savior. The story seems to build up to this climactic finish, in which the mediator will give His life for the life of the people, but it did not work that way. Why not? Moses could not die for the people because he himself was a sinner. Ryken says, "God is willing to let someone die for someone else's sin, but the only sacrifice he can accept is a perfect sacrifice, unstained by sin. So Moses could not do it. He came close—perhaps closer than any man had ever come—but he still couldn't make atonement for sin" (*Exodus*, 1015). This whole chapter points us to one great reality: we need a perfect substitute. And we have One!

We have One who would come from this very people. He would ascend to the cross and bear the punishment that we idolaters deserve. He took the punishment in our place, in order for our sins to be covered. Jesus would say, "Take my life, that they may live." "The good shepherd lays down his life for the sheep" (John 10:11). Because of Christ, our names can be written in the book of life (Phil 4:3; Luke 10:20).

Conclusion

Let me pull it all together. To my non-Christian friend: You need to see Jesus Christ as your substitute who died in your place for your idolatry so that you could be reconciled to God. Turn from your idols to the living God (1 Thess 1:9-10). Apart from Jesus, we just live in Romans 1—satisfying our lusts and exchanging God for created things. Left to ourselves we are idolaters. You need a new life that is made possible through Jesus.

To my Christian friends: You need to see your idols for what they are. They are dumb idols. Properly assess created things. Enjoy and be thankful for and steward created things, but only worship and serve and trust the Creator God (Rom 1:21-25). Put your lusts to death daily (Col 3:5). How? Set your mind on things above (Col 3:1-2). Consider yourself dead to sin and alive to God. Remember that you are new (Col 3:4)!

Let the word of Christ dwell in you richly (Col 3:16). See all of life as an opportunity to worship Christ. Believe that Christ is the best master, the most intimate companion, and the most superior source of satisfaction.

Reflect and Discuss

1. What or whom do your secular friends worship? Are any of those things a temptation for you?
2. Why do people prefer to worship things and people rather than God? What are the stated and unstated demands of each? What does each promise and deliver? What are the eternal rewards of each?
3. How does human pride interfere with obedience to God? Why do we resist worshiping God in the manner He prescribed?
4. What talents has God given you? How could those talents be used wrongly for idolatrous adulation? How could they be used rightly in godly worship?
5. Along with praise and thanksgiving, confession, and prayer for your own needs, what percentage of your prayer time is spent in intercession for others?
6. How would you explain to an adult Sunday school class the way human prayer seems to change the plans of the sovereign God?
7. Have you recently heard requests and prayers that are ultimately selfish? Could those same requests be stated in a way that seeks the will of God and His glory?
8. What is the error in the statement, "Prayer is primarily for the benefit of the one praying"? That is, "The main result of prayer is that the one who prayed feels better afterward about the situation."
9. Give a real or typical example of a child shifting blame. Compare a child's blame shifting with adults' attempts to avoid admitting guilt.
10. Why was Moses insufficient as a substitute to take the punishment for Israel's sins? How would you explain to a child that Jesus Christ was sufficient?

Forward

EXODUS 33–40

Main Idea: The presence of God gives us great hope as we continue on life's journey.

I. **Will We Be Desperate for God's Presence, or Will We Depend on Ourselves? (33:1-17).**
   A. We have a need we cannot overlook (33:1-6).
   B. We have a privilege we must not neglect (33:7-11).
   C. We have an assignment we cannot complete (33:12-16).
II. **Will We Long to See God's Glory, or Have We Seen Enough? (33:18–35:3).**
III. **Will We Be Faithful Stewards or Selfish Consumers? (35:4–36:7).**
IV. **Will We Remain Amazed That God Has Tabernacled among Us, or Will We Grow Cold to the Good News? (36:8–40:38).**

How do you go forward in your faith journey? Maybe you have encountered great loss, are relocating, have graduated recently, or are going overseas soon. How should you handle such transitions? We find divine truth and encouragement from Israel's journey in chapters 33–40.

In the opening words of this section, God commanded Israel to depart and "Go up to a land flowing with milk and honey" (33:3). Then at the end of the book, they continued their journey by God's presence (40:38).

We have seen a lot of amazing things in Exodus. The story opened with Israel being oppressively enslaved to the Egyptians. Then God met with Moses at the burning bush and called him to lead the people out of Egypt. God sent the plagues on Egypt, judging them, but He passed over those who had the blood of a lamb on their doorposts. He did it all so everyone would know that He alone is Yahweh (7:5; 8:10; 8:22). And He did it so Israel could worship Him (7:16). Then God parted the Red Sea, delivered believing Israel, and destroyed the Egyptians. God fed them with bread from heaven and water from the rock. He gave them His law. Israel saw His glory on the mountain, where God gave Moses instructions to build the tabernacle. While Moses was there, however, the Israelites were at the bottom of the mountain worshiping a golden calf. God responded with judgment and mercy: 3,000 died, but the rest were spared and told that they may go on (32:34).

Let us look mainly at chapters 33–34 but also highlight a few points of application in chapters 35–40 (these matters have already been discussed along with chs. 25–31). As we continue to learn from the story of the exodus, I would like to pose four questions on how we may move forward (I am indebted to my friend David Platt for the idea for this outline).

Will We Be Desperate for God's Presence, or Will We Depend on Ourselves?
EXODUS 33:1-17

At first glance, verses 1-3a seem to be good news. Despite their failure, God was going to take the people to the promised land. But then we read of a problem. God said He was not going with them (v. 3b). Why? He said because He would consume them along the way. Notice also that in verse 1 God called them "the people" rather than "My people," and in verse 2 it was just "an angel" rather than "My angel" (23:23). A distance existed between this stiff-necked people and God. God would give them gifts, and the promised land, but He would not go with them.

To Israel's credit, they responded appropriately (vv. 4-6). When they heard of this bad news, they "mourned and didn't put on their jewelry" (v. 4). Indeed, they left their jewelry off from this point forward (v. 6). By removing these ornaments, they demonstrated contrition and repentance. They wanted to be right with God. They said it was time to leave the superficial trappings of this world and long for the supernatural glory of God.

We can learn from Moses' and Israel's desperation for God's presence. Let me mention three applications.

We Have a Need We Cannot Overlook (33:1-6)

Israel realized that their greatest need was to have God. If you think about it, what God said to them is actually what a lot of people want. They want the benefits of God but do not care about having God Himself. They want the blessings but not necessarily the Blesser. They want to go to the promised land, heaven, but it does not really matter if

God is there. Sometimes people even present the gospel like this: "Pray this prayer, and you can be forgiven and go to heaven when you die." While there are wonderful benefits in the gospel, do not forget that the greatest gift you receive when you become a Christian is that you get God Himself! You enter a relationship with God. Knowing God is better than anything else. How sweet it is to have communion with God! The psalmist asked, "Who do I have in heaven but You?" (Ps 73:25). Let me ask you, do you want the promised land without a personal relationship with God? Consider your desire, my friend. To Israel's credit, they said no. We have a need we cannot overlook.

We Have a Privilege We Must Not Neglect (33:7-11)

Moses entered the tent of meeting. This should not be confused with the tabernacle, which was not built yet. Both were places to meet God. But this tent was Moses' own private tent to meet God. This tent was also outside the camp, whereas the tabernacle would be in the center.

Catch this scene: Moses would leave the camp to go to the tent. Then the people would stand. They would watch their mediator go inside the tent to meet with God. When he went in, the cloud would come down and hover over the entrance. What happened inside? Moses talked with God. It says that God spoke with Moses "face to face, just as a man speaks with his friend" (v. 11). This does not mean that Moses could see God. Later we read, "no one can see Me and live" (v. 20). What it means is that Moses and God shared direct communication. This was an intimate relationship. Moses and God were friends, like Jesus said He and His disciples were (John 15:15). There was hope for Israel. While God said He would not go with them, God was at least talking to their mediator.

Let us not leave this in the Old Testament. Think about the marvelous privilege we share today. How can we meet with God? We do not have to go somewhere. We do not have to pitch a tent. As believers in Jesus Christ, we have immediate access to God thorough the Spirit (Eph 2:18). You are the tent! You take the tent everywhere you go because God's presence is in you as a believer. We can commune with God. He speaks to us directly in His written Word, and we speak to Him through worship and prayer. Paul prayed for the Ephesian Christians that they would "be strengthened with power in the inner man through His Spirit" (Eph 3:16). Communion with God—what a privilege!

We Have an Assignment We Cannot Complete (33:12-16)

They were desperate for God's presence because without Him, they could not go on. In verses 12-13 Moses asked God for help in leading the people. What he said was essentially, "We do not have the resources to fulfill this mission." Moses asked to know God and His ways: "Please teach me Your ways, and I will know You," (v. 13). Moses realized now what Jesus said later: "you can do nothing without Me" (John 15:5). Moses used his favorable standing with God to make such a bold request. God answered Moses' prayers. King David wrote, "He revealed His ways to Moses" (Ps 103:7).

God promised to stay with Moses: "My presence will go with you, and I will give you rest" (v. 14). The text literally says, "My face will go," which refers to the closeness of God's presence.

In our journey of faith, there will be times in which all of us say, "Lord, You are all we have." We realize then that He is all we need. Like Israel, when you are living by faith, you experience intimacy with God—His face goes with you.

Then it looks like Moses was not paying attention. God had just said His presence would go with him, but now Moses said that if His presence does not go, he does not want to be made to go (v. 15). Moses seemed to do what some of us husbands do when our wives are talking: check out! Then when we chime in, we sound like idiots because we were not paying attention at all, proving it by repeating what was just said! Is this what Moses was doing? Actually, he paid close attention. Moses realized that God promised to be with *him* individually ("you"), but what about everyone else? Verse 15 shifts to the plural. Moses pleaded with God to go with *the people* ("us," v. 16). He added that God's presence in the midst of them was what made them distinct. Moses proclaimed that they could not go one step without God.

In our lives, we need God to go with us as well. We must have God's presence to fulfill His mission. What distinguished Israel was not their land (they did not have it yet). It was not their wealth (they had been slaves). It was not their culture (it was not fully developed yet). It was not their righteousness (they had just bowed down to a calf). What distinguished them? It was their relationship with God. Now, too, what distinguishes Christians from others is our relationship with God.

We must not rely on methods, money, or marketing (which can be good things), but rather on God's mighty presence to accomplish our mission. We need God's presence to reach other nations, plant churches, care for orphans, parent our kids, live as godly husbands and wives, and everything else. We must have God! Perhaps the greatest problem with the church today is the attempt to do the work of God apart from the presence and power of God. We can get so good at "doing church" that the ministry becomes mechanical and mundane. We must say, "Lord, we do not want to go another step without You!" What made the early church so powerful? It was God's Spirit working through them (Acts 4:29-31). Let it be true of us as well.

In verse 17 we learn why God decided to be with them: the mediator. Israel was blessed because of their mediator. Our salvation and God's abiding presence is a result of our mediator, Jesus Christ. God the Father was pleased with His Son (Matt 3:17). He confirmed His pleasure in the Son by raising Him from the dead.

If you are not yet a Christian, trust in Christ. Through Christ, you can experience a relationship with God. What distinguishes Christians from others is their belief in Christ and God's indwelling presence. Perhaps you think, "God could never be pleased with me." It is not about you. If you trust in Christ, you are united with Christ, and God is pleased with you because He is pleased with His Son.

Let us be desperate. We have a need we cannot overlook. We have a privilege we must not neglect. We have an assignment we cannot complete.

Will We Long to See God's Glory, or Have We Seen Enough?
EXODUS 33:18–35:3

In verse 18 we find a request. Moses did not stop! God just promised Moses what he asked for, but then Moses made this audacious request: "Please, let me see Your glory." Spurgeon said, "Why, it is the greatest petition that man ever asked of God" ("View"). Moses wanted to see the radiance and splendor of God. Think about it! He had already seen glory. He saw it at the burning bush, with the 70 elders, on the mountain top, in the tent of meeting, and through all the miracles. Yet Moses longed to see more. Had he not seen enough? No. He had a taste of glory, and it made him long for more.

God responded in verses 19-23. He responded with a yes and a no. He would show Moses a glimpse of His glory, but He could not show him it fully or else Moses would die. He first gave Moses a gracious manifestation (v. 19). He said that He would make His *goodness* pass before him. It is interesting that He chose "goodness." He said that He would give Moses a glimpse of the brightness and loveliness of Himself.

Then He said that He would manifest His *glory* by preaching a sermon to Moses. He said, "I will proclaim the name Yahweh before you'" (v. 19). We will see how He does this in the next chapter (34:6-7).

Next He manifested to Moses His sovereign *grace.* God said that He was bound to no one and was absolutely free to show mercy and grace to whomever He pleased (33:19). He was not obligated to do what Moses asked. Paul quoted this verse in Romans 9:15 in explaining the doctrine of election. God is God. If we know God, it is because of His free grace, and we should bow down and glorify His holy name.

In verses 20-23 God gave Moses a gracious covering. God told Moses that he could see His "back," that is, a glimpse of His glory, and that He would protect Moses by placing him in the cleft of the rock. "Moses was protected from God by God," as Ryken says (*Exodus,* 1035).

Do you want to see His glory? I believe this is the cry of every human heart, either consciously felt or not. We are made for glory. Unfortunately, many substitute created things for the glory of God. Jesus said, "The pure in heart are blessed, for they will see God" (Matt 5:8). We see Him now through the eyes of faith, but later, we shall see Christ. I love how Stephen saw glory in Acts 7. The psalmist said, "But I will see Your face in righteousness; when I awake, I will be satisfied with Your presence" (17:15). To see Christ is to behold God. Jesus told Philip, "The one who has seen Me has seen the Father" (John 14:9). Paul spoke of "God's glory in the face of Jesus Christ" (2 Cor 4:6). And "now we see indistinctly, as in a mirror, but then face to face" (1 Cor 13:12). John said, "we will see Him as He is" (1 John 3:2). In longing to see God's glory, we are saying that we want to know Him intimately.

I remember hearing a friend talk about Exodus 33:19 in light of his ministry at a pristine university. He said that the students and faculty "have no felt needs." Their righteousness is found in the university. His hope in ministry at the university comes from his belief that God will show mercy to some. He believes that God can convert the hardest of people. If God chooses to manifest His sovereign grace, that would be a display of His glory.

Do you long to see God's glory displayed in the salvation of unbelievers—in your family, in your neighborhood, among the nations?

If you have experienced God's sovereign grace, it should absolutely humble you and cause you to worship. When you display arrogance as a Christian, you have not worked God's amazing grace down deep into your soul.

John Piper summarizes the practical implications of God's sovereign grace with four points: (1) humility for the best of saints; (2) hope for the worst of sinners; (3) help for the cause of missions; (4) homage for the name of God ("I Will Be Gracious to Whom I Will Be Gracious").

In chapter 34 God gave Moses a fresh copy of the law and He revealed to him His great name. Know this: we get a glimpse of God's glory when we get an understanding of His name.

Notice what we learn about His law (34:1-4). Moses returned for a copy of the law. This shows us another picture of God's grace. It is a bit different from the first, not in what it says, but in that this time Moses brings the stones, rather than God providing them (24:12). Perhaps the man-made tablets were to remind Israel of their previous breaking of the covenant. Nevertheless, it was a picture of grace: God giving them the law again, which He Himself wrote again.

Then notice what we see about His name (34:5-9). Moses wanted to know God's glory more, so God proclaimed His name to him. This shows us that to know God's glory, we must know something of God's attributes, God's perfections, God's nature—as He has revealed them to us in His Word.

It is no exaggeration to say that Exodus 34:6 is one of the most important verses in the Bible. It is repeated numerous times in Scripture (Pss 86:15; 103:8; 145:8; Joel 2:13; Jonah 4:2). When someone wanted to know what God was like, they could quote this verse. After saying His sacred name "Yahweh," which God revealed to Moses at the burning bush—denoting His self-sufficiency and self-existence—He explained the meaning of that name more fully by highlighting several attributes of Himself. This could be a sermon in itself, but just consider them briefly for now.

To those in need, God is compassionate (or merciful). God cares about His children. David said, "As a father has compassion on his children, so the LORD has compassion on those who fear Him" (Ps 103:13). Like Israel, we need a compassionate God. It is no surprise that when Jesus came along, Matthew said He looked at the crowds, and "He felt compassion for them, because they were weary and worn out, like sheep without a shepherd" (Matt 9:36). Praise Him for His compassion.

To those who cannot measure up, God is gracious. This means unde-served favor. Sometimes students who do not have their assignments finished ask, "Dr. Merida, can I get some grace?" I want to say, "That is really not grace. Grace would be more like me saying, 'I will write your paper for you, and you will get an A+ as a result.' But that is not happen-ing in my class!" See, grace is not you doing your part, earning favor, and then asking God to do the other part. It is not a 50/50 deal. Grace is one hundred percent God's favor on the undeserved. Praise God that Jesus, full of grace and truth, has done the work for us and made us right with God—not because we deserved it, or because we did part of it and He agreed to do the other part, but because of His grace.

To those who are rebellious, God is slow to anger. This speaks of the patience of God. Are you glad that God is slow to anger? Israel needed a patient God. They murmured and complained and rebelled, but God was patient. He has not changed either. We need a patient God. Praise God we have one.

To the unfaithful, God abounds in faithful love and loyalty. This speaks of the covenant nature of God's love. God is loyal. God always follows through. His faithful love is boundless. Israel needed a covenant-keeping God! In their fickleness, God remained faithful and loving to them. Exodus 34:7 repeats "faithful love." This is the same word in verse 6 *(chesed)*, which we really do not have a good English word for. Some translate it as "steadfast love"; some "loyal love"; some "loving-kindness." Notice how His covenant love goes on "to a thousand generations."

To the guilty, God is forgiving. This word means "lift" or "carry." This is what God does with our sins; He lifts the guilt off our shoulders and carries it away. Of course Israel needed a forgiving God, just as we do. Notice three things God forgives: (1) wrongdoing (turning aside from what is good and right); (2) rebellion (betraying the covenant with the King); (3) sin (any type of moral failure). Moses earlier prayed, "forgive their sin" (32:32). When the paralytic came to Jesus, He could look and say, "Son, your sins are forgiven" (Mark 2:5). Jesus has the authority and compassion to lift your wrongdoing, your rebellion, your sin, your guilt off of you. But we cannot stop with these attributes.

To the unrepentant, God is just. This reminds us of the second com-mandment (Exod 20:5). We cannot pick and choose which attributes of God we want, as if we were at a buffet. Those who choose to reject God will be held accountable. Just because God is compassionate and gra-cious does not mean the guilty who remain unrepentant get a free pass.

The mention of God's consequences on several generations does not mean that grandchildren will be punished for something their grandparents have done. It means that as sin continues, God's justice continues. How do you reconcile His justice and His love? It is reconciled at the cross. There, God poured out justice and at the same time displayed love. He was the just One and the justifier (Rom 3:26). God will judge and punish sin. Either Jesus received your judgment at the cross, or you will face God's just judgment on your own.

With God's just judgment in mind, Moses responded with worship and prayer (Exod 34:8). Moses bowed down. This is how you respond to the glory of God. Then he offered a prayer, but only after he worshiped. Adoration precedes supplication. This prayer was about the fifth time he had prayed since the golden calf incident. This prayer sounds familiar. The repetition serves as a good example for us. We pray for all kinds of things repeatedly: provision, forgiveness, God's glory to be known, and more.

Here we also see the covenant renewed (see 23:10-33). God granted Moses what he asked for. God said that He would be faithful to His covenant. He renewed the covenant in verses 10-28. God promised to drive out the enemies, and the people should destroy their idols (vv. 10-16). They were to be wary of making any covenants with the enemies, and they were to destroy all signs of idolatrous worship, for God is jealous (v. 14; cf. 20:5). The idea of prostituting created the picture of the Israelites breaking their vows to God if they succumbed to worshiping false gods.

Next God provided instructions on true worship (vv. 17-28). In verse 17 the command to worship God alone was again emphasized (cf. 20:4). Then God reiterated His commands regarding the Festival of Unleavened Bread (v. 18; cf. 23:15; 13:3-10); the consecration of the firstborn (vv. 19-20; cf. 13:11-16; 23:15); the Sabbath (v. 21; cf. 20:9-11); the Festival of Weeks, the firstfruits of wheat harvest, and the Festival of Ingathering (v. 22; cf. 23:16-17,19); the appearance of males before the Lord (v. 23); the divine promise to drive out the inhabitants of Canaan (v. 24; cf. 23:27-30); sacrifices (v. 25; cf. 23:18); firstfruits (v. 26a; cf. 23:19); and the command against boiling a goat in its mother's milk (v. 26b; cf. 23:19). God then told Moses to write down the commands for the people as a confirmation of the covenant (v. 27). By writing it down, they were "setting it in stone," literally.

During this time Moses was fasting, a sign of total dependence on God. He did this for 40 days and 40 nights (cf. 24:18). Later, another mediator came along and experienced a 40-day fast: Jesus Christ, who reemphasized that man should not live by bread alone but by every word that proceeds from the mouth of God.

In 34:29–35:3 Moses displayed God's glory. After this exchange with God on the mountain, Moses came down. When he came down, he brought the law with him. He also brought a glow with him. He radiated the glory of God. Why? He had been talking with God. Moses first called Aaron and the leaders together to review the covenant. Then he called all the Israelites together. After he finished, he had to put a veil over his face. This was because Moses had been with God—though after a period of time, the glory would fade (see 2 Cor 3:13). This happened every time Moses met with God. David said, "Those who look to Him are radiant with joy; their faces shall never be ashamed" (Ps 34:5).

For us, when we are with God, we will shine. Remember what they said about Peter and John in the early days of the church? When they saw their boldness, Luke said, "When they observed . . . they were uneducated and untrained men, they were amazed and knew that they had been with Jesus" (Acts 4:13). Do people know you have been with Jesus?

We are also transformed as we gaze on Christ. In 2 Corinthians 3:7-18, Paul explained that the glory of the New Covenant is superior to this Old Covenant glory that Moses knew (see also Matt 11:11). How so? The Holy Spirit is indwelling believers. Paul said in verse 18,

> We all, with unveiled faces, are looking as in a mirror at the glory of the Lord and are being transformed into the same image from glory to glory; this is from the Lord who is the Spirit.

Through Christ and in Christ we gaze on the glory of God. As we behold Jesus, we are transformed. This is the privilege we share. We are not transformed by talking about transformation. We are transformed as we behold Jesus. We become like that which we worship.

Will We Be Faithful Stewards or Selfish Consumers?
EXODUS 35:4–36:7

Chapters 25–31 explain the instructions for building the tabernacle. Then chapters 35–40 show the implementation of building it. A large percentage of the material repeats, either verbatim or virtually verbatim, what was already stated, though not in the exact order. Since we already covered these details, I am simply going to highlight a few things.

Remarkably, some twenty times we read that the Israelites did exactly what God commanded them to do (See 39:1,5,7,21,26,29,31,32,42,43; 40:16,19,21,23,25,26,27,29,32). We see Moses' and the people's total obedience to God's instructions.

While we are not building a tabernacle, our mission is to make God's glory known as well. Jesus told us to make disciples of all nations—fill the earth with worshipers. We too must do "just as the Lord commanded."

Allow me to raise two questions from these two chapters. But before I pose them, consider what is going on. In 35:5-19 the supplies needed for building the tabernacle and making the priests' garments were listed. There was also a call not just for supplies but for the craftsmen also. All the people were told to contribute their possessions to execute the mission. Notice the repeated emphasis on the people's desire to contribute. "Everyone whose heart was moved and whose spirit prompted him" was called to give (v. 21). This involved "all who had willing hearts" (v. 22), "whose hearts were moved" (v. 26), and "whose hearts prompted them" (v. 29).

Then, in 35:30–36:1, we read about Bezalel and Oholiab and other craftsmen. They oversaw the designs and construction of every aspect of the tabernacle. As mentioned earlier in our study, attention is given to the fact that the Spirit of God empowered them for this task (35:31). They were blessed with skill and intelligence as craftsmen. Moses called for the craftsmen, and "everyone whose heart moved him" came to do the work (36:2-7).

Finally, we see the magnificent picture of generosity: "the people continued to bring freewill offerings morning after morning" (36:3). Moses had to tell them to stop giving after he had received sufficient resources (vv. 6-7).

The first question we must address from this passage is this: *Where is your heart?* Paul said, "Each person should do as he has decided in his heart—not reluctantly or out of necessity, for God loves a cheerful giver" (2 Cor 9:7). We need this kind of heart. The Israelites lived this out. The scene was amazing! The people willingly gave their possessions. Generous giving only comes from a heart that has been moved by God's grace. God gives us a new heart as believers, and one of the inevitable results of that new heart is generosity. Robert Murray M'Cheyne once perceived a lack of generosity in his people and said this:

> I am concerned for the poor but more for you. I know not
> what Christ will say to you in the great day. . . . I fear there

are many hearing me who may know well that they are not Christians, because they do not love to give. To give largely and liberally, not grudging at all, requires a new heart; an old heart would rather part with its life-blood than its money. Oh my friends! Enjoy your money; make the most of it; give none away; enjoy it quickly for I can tell you, you will be beggars throughout eternity. (Ryken, *Exodus*, 1085)

When we give, we show that we have been moved by His grace and favor. Those who understand grace, freely give (2 Cor 8:9). Yes, generous giving comes from a heart that has been changed. Has yours?

The second question is this: *What will you give?* There are any number of things that one may give. For instance, we can give treasures such as money and materials. What were the Israelites giving? They were giving what God gave them: gold and fancy threads that they had received from Egypt. When we put our offerings in the box, we simply give back what God has given us.

Another gift to be given is time. It took time to do all of this work! So it is with us; the most precious thing we have is time. We should spend it wisely on things that matter. The Scripture says, "Teach us to number our days carefully so that we may develop wisdom in our hearts" (Ps 90:12).

Another gift involves our talent. People who were blessed with certain skills built the tabernacle, both men and women (see the women serving faithfully in 35:25-26). Likewise, God gifts believers to build up the body. We must use what we have for the mission of God and for the glory of God. May we be faithful stewards of our treasure, time, and talent; and may God help us avoid becoming selfish consumers.

Will We Remain Amazed That God Has Tabernacled among Us, or Will We Grow Cold to the Good News?

EXODUS 36:8–40:38

If we had never heard the story of the exodus, this section would not really appear redundant. There would actually be suspense. Would God dwell among a sinful people in the tabernacle? These final chapters bring the book to a climactic finish.

The craftsmen began by making the curtains. Bazalel attached loops to them with clasps of gold. Then he made more curtains out of goats' hair and attached loops with bronze clasps to them (36:8-19). As the story continues, Bezalel made the upright frames and bars out of acacia wood. These would serve as the structure for the tabernacle (vv. 20-34). Then he made the veil of blue and purple and scarlet yarns and fine linen. For the veil, he made pillars of acacia wood that were overlaid with gold. This also had a screen for the entrance. This was the most holy place (vv. 35-38).

Next Bezalel made the ark and its poles. It was made of acacia wood overlaid with gold. On the ends there were cherubim; in between them was the mercy seat on which the high priest would sprinkle blood (37:1-9). Bezalel also made the table from acacia wood, also overlaid with gold. This had dishes that were made of pure gold (vv. 10-16). Then he made the lamp stand of pure gold. Even with the numerous branches and extensions that came out of the main pole, it was one solid, hammered piece of pure gold (vv. 17-24). The altar of incense was made out of acacia wood and overlaid with gold. Bezalel, the multi-skilled man that he was, also made the holy anointing oil and perfumes (vv. 25-29). He then made the altar of burnt offering out of acacia wood. This was overlaid with bronze rather than gold, as were the pieces that went with it (38:1-7). He made the bronze basin along with its stand (v. 8). Then he finally made the court, which contained numerous pillars, bases, hangings, and more, all being made of bronze and silver (vv. 9-20).

We are also provided with a record of who helped in building the tabernacle and the amount of supplies that went into building it (vv. 21-31). This included around 2,193 pounds of gold. This was and is massive wealth! While some may say that this argues against the historicity of the account, much larger amounts have been found in the East, in both ancient and modern times (Keil and Delitzsch, *Pentateuch*, 251).

The final thing prepared for the tabernacle involved the priestly garments. This included the ephod, breastplate, overcoat, body-coat, turban, and undergarments (39:1-31). This provided the conclusion of the building of the tabernacle. The items were delivered to Moses. After inspecting them, Moses found that the people had made what Yahweh required. As a result, Moses blessed them (vv. 32-43). God then instructed the people when to erect the tabernacle (40:1-15). Moses obeyed God's instruction. He erected the tabernacle and completed the work (vv. 16-33).

"The glory of the LORD filled the tabernacle" (vv. 34-38) when the work was completed. The Lord would remain there until it was time for the people to move. While the cloud and the glory were stationary, they met together in the tabernacle. When the cloud of glory left, the people left. God provided them with direction. They could not mistake when the Lord wanted them to stay or go.

Moses did not see the glory of God head-on in Exodus. He saw glimpses of glory—he saw more than anyone else—but it was not until later that Moses saw the glory of God in the face of Christ. Look at Luke 9:28-36:

> About eight days after these words, He took along Peter, John, and James and went up on the mountain to pray. As He was praying, the appearance of His face changed, and His clothes became dazzling white. Suddenly, two men were talking with Him—Moses and Elijah. They appeared in glory and were speaking of His death, which He was about to accomplish in Jerusalem. Peter and those with him were in a deep sleep, and when they became fully awake, they saw His glory and the two men who were standing with Him. As the two men were departing from Him, Peter said to Jesus, "Master, it's good for us to be here! Let us make three tabernacles: one for You, one for Moses, and one for Elijah"—not knowing what he said. While he was saying this, a cloud appeared and overshadowed them. They became afraid as they entered the cloud. Then a voice came from the cloud, saying: This is My Son, the Chosen One; listen to Him! After the voice had spoken, only Jesus was found. They kept silent, and in those days told no one what they had seen.

Jesus unveiled His glory at the Mount of Transfiguration to Peter and John and James. His face was altered, His clothes were dazzling white, and the cloud appeared, and who got to see Him? Moses (and Elijah)! Previously, Moses could not see God's face, but now, he beheld Him. Now God could say, "You want to see My glory? Here you go." Moses was talking with Jesus face to face as a man speaks to his friend. Luke even added that they were discussing Jesus' "death," literally His "departure," which is the Greek word for "exodus" (Luke 9:31). Jesus was about to lead the ultimate exodus through His death and resurrection. The disciples did not understand it for they thought there should be a tent of meeting for each of them. But the Father said, you do not need a tent; you need to listen to my Son. He told them they were dwelling with God in Christ.

Moses saw the glory of God in Christ as Jesus dwelt among them. It is what we see as well, though through a dark glass. Later, we will see face to face. This gives us great hope! The tabernacle and all its glory point to the glory of God in Christ. The author of Hebrews picked up this point powerfully, and so did the Apostle John when he wrote in John 1:14,

> *The Word became flesh and took up residence among us.*
> *We observed His glory,*
> *the glory as the One and Only Son from the Father,*
> *full of grace and truth.*

What is the tabernacle about? It is about the gospel. Will we continue to stand amazed at Christ—our tabernacle—or will we become indifferent to the good news? Let us continually marvel at grace. Let us continually adore Christ.

Conclusion

In the Lord of the Rings, Sam asks Mr. Frodo, "I wonder what sort of a tale we've fallen into?" (Tolkien, *The Two Towers*, 362). Everyone wants to know the answer to this. The book of Exodus shows us. We are in *the* story, the grand redemptive story, the true story of the whole world. We look back at Exodus and see the good news, and Exodus points ahead to Christ, and Exodus looks to the end (which is only the beginning).

We began our study and said that we were going to see the gospel and how the story of Exodus, in a sense, is our story. Once we were in bondage to sin, enslaved, under the sentence of death, but by taking shelter under the blood of the Lamb, God has delivered us. Now God is with us, leading us to the promised land. We will face challenges, obstacles, and temptations, but we know that God is faithful to His redeemed people. While we journey, we live by grace and forgiveness found not in a tabernacle but in Christ. One day we will see Jesus Christ, and there we will behold the glory of God forever. Everyone who trusts in Christ has this hope. Now let us move forward in this faith journey!

Reflect and Discuss

1. What would you rather have, God's blessings without His presence, or God's presence without His blessings? How is your stated preference reflected in your prayers and in the choices you make in life?

2. How might you present the gospel to an unbeliever with an emphasis on the presence of God, rather than on the avoidance of hell and the obtaining of blessings?

3. In what way is the privilege of Christians today greater than that of Moses who spoke with God "face to face"?

4. What gives evidence that a church or ministry is relying on something other than God's presence to accomplish its goals? Is success a valid indication of a godly ministry?

5. Where do you perceive the glory of God? Which best expresses His glory to you: nature, architecture, art, music, poetry, or something else? Can God be glorified in a secular work?

6. What is the connection between the "name" of God and His attributes? What do people think when they hear your name?

7. How would you explain to children in Sunday School that God is gracious, patient, forgiving, and just?

8. How was God's patience and grace expressed to Israel in this chapter? How has God's patience been shown in your life?

9. How have you seen yourself or others acting as selfish consumers of God's blessings rather than stewards who are willing to distribute what belongs to God? What is hardest for you to part with: treasure, time, or talent?

10. How does it show absolutely undeserved mercy when the glory of God in Christ is accessible to every Christian? How does the presence of the glory of Christ provide hope to Christians?

WORKS CITED

Alexander, T. Desmond. *From Paradise to Promised Land.* Grand Rapids: Baker Academic, 2012.

Beale, G. K. *We Become What We Worship.* Downers Grove: IVP Academic, 2008.

Begg, Alistair. *Pathway to Freedom.* Chicago: Moody, 2003.

Boyce, James. *Ordinary Men Called by God: A Study of Abraham, Moses, and David.* Grand Rapids: Kregel, 1982.

Calvin, John. *Commentaries on the Four Last Books of Moses Arranged in the Form of a Harmony.* In Calvin's Commentaries. Volumes 2 and 3. Grand Rapids: Baker, 2009.

Campbell, Iain D. *Opening Up Exodus.* Leominster: Day One Publications, 2006.

Enns, Peter. *Exodus.* In NIV Application Commentary. Grand Rapids: Zondervan, 2000.

Gentry, Peter J., and Stephen Wellum. *Kingdom through Covenant.* Wheaton: Crossway, 2012.

Guiness, Os, and John Seel. *No God but God.* Moody, 1992.

Hamilton, James M., Jr. *God's Glory in Salvation through Judgment.* Wheaton: Crossway, 2010.

————. *God's Indwelling Presence.* Nashville: B&H Academic, 2006.

Hamilton, Victor. *Exodus: An Exegetical Commentary.* Grand Rapids: Baker Academic, 2012.

Haugen, Gary. *Good News about Injustice.* Downers Grove: InterVarsity, 2009.

House, Paul. *Old Testament Theology.* Downers Grove: InterVarsity, 1998.

International Justice Mission. www.ijm.org

Kaiser, Walter C., Jr. "Exodus." In *The Expositor's Bible Commentary.* Volume 2. Edited by Frank E. Gæbelein. Grand Rapids: Zondervan, 1990.

Kiel, C. F., and F. Delitzsch. *Pentateuch.* Biblical Commentary on the Old Testament. Volume Two. Grand Rapids: William B Eerdmans, 1951.

Keller, Tim. *Counterfeit Gods*. New York: Dutton, 2009.

———. *Generous Justice*. New York: Riverhead, 2010.

———. "Getting Out." Plenary Session, The Gospel Coalition 2011 National Conference, April 12, 2011.

Lee, Robert G. "Pay-Day Someday." Sermon. Grand Rapids: Zondervan, 1957. http://www.sbc.net/aboutus/sbvoices/rgleepayday.asp (accessed November 27, 2012).

Lloyd-Jones, Sally. *The Jesus Story Book Bible*. Grand Rapids: Zondervan, 2007.

Merida, Tony. *Faithful Preaching*. Nashville: B&H Academic, 2009.

———, and Rick Morton. *Orphanology*. Birmingham: New Hope, 2011.

Metaxas, Eric. *Bonhoeffer*. Nashville: Thomas Nelson, 2010.

Moore, Russell. *Adopted for Life*. Wheaton: Crossway, 2009.

———. "Exodus 1:1–2:10" in Sermon Series "Exit Strategy." Delivered January 27, 2007. http://www.russellmoore.com/resources/exodus (accessed February 1, 2012).

———."The Blood-Splattered Welcome Mat: Finding Belonging with the Passed Over." Sermon, March 22, 2009. http://www.russell moore.com/2009/03/22/the-blood-splattered-welcome-mat-find ing-belonging-with-the-passed-over (accessed November 27, 2012).

Newton, John. *Out of the Depths*. Revised and updated by Dennis R. Hillman. Grand Rapids: Kregel, 2003.

Nichols, Stephen J. *Martin Luther*. Phillipsburg, NJ: P&R, 2002.

"Not for Sale." Notforsalecampaign.org (accessed November 27, 2012).

Owen, John. *The Glory of Christ*. 1684. Reprint, Edinburgh: Banner of Truth, 1994.

Piper, John. "Children, Heirs, and Fellow Sufferers." Sermon, April 21, 2002. http://www.desiringgod.org/resource-library/sermons/children -heirs-and-fellow-sufferers (accessed November 27, 2012).

———."I Will Be Gracious to Whom I Will Be Gracious." Sermon, September 23, 1984. http://www.desiringgod.org/resource -library/sermons/i-will-be-gracious-to-whom-i-will-be-gracious (accessed June 1, 2012).

Platt, David. "Exodus 32:1-10, 1 Corinthians 10:6-13." Chapel Sermon, Southern Baptist Theological Seminary, February 16, 2012. http:// www.sbts.edu/resources/chapel/chapel-spring-2012/exodus -321-10-1-corinthians-106-13 (accessed May 25, 2012).

Ryken, Philip Graham. *Exodus*. Preaching the Word Series. Wheaton: Crossway, 2005.

Sailhamer, John H. *The Meaning of the Pentateuch.* Downers Grove: InterVarsity, 2009.

Sproul, R. C. *The Holiness of God.* Wheaton: Tyndale, 1985.

Spurgeon, Charles. *The Power in Prayer.* New Kensington: Whitaker House, 1996.

———. "Marah Better than Elim." Sermon #2301. Delivered March 26, 1893.

———. "To the Saddest of the Sad." Sermon #2026. Delivered June 3, 1888.

———. "A View of God's Glory." Sermon #3120. Published November 26, 1908.

Stuart, Douglas K. *Exodus.* The New American Commentary. Volume Two. Nashville: B&H, 2006.

Tolkien, J. R. R. *The Two Towers.* New York: Ballantine Books. Reprint, New York: Del Rey, 2012.

Tozer, A. W. *A Knowledge of the Holy.* New York: HarperSanFrancisco, 1961.

Wright, Christopher J. H. *The Mission of God.* Downers Grove: IVP Academic, 2006.

———. *Old Testament Ethics for the People of God.* Downers Grove: IVP Academic, 2004.

SCRIPTURE INDEX